"I am greatly encouraged when I read what these young 'reflective practitioners' are writing, for they are the foundation of a rising generation. They are men and women of both action and reflection who are committed to God's truth, obedient in the power of God's Spirit to the Great Commission in all of its fullness; servants who are global in perspective; citizens of their own culture and of the world; leaders who are passionate of heart and who reflect the heart of Christ."

William D. Taylor, Ph.D.
Director, World Evangelical Alliance
Missions Commission

"This book is unique as it expresses the thinking and passion of a new generation of creative practitioners and scholars. It covers a wide variety of topics ranging from the biblical and theological foundations of missionary training, and how to involve the local church in intercultural development. Furthermore, it offers various models of recruiting, training, equipping, funding and dispatching intercultural leaders. Dr. Miguel Alvarez, a seasoned missionary, provides an important dimension to the discussion of training leadership for intercultural service. This book is a significant addition to the knowledge base of intercultural studies in the 21st century."

Willie Tjiong, D.Min.
Director, Doctor of Ministry Program
School of Divinity, Regent University
Virginia Beach, Virginia

"It is obvious that God raised the churches of the Non-Western world to join their Western counterparts in His great plan—reaching out to the people of their continents. Henceforth, as the new century unfolds before us, we have begun to see a passionate new leadership emerging with great creativity and innovation. Indeed, this is the work of the Holy Spirit! This unique collection of studies in the area of intercultural leadership represents a groundbreaking action that will help build the foundation of the future of Christianity. The contributors are not well known, but this is exactly what this book is trying to represent—the emergence of new intercultural leaders from non-traditional turf. If anyone envisions leading in an intercultural setting, I would like to strongly recommend the reading of this book."

JULIE C. MA, PH.D.
Lecturer of Intercultural Studies
Asia Pacific Theological Seminary,
Editor, *Journal of Asian Mission*
Baguio City, Philippines

A World of Opportunities

Training Leadership for Intercultural Service

Miguel Alvarez, Editor

ASIAN CENTER FOR MISSIONS AMERICA
VIRGINIA BEACH, VIRGINIA

A World of Opportunities:
Training Leadership for Intercultural Service
Miguel Alvarez, Editor

Asian Center for Missions America
P.O. Box 64548
Virginia Beach, Virginia 23467

Published by
TCM Publications
PO Box 64295
Virginia Beach, Virginia 23467
USA

ISBN 0-9742360-4-7 (pbk)
ISBN 0-9742360-5-5 (ebk)

Cover design by Nixon Na
Page design by Aileen Barrongo

Printed in the Philippines

Dedication

To the Asian Center for Missions (ACM) family, for their inspiring commitment and dedication to advancing the testimony of Jesus Christ among countless people-groups.

On behalf of the contributors of this volume, I would like to express our gratitude for such passionate and tireless intercultural service. Much of what is in this book has to do with your experience and heart, as a new generation devoted to world evangelization.

Contents

Foreword

DR. L. GRANT MCCLUNG, JR.
Field Director
Church of God Europe
Western/Mediterranean/Middle East
Church of God World Missions
Associate Professor
Missions/Church Growth
Church of God Theological Seminary
Cleveland, Tennessee

"Rome, we have a problem."

Reading the creative articles assembled by Dr. Miguel Alvarez and his student colleagues reminds me of the historical anecdote of a Roman commander. He and his troops had gone beyond the known limits of the Roman Empire. They were in the northwest reaches of what we now call Great Britain far beyond Hadrian's Wall and other Roman-built markers. His frantic dispatch back to Rome was, "Send new orders—we've marched off the map" (in my *Globalbeliever.com: Connecting to God's Work in Your World*, Pathway Press 2000).

A World of Opportunities: Training Leadership for Intercultural Service is a refreshing demonstration that a class project can get students "out of the books and into the boots" for missions service. New missions thinking takes us off our traditional maps. Clearly, what is needed today is less musing and more marching. This book is a welcome affirmation that Christ's missionary mandate has been embraced by yet another new generation ready to march.

The chapters are arranged around three guiding themes: (1) Biblical and theological foundations; (2) The indispensability of the local church in recruitment and training, and; (3) Strategic initiatives and needed components in intercultural training. These themes all focus on the goal of church planting among unreached people groups.

Under the experienced guidance of Alvarez, what surfaces is emphasis upon the need for intercultural training. Could it be that the synthesis of the separate disciplines of leadership training and intercultural communication (i.e. "missionary anthropology") may eventually be synergized into a new and needed sub-discipline in missiology: *Intercultural Training*?

I'm grateful for the insight and vision of my friend, Miguel Alvarez. Some 20 years ago, our paths crossed when he arrived from Honduras, already an experienced church leader, to the classrooms of the Church of God Theological Seminary. Over the years we have partnered in various projects, consultations, and missions. I have been impressed with his charismatic skill of mobilizing a team of fellow "global believers" around him, especially young people from the "Southern World."

While reflecting upon this Foreword, I received my copy of the May-June 2003 issue of *The Commission* (from the Southern Baptist International Mission Board). On the cover was an MTV style photo of "Twenty-something" from Generation X. He was not hanging out at the mall but trekking across remote parts of China sharing Christ and gathering data. In the lead story, "Taking the Gospel to the X-treme—Backpacking Across China," this new generation missionary revealed his heart and lessons learned in the praxis of the backroad:

> God showed me it is about Him. He basically said, 'Get over the stuff. You don't need Mountain Dew and Papa John's to survive.' All this changes your perspective. I mean, when we come to an isolated village and pray for some guy who is 80 years old, and then I know that I am probably the first Christian to ever pray for him, that is a pretty awesome thought. Dude, that's humbling.

May your reading of these reflections and projections bring you again to the realization of the high privilege we share as Christ's ambassadors trekking with Him to the nations.

Dude, that's humbling.

Acknowledgment

There are several scholars to whom I am deeply thankful for the time and effort they have devoted to this manuscript. First of all, I would like to thank the students of my course on Training Intercultural Leadership at Regent University. Their commitment to write such high quality papers helped set the foundation for this book. Among all of them, George Mitchell did the most difficult part. He was the assistant editor and was instrumental in the preparation of the initial text.

Thank you also to Ron DeBerry for helping proofread the final manuscript. A word of gratitude to Justo Roberto Navarro, my Graduate Assistant and co-editor. He was able to effectively facilitate the process from his post at the Asian Center for Missions (ACM) US Office. We are also grateful to Christina Shawe for assuming the last part of the process and working out all the details for the proper publication and promotion of this book.

General Introduction

MIGUEL ALVAREZ
Vice President
Asian Center for Missions US Office
Adjunct Professor of Intercultural Studies
Regent University
Virginia Beach, Virginia

There is no other book quite like this! It started as a class project for the course on *Training Intercultural Leadership* at Regent University. In the process, professor and students assumed the assignment with enthusiasm and developed a complete research text for publication.

A World of Opportunities: Training Leadership for Intercultural Service aims to contribute to missionary training, as it is understood and practiced in the 21st century.

This book is unique because it contains specialized research done by young missiologists and practitioners. Yes, most of them are Generation Xers, young scholars who are now making remarkable contributions to the missionary training discipline. Traditional missionary scholars have documented their experience, causing great impact in the selection and training of missionaries: This time, these young scholars are reflecting over the same principles and methods of missionary training but with the mind and the heart of a new generation. They represent a new breed of scholarship at the service of the Church of this century. The current order of events in the world has challenged young scholars to rethink and reorder their missiology. Consequently, this foundational book lays out new opportunities for a younger generation, eager to assume its responsibility in the proclamation of the Gospel to every people group.

Besides its profound missiological reflection, this book provides practical applications to the intercultural service most missionaries are experiencing today. It begins by establishing biblical and theological foundations for intercultural training. The book then focuses on the methods of involving the local congregation in the process. Training leaders for intercultural service begins at childhood and continues through the youth and adult church life. Finally, this book presents the most current models of recruiting, training, equipping, sending and funding intercultural leaders.

Christian mission transcends gender, race, culture, and social differences. It is the responsibility of the body of Christ to proclaim the Gospel to every people group on earth. Such action enables the Church to fulfill the Great Commission as ordered by the Lord Jesus Christ in the New Testament. With those implications in mind these Generation Xers are challenging the theory, method, and practice of missionary training; thus, this initiative is also an attempt to make intercultural training a fully practiced discipline, with the goal of equipping the leadership that should reach this present multicultural generation effectively.

Part One
BIBLICAL AND THEOLOGICAL FOUNDATIONS

1. Training Leadership for Intercultural Service: A New Paradigm

MIGUEL ALVAREZ

"We have a gospel, given to us at a great cost, which has turned our lives around, given us hope and joy. Do you remember what Jesus' last command to His disciples was before He ascended into heaven? It was to go into the entire world and to make disciples of all people groups on earth. That is why you can't just shrug this off and say, 'It's no concern of mine. I have enough to do here at home.' It is your Father's concern, it has to be yours."[1]

Introduction

The discipline involved in training leadership for intercultural service has long been recognized and accepted not only in religious circles but also by a broad range of individuals and organizations that operate cross-culturally. Recent intercultural training programs have attracted fresh attention from field missionaries, churches and professional mission leaders who do cross-cultural service. However, in the past, traditional Christian leaders treated intercultural training merely as a field that only required emergency proceedings. If one decided to become a missionary, then some kind of training was to be provided, but there was not much consistent strategic planning to facilitate such training. Reflecting on this, Titus Loong said,

> "It has been like having a brand new car and not knowing any thing about mechanics. Whenever there was a problem, the owner learned spontaneously about the affected part of the car."[2]

The time has come for the missionary leadership of the church to provide adequate training for intercultural service.

In this article I intend to address the issue of intercultural training as a natural discipline and responsibility of the Church. Christian organizations should assume this responsibility and take this discipline as an active part of the ministry of the Church. I also urge the need for this training endeavor to be practiced by all Christian organizations not only at the grassroots but also at the top level of leadership.[3]

Early 21st century Christian organizations have grown extensively as organized religious systems; consequently, they need to revise and adjust their vast structures to the new realities of world evangelization.[4] For an international Christian organization to delegate its missiological responsibility to a missions department may not be the solution to a monumental task. Eventually, the specialized missions department could hinder the entire organization from becoming actively involved in the challenge of intercultural service. For that reason, it must be emphasized that the whole organization, including its leaders, must be decisively engaged in intercultural mission. The task cannot be relegated to a specialized missions department.

Furthermore, I am also suggesting a revised definition of missiology that could be applied to the discipline of intercultural training. This conceptual framework may contribute to justifying the need to dedicate concentrated denominational and cooperative efforts to the training of intercultural workers. On that account, and as a matter of practical commitment, I suggest, among many other efforts, a model intercultural training program that would offer alternatives to the traditional models. It is my interest to initiate a dialogue that would convey academic and professional insights to the discipline of intercultural training as we head towards the future.

In addition, I suggest that intercultural trainers from the Southern Hemisphere[5] may benefit greatly by learning from the current intercultural structures (or networks) already operating in the world.[6] Likewise, intercultural leaders from the Southern Hemisphere may provide a wider variety of new models on training that should be carefully considered and studied in the Northern Hemisphere. Intercultural training today demands strong bonds of fellowship and the creation of new ways to exchange ideas and resources. Trainers must share their teaching load and multiply themselves by equipping new trainers as well. These are new trends that affect world evangelization in the 21st century and networking efforts and cooperation heavily saturates them. We cannot ignore this reality, particularly as the church faces the needs of 21st century missions service.[7]

Missiological Basis for Intercultural Training

Missionary training is both an academic discipline and a practical commitment. Jan A. B. Jongeneel has written an extensive article addressing missiology as an academic discipline. After a review of historical and theological research, he concludes that as a discipline, missiology involves both methodological connection and methodological commitment to the mission of the Church. The combination of these two elements provides natural identity to a theology of mission.[8] In his article, Jongeneel renders a definition of missiology that could well fit the interest of intercultural training as a formal discipline.

> "Missiology is the academic discipline, which from a philosophical; empirical; and theological point of view, reflects upon the history, theory and practice of world mission. This, as a means for both preaching the Gospel, healing the sick, casting out evil spirits, and idolatry, for the glory of God and the well being of all human beings."[9]

Allan R. Tripplett defines missiology as "the discipline or science which researches, records and applies data relating to the biblical origin, to history, and to the use of anthropological principles and techniques as well as the theological base for the Christian mission."[10] One may observe in this definition that Triplett includes methodology and the data bank. In this case, these elements are particularly directed towards the process by which Christians communicate the message. This definition includes the incorporation of converts into local congregations. The latter will measure the growth and relevance of the local church's structure and the fellowship this provides to the new members.[11]

Missiology, then, is the study of individuals being brought to God throughout history. Therefore, if there is an observable discipline of missiology in the cross-cultural extension of the Christian movement, then intercultural training becomes indispensable for the Church to continue to extend itself even unto the uttermost parts of the earth as stated in the Great Commission (Matthew 28:18–20). Intercultural missionary training must therefore be a natural discipline in the educational nature and expansion of the Church.

The Learning Domains of Intercultural Training

Jonathan Lewis identifies the desired outcomes, methods, and context of missionary training. He presented the three domains that must characterize the training task for this to be effective:

(1) *Cognitive* outcomes produced through *formal* methods in a *school* context.
(2) *Skill* outcomes produced through *non-formal* methods in the *workplace* context.
(3) *Affective* outcomes produced through *informal* methods in a *community* context.[12]

Lewis argues that the best missionary training models combine all three domains, use all three methodologies intentionally and provide all three contexts together. He also states that if intercultural training is to be effective, this will have to focus on the true objective of training—the equipping of godly and effective intercultural workers.[13]

Training Movements at the Northern and Southern Hemispheres

A review of the history of Western missionary movements will reveal that commitment to intercultural service has been the result of a simple and direct act of obedience to the Great Commission of the Lord Jesus Christ. There is no evidence that intentional efforts were made to establish effective intercultural training programs in the churches. Therefore, the character of a missionary was often shaped at a young age, at home and at church, not at a training center established for this purpose. Whenever missionaries returned home after a long-term service on the field, they lived and served among their Christian community. Homes and pulpits were the only venues of leadership training opened to them.

Similarly, as the Southern Hemisphere missionary movement emerges, the home and the church have also become the first training ground for the development of a missionary character. Although the home element is basic in the formation of a missionary character, the church must also be educated in the raising, development and training of new and qualified missionaries. In this way the congregation should actively participate as a full partner in the training of the next generation of intercultural workers. One Asian missionary trainer suggested that "missionary training programs in the Two-Thirds World should have more nationals as trainers, for they know the culture of their people."[14] This component, then, includes not only the participation of the entire church but also the employment of nationals as trainers to ensure an objective intercultural formation.[15]

Most missionary trainers agree that the church of the Southern Hemisphere has come of age. Asian churches, for instance, are now mobilizing a great number of members to engage in either long- or short-term missionary service. These Asian Christians understand the costs and challenges of intercultural ministry.[16] They are now learning about missions at any regular Sunday service, during praise and worship, and even at prayer meetings. Task groups are also encouraged to organize mission-exposure trips. Moreover, when the church grows larger, they appoint a mission pastor who will design the training programs for the church. The mission pastor will also encourage individual and corporal commitment to support the intercultural movement through the regular programs of the church.

Intercultural Training

By intercultural training, we mean the ability to provide instruction in the cross-cultural discipline. Such instruction includes spiritual foundations or practices which impart proficiency to undergo the missiological task. This training is driven to develop proper missionary skills, such as behavior, spiritual habits, and mental attitude.

Concerning the philosophy of training, Richard L. Hopkins states that intercultural training must be planned and managed; it does not just happen. Ad hoc training is never the most effective training.[17] Hence, training also involves a technology. The trainer has an understanding of the learning process, and has knowledge of and ability to draw upon a variety of appropriate training techniques and exercises. The trainer knows the components that are effective in training. These components are designed to increase knowledge skills and modify attitudes.[18]

The trainer's expertise is training. Training should cause a change. Those changes should be specified beforehand in learning objectives, and whenever possible, the learners should have an input in planning their own training.[19]

Henceforth, training should be action-oriented and involving. It should emphasize relevance and make learning meaningful. When possible, training should be individualized, because everyone learns in different ways and because entry-level skills and competencies vary widely.

Lastly, trainers should function as facilitators, coaches, consultants, guides, and stimulators.

Intercultural Training in the 21st Century

The last decade of the 20th century witnessed a systematic approach to intercultural training, particularly as worldwide evangelization intensified. International movements, such as AD 2000 and Beyond, created a remarkable mobilization of the Church worldwide towards the evangelization of the earth before the end of the century.[20] Also, the World Evangelical Alliance Missions' Commission provided systematic service on missionary training. It facilitated national, regional and global consultations and produced academic and training materials focused on intercultural evangelization.[21] This Commission's focus on intercultural trainers, critical in properly equipping the trainees, became determinant in its agenda. Likewise, other major prayer movements began operating across the world. These and other actions kept Christians increasingly aware and mobilized for world evangelization at the end of the 20th century.

Moreover, at the sunset of the second millennium, cooperation became the common language among international mission agencies. Now, early in the third millennium, networking and cooperation are the common language for the globalization of missiology. Training for intercultural workers has become a necessity. Furthermore, the church is now engaging a complex world where trainers and trainees must become expert and knowledgeable to be able to carry out the missiological task.

Effective Intercultural Training

If the church of the future wants to continue to be effective in reaching out to the lost world, intercultural training and equipping of its leaders must take place at all levels.[22] Christian organizations will have to open their doors to new and fresh input from other sister organizations. Twenty-first century missiology demands interdependent relationships within the entire body of Christ, particularly in the training of intercultural leadership.

The most important element in missionary service is personnel. How could the Church be more effective in training intercultural leadership and personnel? As we answer this question, we realize that the chief problem today is the lack of qualified personnel for intercultural service. There is a genuine need to develop creative missionary training programs among the Christian community. Consequently, missionary training and sending organizations could become more effective if they would invest heavily in intercultural training. This action would also lessen the levels of missionary attrition.[23]

Models of Intercultural Training

As previously stated, Asia has now become a key participator in world evangelization. It is not only because of its location within the so-called 10/40 Window, which comprises the neediest geographical area of the world, but also because of the great number of missionaries arising from the same area. David Harley conducted a survey among six missionary training centers in the Southern Hemisphere to identify the most important theological issues that need to be addressed by students in their own missionary context. Out of those six centers, three are located in Asia: the Global Ministry Training Centre (GMTC) in Korea, the Outreach Training Institute (OTI) in India, and the Asian Cross-Cultural Training Institute (ACTI) in Singapore.[24] Now for the purpose of this paper, I would also like to mention the Asian Center for Missions (ACM), along with the Great Commission Missionary Training Center (GCMTC) and the Living Springs International (LSI) in the Philippines. These are only a few among many other training centers that have emerged lately as specialized in equipping and sending intercultural workers to the world.

The Asian Center for Missions

At this point, I will discuss the model of training developed by the Asian Center for Missions (ACM) in the Philippines. ACM leads the way in recruiting, training, and sending intercultural workers into the least evangelized regions of the world. Since its beginning in 1995, ACM has offered a unique model of training which calls for cooperation among all the Christian organizations involved in the intercultural training process.[25]

The Asian Center for Missions began as a cooperative effort[26] of six major Christian organizations in the Philippines.[27] They have been working in partnership to fulfill the command of the Lord Jesus Christ to "Go, and make disciples of all nations [people groups]" (Matthew 28:19). ACM aims to network and develop partnerships with churches and Christian organizations in the Asian region to fulfill its vision and purpose: training, equipping and sending Asians to preach the Gospel to Asians.[28]

Instead of a traditional missionary training by calendar year, ACM offers an intensive modular training program. This is composed of four months of classroom instruction and group interaction, and a one-month missions-exposure trip to the selected place of service. ACM core groups are organized around teams of missionaries who are already bound to a particular people group. Teams study the language and the culture of their selected community. ACM students are also equipped in preaching, evangelism, church planting, discipleship, cell-dynamics and counseling by missiologists and mission leaders.[29] The curriculum is designed to equip the candidate missionary with enough information and ministry skills to perform effectively in a foreign intercultural setting.[30]

An ever-growing network of Asian churches has been established to help direct the missionary teams to specific people groups. ACM seeks to place its graduates where the local churches need workers most. The support of indigenous churches, and existing missionary efforts on the field, help to provide fellowship and prayer support for the teams. ACM missionaries raise their own financial support, and the center is working to build a worldwide network of churches and individuals who are willing to provide additional funding to keep these missionaries on the field.

ACM has grown from one training center at its 1995 inception to ten regional training centers in the Philippines and several others in Indochina and West Africa.[31] By the year 2003, ACM had successfully trained and mobilized intercultural workers from Latin America as well. As a result of ACM efforts, many church plants have started taking roots in Hindu, Buddhist, and Islamic strongholds across Asia, North Africa and the Middle East.

ACM's success in training intercultural workers should not disregard the fact that this is still a young model and its leaders are still learning to cope with the weaknesses and limitations typical of the nature of the program. On one hand, the strength of ACM can be found in the relationship of cooperation that has been established among several Christian organizations in the Philippines and Asia, needless to mention its developing partnerships in North, Central and South America.[32] On the other hand, ACM's major weakness is its lack of experience in the training discipline. Its graduates are yet to be evaluated after a long-term commitment. Moreover, stability and consistency in the training process are still issues that ACM will have to face soon.

The Desired Outcomes of Intercultural Training

After looking closely at the ACM model, one comes up with some questions that need objective answers. What makes an intercultural training program successful?[33] One simple answer would be that a good training program effectively prepares a person to fulfill his or her calling as an intercultural servant of Christ. But how can this effectiveness be measured, that is, what makes an intercultural worker effective?

Although a different set of criteria may need to be developed, there are certain qualities and skills that a trainer must consider in order to answer those questions. What are they?

1 Intercultural workers of Christ must be mature Christians, humble and adaptable, willing servants, flexible and teachable.

2. They must be good team players, able to do personal evangelism, to teach, and to practice sound pastoral care with new believers.
3. Intercultural workers should be committed to learning the language and culture of the target people, and willing to accept and learn from nationals.
4. They must be committed to doing Christ's will. They need to learn to cope with stress, and know how to strengthen themselves spiritually.
5. They should be people who have faith, who know how to pray and to rely on God alone. They are prepared for setbacks, disappointments and unanticipated events that may occur in the mission field.
6. Intercultural servants must also know how to relax and laugh, and are careful to maintain physical fitness through appropriate recreational activities.
7. They should also know how to set up a house in their adopted culture that will be truly home for their family, yet also a place where the nationals will feel comfortable when visiting.

The training described here provides instructions appropriate to the different situations missionaries will face in the place of service.[34]

The Selection Process at ACM

The missionary candidate is prayerfully chosen through a rigorous process of selection. A committee then carefully evaluates the candidate based on the kind of characteristics needed in the field. A review of an objective selection process indicates that there are some consequential elements to be considered in the screening of candidates. For instance, they are to be considered according to their spiritual maturity. Missionaries must be committed Christians with a personal and growing relationship with God. They must have a strong desire for others to come to know Christ. This element is necessary to confirm his or her call. They need a conviction that being a missionary is God's will and call for them.[35]

Their academic records and intellectual ability need to be considered. A degree is not an essential requirement for an intercultural worker, but the ability to learn is definitely essential. Likewise, interpersonal skills and physical and mental health are also crucial in the selection. The candidates may have to face heavy physical, emotional, and spiritual pressures in the future, and may do so in an isolated situation.

Theological and doctrinal beliefs and experience in Christian service are also observed. Since the candidates are to be trained to serve in other cultures and with Christians from different traditions, they must know and accept that there are also Christians from other traditions. Consequently, even though they hold firm theological and doctrinal commitments, they should not impose their position on others.

Conclusion

I have addressed the importance of embracing intercultural training as a natural discipline and responsibility of the Church. And I have concluded that Christian organizations should assume this responsibility and take this discipline as an active part of the ministry of the Church. Training therefore should be practiced by all Christian organizations, not only at the grassroot but also at the top level of leadership. The fact that early 21st century Christian organizations have grown extensively pinpoints the need to revise and adjust their vast structures to the new realities of world evangelization.

I have also suggested new definitions of missiology that may serve in the discipline of intercultural training. I do hope that these ideas will contribute to underlining the need to dedicate larger denominational and cooperative efforts to training intercultural workers. I suggested ACM as a model of effective intercultural training. In addition, I recommended that Southern Hemisphere trainers could benefit greatly by learning from current intercultural structures or networks already operating in several regions of the world.

Furthermore, I intended to initiate a dialogue that may convey academic and professional insights to the intercultural training discipline as we head towards the future in a world dominated by globalization and its cost.

Finally, may I say that there are various ways an individual may arrive at his or her conviction that God is calling him or her to become an intercultural servant. A thorough study of the experiences of men and women in the Scriptures will teach us that God dealt with each one differently. Abraham heard God speaking to him (Genesis 12:1). Moses saw a burning bush (Exodus 3:2), Isaiah saw a vision (Isaiah 6:1), Amos had a growing inner conviction (Amos 3:8), and Paul had a vision (Acts 16:9). Some were guided by unusual or supernatural events. Others were convinced through prayer, the reading of the Word, the advice of others or through circumstances, that the Holy Spirit was guiding them to a particular area of Christian service.

There is no such thing as a pattern for guidance. Hence, it may not be necessary for God to speak to somebody in a spectacular way. However, it is important that the guidance of the Holy Spirit be clear and the person be certain that this assignment is God's will for his or her life. Intercultural servants will face many difficulties and even discouragement; yet, if they are convinced that they are in the right place, it will help them to strengthen their hearts.

Once an individual reaches the point of full conviction that the Lord has called him or her to be an intercultural servant, the next step is to receive the confirmation of the church and then the proper training for his or her mission assignment. Here is where effective training can make a tremendous difference in the life and ministry of a missionary. The church or Christian organization must then pay close attention to establishing a program that properly responds to the needs of the intercultural worker.

Miguel Alvarez, D.Min. (Ashland Theological Seminary), is a missionary from Honduras serving as Vice President of the Asian Center for Missions and Adjunct Professor of Intercultural Studies at Regent University. He is also Chancellor and former President of the Asian Seminary of Christian Ministries in Manila, Philippines. Dr. Alvarez is an Ordained Bishop with the Church of God (Cleveland, TN), and has served in several capacities within his denomination as youth leader, pastor, missionary and educator. He is a specialist in Intercultural Studies (Cross-Cultural Missions) and Missionary Training. Dr. Alvarez is also a consultant of Church Growth and Cell Church Development.

NOTES

1 Winters, Roberta H. *Once More Around Jericho* (Pasadena, CA: William Carey Library, 1978) p.66.
2 In an abstract from of his plenary presentation at the Asia Missions Congress II, Pattaya, Thailand, in September 29–October 3 1997, Titus Loong addresses issues related to the expansion of missionary training and mission education. See Titus Loong, "Equipping the Next Generation of Missionaries," *Asian Mission* 1 (July 1998), pp. 7–10 (9).
3 On the issue of denominational management as it relates to missionary training, see Raja B. Singh, "What Does Missionary Training Stand for?," in *The Management of Indian Missions*, ed. Ebenezer Sunder Raj (Madras, India: India Missions Association, 1992), pp. 185–187.
4 See Samuel Escobar, "The Global Scenario at the Turn of the Century" *Global Missiology for the 21st Century. The Iguassu Dialogue*, ed., William D. Taylor (Grand Rapids: MI: Baker Book House, 2000) pp.25–46.
5 The term "Southern Hemisphere" has been used recently to refer to that part of the Christian movement other than Western Europe, North America, Australia and New Zealand, that are traditionally know as the "Northern Hemisphere" in the world Christian movement.
6 See for instance, Howard L. Foltz, *For Such a Time as This: Strategic Missions Power Shifts for the 21st Century* (Pasadena, CA: William Carey Library, 2000).

7 See Loong, p. 9. See also Robert Ferris and Lois Fuller, "Transforming a Profile into Training Goals," in *Establishing Ministry Training*, ed. Robert Ferris (Pasadena: William Carey Library, 1995), pp. 242.

8 Jongeneel, Jan A. B. "Is Missiology an Academic Discipline?" *Exchange* 1 (1998), pp. 208–211.

9 Jongeneel, p. 210.

10 Triplett, Allan R. *Introduction to Missiology* (Pasadena, CA: William Carey Library, 1987), p. xiii.

11 Triplett, p. xiii.

12 Lewis, Jonathan. "Matching Outcomes with Methods and Contexts" in *Training for Cross-Cultural Ministries*, ed. Jonathan Lewis, Occasional Bulletin of the International Missionary Training Fellowship (Wheaton: WEF, 1998), pp. 1–3. Italics are mine

13 Lewis, "Matching Outcomes," pp. 2–3.

14 Castillo, Met. "Missiological Education: The Missing Element in Mission Strategy," *Asia Pulse* 1 (1973), pp. 2–5.

15 Castillo, p. 5. See also, Neuza Itioka, "Third World Missionary Training: Two Brazilian Models," in *Internationalising Missionary Training: A Global Perspective*, ed. William D. Taylor (Exeter, UK: Paternoster Press, 1991), pp. 111–118. More information on the subject can be found on Sunder Raj, Ebenezer, "The Philosophy and Ethos of OTI Training," in *The Management of Indian Missions*, ed. Sunder Raj, Ebenezer (Bangalore, India: Indian Evangelical Mission, n.d.), pp. 1–2.

16 See some selected readings on this issue in Daniel Rickett and Dotsey Welliver, eds., *Supporting Indigenous Ministries* (Wheaton, IL: Billy Graham Center, 1997).

17 Hopkins, Richard L. "Philosophy of Training" in *Training for Cross-Cultural Ministries*, ed. Jonathan Lewis,

Occasional Bulletin of the International Missionary Training Fellowship (Wheaton:WEF, 1998), pp. 5-6. See also Kohls, L. R. with H. L. Brussow, *Training Know-How for Cross-Cultural and Diversity Trainers* (Duncanville, TX: Adult Learning Systems, 1995), p. 60.

18 Ibid.

19 Ibid.

20 Extensive information about the AD 2000 and Beyond Movement is found at http://www.ad2000.org/.

21 For more information on the World Evangelical Alliance Missions Commission click on http:/www.world evangelical.org/missions.html. More information could be found at http://www.globalmission.org/.

22 In cross-cultural training of denominational leaders at all levels, I also include the top executive officers. Recent surveys reveal that most denominational leaders lack proper understanding of the missionary enterprise, and most of them are not actually committed to cross-cultural involvement. This could be due to the fact that they have not been provided missionary training for their level of capacity. More information on this issue can be found in Paul E. Pierson, "A North American Missionary Trainer Responds to Two-Third World Concerns," in *Internationalising Missionary Training: A Global Perspective*, pp. 193-196.

23 Extensive information on missionary attrition has been documented by John Kayser, "Training and Missionary Attrition," in *Training for Cross-Cultural Ministries*, ed. Jonathan Lewis (Wheaton: WEF, 1997), pp. 6–7. See also William D. Taylor, ed., *Too Valuable To Lose. Exploring the Causes and Cures of Missionary Attrition* (Pasadena, CA: William Carey Library, 1997).

24 Harley, David. *Preparing to Serve Training for Cross-Cultural Mission* (Pasadena, CA: William Carey Library, 1995) p. 137.

25 More information on the ACM story can be found in Miguel Alvarez, "Missionary Training: A Discipline," *Journal of Asian Mission* 2:1 (March 2000) pp. 91–102 (98).

26 On the issue of strategic cooperation see Daniel Rickett, *Building Strategic Relationships: A Practical Guide to Partnering with Non-Western Missions* (Pleasant Hill, CA: Klein Graphics, 2000).

27 The six ACM partner organizations are the Philippine Council of Evangelical Churches (PCEC), the Philippine Missions Association (PMA), the Philippines for Jesus Movement (PJM), the Asian Seminary of Christian Ministries (ASCM), CBN Asia, and the Jesus Is Lord (JIL) Church. ACM was organized in 1995.

28 According to a report of Russell G. Shubin, "in the four brief years since its founding, the Asian Center for Missions (ACM) has become the Philippines' largest agency sending workers outside the Filipino archipelago." See Russell G. Shubin, "The Escalating Filipino Force for the Nations," *Mission Frontiers* 20 (September–December 1998), pp. 38–40.

29 Concerning the effective participation of missionary educators, see the article of Lois McKinney, "New Directions in Missionary Education," *Internationalising Missionary Training: A Global Perspective,* pp. 241–250.

30 Learning through a modular approach in contrast with the traditional model can be effective in the training of new missionaries. See David Harley, *Preparing to Serve Training for Cross-cultural Mission* (Pasadena, CA: William Carey Library, 1995), p. 97. Also see Barbara

H. Burns, *Teaching Cross-Cultural Missions Based on Biblical Theology: Implications of Ephesians for the Brazilian Church* (Deerfield, IL: Trinity Evangelical Divinity School, 1983), p. 73. A thesis for the Doctor of Missiology degree.

31 *Catalog of the Asian Center for Missions* (Manila, 1999), p. 2.

32 For extended information on different partnership models, click on http://www.interdev.org/.

33 I answer this question in my article "So, What Makes and Intercultural Training Program Successful?" at the last chapter of this book.

34 Met Castillo identifies some areas of concern related to the lack of adequate training. The untrained may end up frustrated and defeated. See Met Castillo, "Let's Think Clearly about Missionary Training," *Bridging Peoples* 8:1 (1991), pp. 2-4.

35 See Harley, *Preparing to Serve Training*, pp. 60–66.

2. Getting in Cadence with God: The Goals and Objectives of Missionary Training

GEORGE MITCHELL

"This Gospel of the Kingdom will be preached . . ."[1]

Introduction

The words "goal" and "objective" do not appear in the *King James Bible.* However, the word goal does appear in other Bible versions, but not in the context of missionary training. Let's define these words first from the dictionary and then attempt to narrow our focus to see God's desired purpose in intercultural leadership training. By dictionary definition, these two words are virtually synonymous. According to the *American Heritage Dictionary*, a goal is "a desired purpose, objective or the finish line of a race." An objective is something "uninfluenced by emotions or personal prejudices, something worked toward or striven for, or a goal."[2] We will use some of these definitions at different points within this chapter, and also attempt to draw some analogies to help us see what God's perspective is for His church and the training of intercultural leaders.

Now that we have defined the meaning of goals and objectives, let's try to describe the heart of God and His desired purpose, so that we can get in step with Him. I spent 26 years in the military and understand the criticality of a synchronous response to the cadence call. By definition, cadence is a balanced, rhythmic flow, as of poetry, the beat of movement, as in marching.[3] I was never very adept at marching or keeping in proper cadence with the rest of the group. In fact, the flight leader once declared, "everyone but Mitchell, change step." There are many reasons why everyone within the intercultural leadership training process must be in cadence with our Lord.

Getting out of cadence with God was a major difficulty with the disciples and the early church. For example, it was just before Jesus' death, resurrection and ascension; the disciples had walked with Jesus for quite some time. Luke 9 tells the story. The Lord sent messengers ahead to a Samaritan village to get things ready for His arrival.[4] In other words, the Lord sent angels to prepare the harvest field in Samaria.[5] I believe what we see here in the passage of Luke is a divine opportunity for the disciples to transition into cross-cultural ministers. Unfortunately, they were completely out of cadence with the Lord Jesus. They displayed a wrong spirit. They requested the Lord to call down fire from heaven on that Samaritan village. Jesus therefore rebuked the disciples for their wrong attitude. As we all know, God knew that the time was not yet for intercultural leaders to come on the scene. The disciples were not ready for intercultural leadership ministry until after Pentecost.[6]

Remember the "messengers" mentioned earlier? God knows how to prepare the harvest; our part is to pray! In Luke 10:2, Jesus said, "The harvest is plentiful, but the workers are few. Ask the Lord of the harvest, therefore, to send out workers into his harvest field." Our part is to pray to the Lord of the Harvest regarding who shall go, not if someone should go. Our task then should be listening and heeding the call to go. An older missionary man whom I met in the early 70s in Nova Scotia once told a fellow summer missions friend of mine that "Jesus already told us to go, so why would you pray about whether you should go or not?" The missionary was for the most part correct. The Great Commission was given to those that were disciples and those that would become disciples. "Therefore, go and make disciples of all nations."[7] This is our story and this is the goal and objective of all believers in Jesus Christ.

You might say: "But that was to the disciples at that particular period of time. Not so, let me direct you to John 17:20, when Jesus prayed to the Father just before His arrest, "My prayer is not for them [current disciples] alone. I pray also for those who will believe in me through their message."[8]

Purpose of Goals and Objectives

Establishing a training program without well-defined goals and objectives is like jumping into a taxicab and saying, "take me there!" We need mile markers and a well-drawn up road map to get us to where we are going. Setting goals without a well thought-out plan will get us nowhere. Goals of a successful training program must have subordinated milestones in order to check our progress towards reaching our end.

Let's tread lightly for we must be careful when planning programs for God. God is a God of love and is longsuffering and forbearing when it comes to His children, however, Paul warns us in 1 Corinthians 3:10–15:

> "By the grace God has given me, I laid a foundation as an expert builder, and someone else is building on it. But each one should be careful how he builds. For no one can lay any foundation other than the one already laid, which is Jesus Christ. If any man builds on this foundation using gold, silver, costly stones, wood, hay or straw, his work will be shown for what it is, because the Day will bring it to light. It will be revealed by fire, and the fire will test the quality of each man's work. If what he has built survives, he will receive his reward. If it is burned up, he will suffer loss; he himself will be saved, but only as one escaping through the flames."[9]

We could spend a lot of time on this passage, but I will pick just one phrase from this important building instruction passage, and that is "the fire will test the quality." As a quality team builder by experience, I understand the importance of keeping our purposes and goals simple, understandable, and achievable by all our personnel. There is the expression "if you take care of your people, they will take care of your mission." We would do well to heed this in training our intercultural leaders for the field.

In the Air Force, we had doctrine that we could not stray from. It was clear that we could write new lower level procedures and operating instructions, however, they all had to comply with the the standards and scope of our overall Air Force doctrine. In the same manner, we as church builders, planters, and intercultural leader trainers and program developers, must not err from the holy doctrine, the Scriptures when building a training program.

We have a handbook that explains how we build upon foundations within our intercultural leadership training structure; it's called the Bible! The quality of how we build depends upon our relationship to the master founder, Jesus Christ. Our one and only true guide for viable intercultural training goals and objectives is the inerrant Word of God.

The Purging of Goals

Nothing stays the same. Technology, trends and postmodernity need to be factored into our setting of goals and objectives if we are to stay ahead of the game. David Wilkerson once said, "The new morality is the old immorality!" This is no less true today. The paragraph below is from the book *Toward the 21st Century in Christian Missions*, in a chapter entitled "Developments Affecting the Teaching of Mission."

> "Given the reservoir of knowledge we already have about the world and its people, about teaching and learning, about history, anthropology, the Bible, culture, world religions, theology, linguistics, and communication, together with the vastly increasing amount of new information, we should

> now be in a better position to prepare people for engagement in mission than at any time in the past. But just when we have more experience, knowledge, and tools, the future is more problematic and less predictable. Social, political, economic, and ideological changes in the world are occurring at a breathtaking rate."[10]

A constant re-evaluation of our training goals and objectives, in light of the above, is critical. This reevaluation should be done at least annually or as socio-political or ideological changes occur. We must be flexible and adaptable as program developers.

Furthermore, as we hold up our training goals and objectives in light of the Scriptures, "Let us throw off everything that hinders and the sin that so easily entangles, and let us run with perseverance the race marked out for us. Let us fix our eyes on Jesus, the author and perfecter of our faith."[11] It's the "throwing off" that we need to perfect in our disciples if we are to finish the race set before us. Remember that our definition of a goal was the "finish line of a race." I've always been mindful of Jesus' parable of the wise and foolish builders in Luke 6:48.[12] When we build training program goals and objectives, we are to dig deep. The reason for digging deep before laying a foundation is to clear away the frivolous layers of the ground to ensure a solid foundation upon which to build. It is clearing away of unnecessary layers to establish a firm foundation. We need to throw off, clear away and then run with God's plan, looking unto the master builder for the next step in the building process. There must be a constant purging of our programs to ensure the frivolous layers are cleared away, and that we are on a solid biblical foundation; one that can stand the test of Scriptures.

Objectives of Training

A major objective within a missionary leadership-training program would be to present the best possible model to missionary candidates of what a true missionary should be and do. Issues such as how to handle hardships, when to ask for help, who to ask for help, what's expected of a missionary and many other items should be addressed.

Our candidates deserve our best effort in developing training methodologies. One methodology I call "modeling" has worked well. While serving in the military within diplomatic programs in unusual assignments such as Tel Aviv, Israel and Lagos, Nigeria, I was provided a training called "model office." The trainee experienced the actual stress and complications of managing multiple tasks in a simulated, albeit realistic setting. The pressure to accomplish tasks under real deadlines and combat stress, greatly enhanced our preparedness for the field. In fact, we performed most of the tasks via exercises faced in real scenarios. We required comprehensive background knowledge of all aspects of the profession in order to accomplish the mission under this modeling style of learning.

It would behoove us to adopt such unorthodox training techniques within our missionary training centers. However, the only way this methodology will work is to use missionary "patterns." To be effective, we must have men and women of God who have the experience and background and are able-bodied veteran "disciplers" for young missionary candidates to emulate.

Therefore, as those who are to make disciples, seasoned veterans of Foreign Service must be living the abundant Christian life; a life that's been disciplined by the Holy Spirit and set apart by God. Hence, the pillar of all successful training programs is the trainer himself. Dr. Miguel Alvarez, professor of Intercultural Studies at Regent University states, "You *are* the mission's seminar!"[13] We can't separate the program from the program developer or trainer.

Paul charged Timothy (2 Timothy 3:10–14) by these words: "You, however, know all about my teaching, my way of life, my purpose, faith, patience, love, endurance." Note that Paul didn't say you know all about my teaching *on* all these subjects. Paul was talking about himself! He went on to drive home his point to Timothy in verse 14, "But as for you, continue in what you have learned and have become convinced of, because you know those from whom you learned it, and how from infancy you have known the holy Scriptures, which are able to make you wise for salvation through faith in Christ Jesus."[14] Timothy was Paul's son in the faith (1 Timothy 1:2). He knew that it was Paul that gave his faith away to him and that by way of holistic knowledge, life, goals and deed (fruit), he was made a disciple in good standing. Are you seeing the picture? It was once said that when you disciple someone, you make them exactly what you are.

In contrast, Jesus described the worst scenario of those that proselyte in intercultural arenas and make a mess of lives, when speaking to the Pharisees, "Woe to you, teachers of the law and Pharisees, you hypocrites! You travel over land and sea [intercultural] to win a single convert, and when he becomes one, you make him twice as much a son of hell as you are."[15] We have to ensure our trainers of intercultural leaders, who offer themselves to be "models" or "patterns" within the scope of missionary training, are strongly established in the faith, are patient teachers, and most importantly have a Holy Spirit-filled capacity to "fill up that which is lacking"[16] in our missionary candidates, before allowing them to make replicas (disciples) of themselves!

Practical Issues for Trainers

When I was getting ready to go to Nigeria as a diplomat within the defense structure of the U.S. Embassy in Lagos, I was a full-time student at a college in the District of Columbia. The school had an office that was supposed to process our passports and visas in order to facilitate a smooth entry into Nigeria. Because of my intense study and preparations, I thought nothing of looking at my passport to ensure the visa was stamped there when they called me to pick up the passport. Unfortunately, I found out that I didn't have the visa stamp for Nigeria after I arrived at Muhrtahla Muhammed International Airport in Lagos. My wife and I were detained and questioned and endured 100 plus degree Fahrenheit temperatures for four hours. Practical preparation plays a significant role when setting objectives for a good intercultural training program.

More importantly, in light of missionary work in some restricted countries, one could find himself in the middle of a religious difficulty or even a coup d'état. Tentmaker Levi Keidel found himself in a Muslim fundamentalist prison for preaching the Gospel. In his book *Conflict on Connection: Interpersonal Relationships in Cross-Cultural Settings*, he asked, "What things were in place prior to your departure that proved very important?" His answer was, "First, having a business manager [he was a tentmaker] in the States. The role of our business manager, Bob, was primarily secular. He gave our business a legitimate identity. He facilitated its function and development. He lived in Washington, D.C., where he could build bridges to key persons in government."

Some other good recommendations in his book are:

1) If in a restricted country, make sure you're not identified as an evangelist or church planter. That country's state department will wonder how you got in if it is restricted to missionaries.
2) Have someone intercede on your behalf with a congressional representative.
3) Have a large network of people to pray for you and to participate in a letter-writing campaign.
4) Have an encrypted email messaging system if possible. In other words what they did was use a program in the States that unscrambled his messages while he was in jail. (Unbelievable! They let Keidel send email, but anything's possible).[17]

Although Keidel was a tentmaker in a Muslim area, there is good advice for all future missionaries in his book. Paul the Apostle was aware of the benefit of using his Roman citizenship (Acts 22:25) as a practical measure to get him out of trouble. A lot could be done with our secular background. God encourages us to be innovative when preparing leaders for the mission field.

Security is another issue. If security isn't being seriously discussed with our intercultural leadership students, it most certainly should be. A good recommendation would be to get information from the U.S. State Department training facility in Arlington, Virginia. For those of you who are not from the United States, you should get security information for your intercultural leadership students. You can for security updates from your respective embassy or consulate or through the Internet. An example of what can happen: While working in the U.S. Embassy in Tel Aviv, Israel, our office had to facilitate the emergency medical evacuation of a major's little girl out of the country. In accordance with State Department policy, U.S. military personnel are required to contact the U.S. Embassy prior to traveling to Israel. This U.S. Air Force major found out the hard way, that it would have been a good idea to comply with this policy. He did not contact the embassy, either out of ignorance or forgetfulness. He came to Israel looking for Lazarus' tomb in Bethany. Little did he know that the area of the tomb was in East Jerusalem, a strongly Muslim fundamentalist area that wasn't safe for travel at that time. After driving around the neighborhood several times, this Air Force Major received a lot of attention by someone with criminal intentions. The perpetrator threw a large piece of a cinder block through the windshield of his car. His daughter later required jaw reconstruction and wiring, and a long healing period. We need to make security plans with loved ones and sending churches or agencies.

The Trend of Change—A Time for Innovation

Dr. Miguel Alvarez, stated that the training goals of intercultural leaders will, and very well should, change with the times. He envisioned sending missionaries using Two-Third World country resources. The age of the Oral Roberts and Billy Grahams is possibly over; God will use the older sending countries (Western countries) to train up a remnant within the grassroots of the Third World.[18] Just because God did it one way a century ago, it doesn't mean that is how He will work today.

God will have to help us accomplish the Great Commission in the face of this new age of globalization. If we pray, He will indeed renew our minds and show us His will in this area. We must completely empty ourselves of all preconceived teachings (not necessarily doctrines) that will do us no good on the mission field. If ever we need to be scripturally open-minded it is in intercultural leadership studies. The missionary will have to adjust his way of thinking if he or she is being called to an urban city ministry. Things don't stay the same. In 1800, 2.5% were city dwellers (21 million); in 2000, 51% were city dwellers (3.3 billion), worldwide.[19]

Consider the demographics of the world when preparing for missionary work. One-third of the world is under age 15; 85% of these young people live in the Two-Thirds World. And, 55% of the Two-Thirds World is under 20 years of age.[20] Today, 11% of all Americans are immigrants, totaling 3 million people.[21] These statistics cause us to re-think our traditional roles in training intercultural leaders. And, our intercultural designates will be dealing with a new trend. "By the year 2000 there were more than 150,000 non-North American, non-European evangelical missionaries originating from overseas churches!"[22] In fact, undoubtedly some of these missionaries have come to the United States to minister to the 11% of immigrants mentioned above.

The leaders of tomorrow must be the humble learners of today. How long have they sat at the feet of Jesus? "The learner role takes time, time taken to learn another culture is ministry. And, beware of: Those who teach before being taught; those who fail to earn the right to be heard by key people."[23]

Goals and Objectives: Holistic Intercultural Ministries

Not much has been said about developing the spiritual gifts of intercultural leaders as a part of their initial training. However, the divine gifts of the Holy Spirit that God provided to the Body of Christ are critical to the success of ministry and personal victory in the cross-cultural arena. It is amazing that so many of our spiritual trainees have a general call and some idea about their spiritual gifting(s), but some need encouragement to stir up their spiritual gifts, using them to bless many in the Body of Christ both in the local church and abroad.

Furthermore, if our goal and objective is to come up with a "new" plan of an educational methodology, we miss the emphasis of scriptures regarding the making of disciples. The writer of this chapter could not find or create a better educational or methodological approach than the holistic discipleship model. Theresa Roco Lua, in her article "Discipleship Ministry Among Filipino Urban Poor Adults in Metro Manila," in the *Journal of Asian Mission (JAM)*, stated:

> "The goal of discipleship is conformity to Christ. Discipleship is the lifelong process of growing into Christlikeness. Jesus is the model of what a disciple should be. The disciple should grow as Jesus did."

And, "Jesus grew holistically—physically, mentally, spiritually and socially (Luke 2:42)."[24]

We have models (examples) of Jesus and His approach to ministry. There was a man lame from birth at the temple gate called Beautiful in Jerusalem. When he saw Peter and John, he immediately begged for money. Peter looked straight at him and Peter told the man "Look at us!" The man expected to receive money from Peter and John. Then in verse 8 Peter said, "Silver or gold I do not have, but what I have I give you. In the name of Jesus Christ of Nazareth, walk."[25] Of course, he walked, leaped and praised God. Why? Because he was ministered holistically! The man had need of sustenance for the body, hence the request for money, however, God through Peter recognized the greater need that kept this man dependent upon others through his whole life. If Peter simply worked with this man along social lines alone, for example, providing for his lowly status as a beggar, this would have meant an ongoing dependency on man. In another example, there was a lame man who told Jesus, "I have no one to help me into the pool." Jesus healed this man's body and he picked up his mat and walked. It wasn't until later in the passage that Jesus met this healed lame man and at that other encounter ministered to his spiritual life.[26]

Outcomes of Our Goals and Objectives

What should we reasonably expect from our missionary protégés upon completion of our Intercultural Leadership Training programs? The sign of a good training program in the military was an airman, soldier, coast guardsman, sailor or marine who could work autonomously without minute-by-minute supervision, and perform at the proficient level. God calls missionaries to the mission field.The church helps them grow and develops them spiritually. We equip them from a program developer and trainer perspective.

Let us be careful that we set goals and objectives for such a training program only through much prayer and wisdom from above.What should be the results of our goals and objectives? What should a trained missionary be able to do and be?

This recommendation will be unpopular; however, every student of intercultural leadership should be required to submit a paper on the Christian—Muslim (or Hindu, or other people group) relations.This paper would document the student's research on the current dialogue within the receiving country. Additionally, each student should produce a paper on his goals, including short- and long-range objectives (time lines), that will guide him to the fulfillment of his goal—the evangelization of the unreached people group to which he has been called. Aid the students in putting their vision down on paper and praying over it.

This comprehensive missions plan will also include how they will organize for a successful mission, using some of the tips mentioned in this chapter as well as others. We should also compile a list of other agencies and fellow missionaries (not necessarily from the same denomination), and seek to engender other cooperative relationships for the purpose of coordinating efforts. This is scriptural in view of Paul's statement to not build on another's work, but to preach to those who have not heard.[27] How many times do we hear of strife on the mission field due to uncooperative relationships and hard feelings? One recent statistic underlines this problem: The average number for early attrition from the mission field, of both Old and New Sending Countries for the reason of "problems with peers," was 5.9%. The same study showed "disagreement with agency" as 4.7%.[28] When added together, these figures show that 10.6% of all missionaries within the study are returning early from the mission field due to uncooperative relationships. To put it into perspective, for every 100 missionaries sent from both Old and New Sending Countries, almost 11 return for uncooperative relationships. Let's work on this *before* we send missionary designates to the field. A wrong ministerial attitude might be to blame.

In addition to cooperative relationships, we must also address our approach to ministry in the cross-cultural setting. In *Conflict or Connection*, Levi Keidel tells of his imprisonment and what helped his team in their very difficult cross-cultural setting among a Muslim fundamentalist people group. Here are some important prerequisites required prior to joining their missionary team:

1) At least five years in the Christian faith;
2) A love for Muslims;
3) A willingness to suffer;
4) A willingness to learn;
5) Submission to the team leader's authority.

The following is worth quoting in its entirety:

> "We aren't here to convert Muslims to Christianity," Tim explained. "We are here to persuade Muslims to become followers of Jesus Christ. A Muslim who decides to follow Christ does not need to extract himself from his Muslim culture

> or his community. In fact, we encourage converts to continue those Muslim traditions which are not incompatible with the Bible. We as team members try to identify with the culture here by adopting these customs ourselves; they can serve to deepen our own spirituality. Our wives dress like Muslim women; that clearly sets us apart from the 30,000 or so Americans here. We have the challenge of modeling for them what we understand a Muslim believer should look like."[29]

It may sound like radical Christianity, but these missionaries are doing what Paul said to the Corinthian church, "To the weak I became weak, to win the weak. I have become all things to all men so that by all possible means I might save some."[30]

"In God's work everything depends upon the kind of worker sent out and the kind of convert produced. On the part of the convert, a real Holy Spirit new birth is vital to his or her relationship with God. On the part of the worker, besides personal holiness and endowment for service, it is essential that he has an experimental [I believe Watchman probably meant "experiential"] knowledge of the meaning of committal to God and faith in His sovereign Providence; otherwise, no matter how scriptural the methods employed, the result will be emptiness and defeat."[31]

Please note the contrast between worldly Christians and the Apostles in 1 Corinthians 4:8–13 (*NIV*) on page 61. Here lie the end results of our goals and objectives of a missionary. Once called by God, Paul made the ultimate commitment to be a true apostle of the faith. In light of Paul's honest confession of his life, let's not pity him, for he knew that his crown of glory was not attainable in this earth. We would have to indict the "claim it—frame it" (the positive confession) attitude because it would mean that Paul the Apostle was a failure based on his negative confession. Those that would aspire to greatness and success in biblical terms must come to grip with this powerful lesson.

Although we don't wish such a lifestyle on our missionaries, we would do well to post this lesson on every reading board in our intercultural leadership training centers and churches, along with the beautiful posters we show our congregations during missionary emphasis periods. In my opinion, we are in error by portraying a poor and grossly inaccurate philosophy and theology of missionary work.

We hope that the results of our sending workers into the ripe harvest fields of the world in order to fulfill the Great Commission would be pleasing to the Lord!

The Enemies of Goals and Objectives

Since I am an American, I will pick on my own culture. There are many reasons for the decline of the church in the United States. One of the indictments from God is due to millions of abortions annually. Another, our rejection of God and worship of idols made with hands. Lastly, the failure of the American church in its devotion to God; it has prioritized its own pleasures ahead of the fulfillment of the Great Commission.

American missionary candidates will have to learn to recognize apathy and lukewarmness that unfortunately has seeped into the church, and fight them as David did the bear and the lion. Paul told Timothy about the end times, which he calls "terrible." Here are a few of the indictments marked out by Paul: Lovers of themselves, lovers of money, ungrateful, unholy, without love, lovers of pleasure rather than lovers of God—having a form of godliness but denying its power.[32] This is not the entire list, but a good sampling of the ones that bear mentioning in light of Paul's emphasis regarding the latter days of the Body of Christ. Take note, that there is a self-seeking, pleasure-driven underlying theme throughout this Scripture. But, do we understand that Paul is not speaking to the unsaved necessarily, but also to the church? Are we guilty as believers of building bigger barns and hoarding the produce for ourselves? Let's open the door to our own heart and ask the Holy Spirit to help us answer this question. We must realize that we fight this end time spirit of selfishness in many arenas. We fight it when attempting to raise money, gather other practical support and even when planting churches.

Furthermore, statistics tell us that much of what Paul and James were saying is what God is saying to all His churches today! Most of us remember what happened to Praise the Lord Ministries (PTL) and Jim Baker in the 70s.[33] There are various reasons for the downfall of PTL, but I believe the most important lesson that came out of it, was that God is telling his children He is about the building of His Kingdom and not the building of pleasures to be enjoyed. How must God feel when we spend so much on pleasures while His precious mission fields are white unto harvest and yet we sit by and aren't crying out to Him in prayer and not monetarily supporting the reaping of the harvest for Him!

God is speaking and we need to listen! The American church must get out of its theme park mentality and take up its cross and follow Him, before she falls into apostasy.

David Bosch, a professor of missiology, stated "Out of compassion flows passion—in the original sense of the word, which means suffering and martyrdom. Mission is not a triumphalist enterprise. It is by definition done in weakness."[34] God's desired purpose (goals/objective) is to see His harvest reaped!

We need to teach our intercultural leaders about the great sacrifice both they and their students will endure for the Cross of Christ! These issues are brought up not to trouble the missionary candidates, but to mentally prepare them for the reality of end times—our goal is the fullness of the stature of Christ!

The Goal of Cooperation

In order to reach our goals and objectives, we must understand that we will most likely be working alongside many cross-cultural missionaries from other nations. Here is a reminder from Levi Keidel.

> "The American leader tends to make decisions independently, and expects his subordinates to comply without raising too many questions. Koreans are probably more hierarchical (top-down authoritarian) than Americans. A Briton would be much more diplomatic in exercising her authority. A European would be inclined to consult with her subordinates towards reaching a leadership decision. Asians, especially Chinese, are more diplomatic than Europeans; hence more time is required to reach consensus. Australians

> have an anti-authoritarian stripe that tends to cut leaders down to size if they try to throw their weight around."[35]

We would do well to teach this to our intercultural leadership students if we want them to be successful in a multicultural team effort.

Thank God that we have His love and we understand the biblical concepts of considering others as more important than ourselves and living at peace with one another. However, we are still humans and our patience, love and adaptability to other cultures and leadership styles will indeed be tested. We need to teach sensitivity and again use good examples of mission field scenarios to prepare them for the inevitable.

Conclusion

We can't run intercultural leadership training programs as a normal business and expect results. I do not advocate a managerial missiological approach; however, God created us with a brain, and we were created in His image and likeness.[36] We are creative beings and we possess the ability to think and plan ahead, with the leading of the Holy Spirit. Otherwise, we would be mindless puppets, manipulated by an imperial, impersonal god.

We are strange creatures. God indeed must have a sense of humor in choosing flawed humans to accomplish such great tasks. Someone once said: "God does not so much desire our capability as He does our availability." The Apostle James tells us that we are to show our faith by our works, and our faith plus our actions justify us.[37]

Therefore, we need to move forward and be proactive in planning the very best intercultural leadership training programs. God grants wisdom; however, wisdom not applied is wisdom denied. We need to get off dead center and move out for God. As an illustration, it is very difficult to steer a parked automobile. You have to start the automobile moving before you can start steering it in the right direction.[38] Some of us are afraid to take a step for God for fear of failure. God wants you to move out! Leave the comfort zones of status quo! Don't do it the way it has already been done. Be innovative, do a new thing for God. Do the best you can! Once you know God wants you to accomplish a great thing for Him, take the first step, and then the second—plan. The Lord orders the steps of a good man [or woman].[39] Endure hardness as a good soldier.[40] Refuse to be denied! Be tenacious! Take hold of God's plan for you with passion. God's purpose when training intercultural leaders is for us to first give ourselves to Him and, then, ask for wisdom and understanding in the knowledge of Him. The battle is the Lord's.[41]

> "He calls His own sheep by name and leads them out [He wants us moving]. When He has brought out all His own, He goes on ahead of them, and His sheep follows Him because they know His voice."[42]

In conclusion, let's never forget what our true goal and objective is, the salvation of souls, for:

> "'Everyone who calls on the name of the Lord will be saved.' How, then, can they call on the one

they have not believed in? And how can they believe in the one of whom they have not heard? And how can they hear without someone preaching to them? And how can they preach unless they are sent? As it is written, 'How beautiful are the feet of those who bring good news!'"[43]

Let's roll![44]

George Mitchell (M. Div. Student) retired from the U.S. Air Force after 26 years. He served four years in Italy in NATO, three years in Israel and two years in Nigeria as a military diplomat. Prior to his military career, he was actively involved in inner city evangelization within the Jesus Movement in the early 1970s. He is strategically placed in the U.S. government for such a time as this.

APPENDIX

Contrast Between Worldly Christians and the Apostles

Worldly Christians	Scripture verse from 1 Cor. 4:8–13	The Apostles	Scripture verse
Kings — Preeminence	Verse 8	Spectacles— Displayed at end of procession	Verse 9
(Blessed) Assumed	Verses 8–13	Condemned to die in the arena	Verse 9
Wise (In the world)	Verse 10	Fools for Christ weak (Strong in Christ)	Verse 10
Strong (Weak in Christ)	Verse 10	Dishonored (by men)	Verse 10
Honored (by men)	Verse 10	Hungry and thirsty	Verse 10
(Full and fed) Assumed	Verses 8–13	In rags Homeless	Verse 11
Rich—Have All they Want	Verse 8	Scum, refuse, Brutally	Verse 11
(Favored by man) Assumed	Verse 8–13	Mistreated by man	Verses 11, 13

Extracted from 1 Corinthians 4:8–13.[45]

NOTES

1. This is a partial quote of Matthew 24:14 *NIV*, "And this gospel of the kingdom will be preached in the whole world as a testimony to all nations, and then the end will come."
2. *The American Heritage Dictionary* (2001), s.v. "goal" and "objective."
3. *The American Heritage Dictionary* (2001), s.v. "cadence."
4. Luke 9:51–46 *NIV*.
5. Let's look at the title "messengers." In Greek, it is *aggelos*, which is an angel.
6. Acts 2:1–4 *NIV*.
7. Matthew 28:19 *NIV*
8. John 17:20 *NIV*
9. 1 Corinthians 3:15 *NIV*
10. Phillips, James J., and Robert T. Coote, eds. *Toward the Twenty-First Century in Christian Mission: Essays in Honor of Gerald H. Anderson*. (Grand Rapids, MI: Eerdmans, 1993). p. 273.
11. Hebrews 12:2 *NIV*.
12. Luke 6:48 *NIV*.
13. Miguel Alvarez is Adjunct Professor of Intercultural Studies at Regent University. The statement was made while teaching the Intercultural Leadership Training course.
14. 2 Timothy 3:10–14 *NIV*.
15. Matthew 23:15 *NIV*.
16. 1 Thessalonians 3:10 *NIV*.

17 Keidel, Levi O., *Conflict or Connection: Interpersonal Relationships in Cross-Cultural Settings.* (Chicago, Illinois: Evangelical Missions Information Service, 1996), p. 78.
18 Miguel Alvarez, lecture to an Intercultural Leadership Training Class at Regent University.
19 Steffen, Tom A., Business as Usual in the Missions Enterprise? (La Habra, CA: Center for Organizational & Ministry Development, 1999), p. 23.
20 Ibid, pp. 23–24.
21 "Lou Dobbs Money Line," CNN. March 10, 2003, 6 p.m.
22 McClung, L. Grant. *Globalbeliever.com* (Cleveland, Tennessee: Pathway Press, 2000) p. 279.
23 Steffen, p. 83.
24 Lua, Theresa Roco. "Developing a Holistic and Contextualized Discipleship Ministry Among Filipino Urban Poor Adults in Metro Manila," in *Journal of Asian Mission 2:1* (March 2000): 46–47.
25 Acts 3:1–8 *NIV.*
26 John 5:1–9 *NIV.*
27 Romans 15:20 *NIV.*
28 Taylor, William D. et al. *Too Valuable to Lose: Exploring the Causes of Missionary Attrition* (Pasadena, California: William Carey Library, 1997). p. 92.
29 Keidel, p. 68.
30 1 Corinthians 9:22 *NIV.*
31 Nee, Watchman. *The Normal Christian Church Life.* (Colorado Springs, CO: International Students Press, 1969). p. 12.
32 2 Timothy 3:1–6 *NIV.*

33 First, I must preclude any comment about Jim Baker, with saying that our job is and always has been one of restoration.The author of this chapter, although troubled by the amount of money placed into a Christian theme park, took part in giving to PTL and its ministry at that time.

34 James and Coote, p. 182.

35 Keidel, p. 22.

36 Genesis 1:26 *NIV.*

37 James 2:18, 24 *NIV.*

38 McClung, Grant. Globalbeliever.com (Cleveland, Tennessee: Pathway Press, 2000) p. 38.

39 Psalm 37:23 *NIV.*

40 2 Timothy 2:3 *NIV.*

41 1 Samuel 17:49 *NIV.*

42 John 10:3–4 *NIV.*

43 Romans 10:15 *NIV.*

44 The late Todd Beamer made the statement on the plane that was hijacked by 9/11 terrorists. He was heard voicing these last words to the other passengers encouraging them to retake control of the plane. It ultimately crashed near Pittsburgh, killing everyone aboard. Beamer and his fellow passengers' courage most definitely saved lives in the Pentagon and the White House, which were the probable targets.

45 This extraction aims to show the contrast between the lifestyle of worldly Christians and that of the Apostles (from Paul the Apostle's perspective), in order to portray to prospective missionary candidates the difficulties of their commitment.

3. Going Therefore to All People Groups: Setting up the Biblical Foundation

CHRISTINA J. BROOKS

"For God so loved the world, that He gave His only begotten Son, that whosoever believeth in Him should not perish, but have everlasting life."[1]

Introduction

Jesus spoke these words to His disciples before He ascended to heaven,

> "All authority has been given unto Me in heaven and on earth. *Go* therefore and make disciples of *all nations* baptizing them in the name of the Father and the Son and the Holy Spirit, *teaching*

> *them* to observe all that *I commanded you*; and lo, I am with you always, even to the end of the age."

The Great Commission is still in effect today, and we must do our part to help bring it about. We are called to go into all nations, this necessitates exposing ourselves to other peoples and other cultures. We are blessed to be alive at this time when technology has advanced at such a rapid rate; it has greatly changed the face of missions. As we are now more advanced technologically and more able to cross geographical and national boundaries with ease and escalating frequency, we may forget that it is the cultural barriers which are the most formidable. We have gotten ahead of ourselves in the field of technology, but unfortunately along the way we neglected our communication skills. This is one of the characteristics of modern civilization. However, we are becoming aware that cross-cultural communication, as in training intercultural leaders, is essential for this new level of mission that the Lord is ushering us into. God is calling for unity in the body of Christ, and we can surely cover a lot more ground by working together—not working harder but working smarter.

Culture is a complex concept; a whole made up of numerous parts. These include linguistic, national, racial, political, social, as well as other elements interacting with each other to create various effects. Louis Luzbetak writes:

> "Culture is a design for living. It is a plan according to which society adapts itself to its physical,

> social environment. A plan for coping with physical environment would include such matters as food production and all technological knowledge and skill. Political systems, kinships and family organization, and law are examples of social adaptation, a plan according to which one is to interact with his fellows. Man copes with this environment through knowledge, art, magic, science, philosophy, and religion. Cultures are but different answers to essentially the same human problems."[2]

Culture is the shared assumptions, values, and beliefs of a group. The combination of these results in characteristic behaviors. Intercultural leadership training will empower the person called by God to be a missionary, by providing the necessary training and instruction in a cross-cultural setting. This instruction includes spiritual drills designed to improve proficiency in performing the missiological task. This training is driven to form proper intercultural skills, behavior, spiritual habits and mental attitudes.

In this chapter, I would like to establish a biblical basis for training intercultural leadership. In order for us to understand the future role of missionaries and the process of training intercultural leaders we must first revisit our biblical examples. The biblical missionaries sent out to teach and mobilize others to spread the Gospel included Jonah; John (3:2, 3); the early church (Acts 8:4); some from Cyrene (Acts 11:20); Paul and Barnabas (Acts 13:1-4); Peter (Acts 15-7); Apollos (Acts 18:24); and, Noah (2 Peter 2:5). We will start in the Old Testament with God's promise to Abram.

God's Chosen Men

Abraham

Christian mission can be understood through the promise God made to Abram, who upon the fulfillment of God's commission became Abraham. Genesis 12:1–4 (*King James Version*) states the main points of God's redemptive plan for the whole of mankind.

> "Now the LORD had said unto Abram, Get thee out of thy country, and from thy kindred, and from thy father's house, unto a land that I will shew thee: And I will make of thee a great nation, and I will bless thee, and make thy name great; and thou shalt be a blessing: And I will bless them that bless thee, and curse him that curseth thee: and in thee shall all families of the earth be blessed. So Abram departed, as the LORD had spoken unto him; and Lot went with him: and Abram was seventy and five years old when he departed out of Ha'ran."

God singled Abram out from among his fellow-idolaters, that he might reserve a people for Himself, among whom His true worship will be done till the coming of Christ. From henceforward Abram and his seed are almost the only subject of the history in the Bible. Abram was tested to see whether he loved God more than all, and whether he could willingly leave all to go with God. Those who leave their sins, and turn to God, will be unspeakable gainers by the choice to follow Him. The command God gave to Abram is much the same as the Gospel call, for natural affection must give way to Divine grace. Sin, and all the occasions of it, must be forsaken, particularly associating with bad company. In Genesis 12:1–4 are some of God's many great and precious promises. All God's precepts are attended with promises to the obedient.

1) "I will make of thee a great nation." When God took Abram from his own people, he promised to make him the head of another people.
2) "I will bless thee." Obedient believers shall be sure to inherit the blessing.
3) "I will make thy name great." The name of obedient believers shall certainly be made great.
4) "Thou shalt be a blessing." Good men are the blessings of their country.
5) "I will bless them that bless thee, and curse him that curseth thee." God will take care that none lose because of any service done for His people.

God chose one man and his family, so that through them, He might bless all the families of the earth. We are by faith the seeds of Abraham, and the families of the earth will be blessed only if we go to them with the Gospel. God's promise to Abraham receives an intermediate or Gospel fulfillment in Christ Jesus. Jesus Christ, our Lord and Savior, is the greatest missionary.

The Lord's Example

One major thrust of Jesus' ministry while walking among men was teaching. Jesus understood the methodology of teaching, even in intercultural situations. He taught both Jews and Gentiles. He had strategy and tactics, as well as objectives and means for attaining them. Without strategy, tactics have no goal; without tactics, strategy has no means of attainment.[3] Jesus' objective was to do the will of His Father.

> "Then said Jesus unto them, 'When ye have lifted up the Son of Man, then shall ye know that I am He, and that I do nothing of Myself; but as My Father hath *taught* Me, I speak these things.'"
>
> John 8:28 (*KJV*)

Jesus Christ—Son of God, Son of Man is our example. The word "teach" is used over one hundred times in the Bible. John 6:45 reads,

> "It is written in the prophets, and they shall be all *taught* of God. Every man therefore that hath heard, and hath learned of the Father, cometh unto me."

Jesus assured us that he would not leave us helpless; He left us with a comforter, a friend and most of all a *teacher*.

> "For the Holy Ghost shall *teach* you in the same hour what ye ought to say."
>
> Luke 12:12 (*KJV*)

> "But the Comforter, which is the Holy Ghost, whom the Father will send in my name, he shall *teach* you all things, and bring all things to your remembrance, whatsoever I have said unto you."
>
> John 14:26 (*KJV*)

In Matthew 5:18–19 (*KJV*), Jesus reminds us of our commission,

> "For verily I say unto you, till heaven and earth pass, one jot or one tittle shall in no wise pass from the law, till all be fulfilled. Whosoever therefore shall break one of these least commandments, and shall teach men so, he shall be called the least in the kingdom of heaven: but whosoever shall do and teach them, the same shall be called great in the kingdom of heaven."

Scripture also notes Jesus' interest in teaching people and how profound his teachings where.

> "The same came to Jesus by night, and said unto him, 'Rabbi, we know that thou art a *teacher* come from God: for no man can do these miracles that thou doest, except God be with him.'"
>
> John 3:2 (*KJV*)

Note here, the order in which the steps of Jesus were written. Before Jesus healed anyone or preached, he taught. I believe this is significant.

> "And Jesus went about all Galilee, *teaching* in their synagogues, and preaching the gospel of the kingdom, and healing all manner of sickness and all manner of disease among the people."
>
> Matthew 4:23 (*KJV*)

Summary

As far as Christians are concerned, the issue of education must be addressed from the divine revelation of the Word of God. The New Testament, which most clearly teaches the divine inspiration of Scripture, also clearly teaches the Bible's role in education.

> "All Scripture is given by inspiration of God, and is profitable for doctrine, for reproof, for correction, for instruction in righteousness: That the man [or woman] of God may be perfect, throughly furnished for unto all good works."
>
> 2 Timothy 3:16–17 (*KJV*)

Paul is concerned not only with imparting knowledge about the Bible or with academic education or the formation of character and spiritual qualities, but also with training which covers all aspects of life and thoroughly equips the Christian "for every good work." If full-time service in the church or in missions is to be worthwhile, the Bible is necessary in preparation for carrying out that service; not only as biblical content, but also biblical instruction on how that content is to be communicated.[4] That is why it is so important that we take our gift, the Word of God, and continue to incorporate it into what He has called us to do in the Great Commission by training intercultural leadership.

We need to ensure that our missionaries are trained and educated properly in every aspect of their lives. The Bible can help us do this. The Bible "is profitable for all purposes of the Christian life. It is of use to all, for all need to be taught, corrected, and reprove. There is something in the Scriptures suitable for every case. Oh that we may love our

Bibles more, and keep closer to them! Then shall we find benefit, and at last gain the happiness therein promised by faith in our Lord Jesus Christ, who is the main subject of both Testaments. We best oppose error by promoting a solid knowledge of the word of truth; and the greatest kindness we can do to children, is to make them early to know the Bible."

Abraham was called and set apart for the Master's use. Jesus was sent to seek and save the lost. Jesus had surrounded Himself with men and women who would continue to do the work that He started. These faithful disciples who had followed Christ as students had become teachers, kingdom builders of the Body of Christ, the Church.

The Mission of the Church

Training intercultural leaders is not an option, but part of the mandate of the Great Commission

Finally, before He ascended back to the Father, Jesus went over the program with the disciples for the last time, showing them how things had to be fulfilled while He was with them (Luke 24:44-45). His suffering and death, as well as His resurrection on the third day, were all according to schedule (v. 46). Jesus went on to show His disciples "that repentance and remission of sins should be preached in His name among all nations, beginning at Jerusalem" (v. 47). And for the fulfillment of this divine purpose, the disciples, were no less a part than their Master. They were to be human instruments announcing the good tidings, and the Holy Spirit was to be God's personal empowerment for their mission.

"But ye shall receive power, after that the Holy Ghost is come upon you: and ye shall be witnesses unto me both in Jerusalem, and in all Judea, and in Samaria, and unto the uttermost part of the earth."

Acts 1:8; cf. Luke 24: 48–49

Clearly Jesus did not leave the work of evangelism subject to human impression or convenience. To His disciples it was a definite command. They received it at the beginning of their discipleship and was progressively clarified in their thinking as they followed Him, until it was finally spelled out in no uncertain terms. No one who followed Jesus very far could escape this conclusion. It was so then; it is so today.[5]

In the 1980s, Keith Green pointed out that 94% of the world's ordained preachers served the 9% of the world's English speaking world. That was an incredible imbalance, with the United States enjoying the service of one full-time Christian worker for every 230 people, while those who had *never* heard the Gospel had one full-time Christian worker for every 450,000 people.[6–7] Some of you are wisely noting, "Those are old statistics. Surely the situation has changed in 15-plus years since they first appeared." It is true that strategies partnering Western churches with indigenous pastors and missionaries may have made some impact in the figures. But even if we have doubled or tripled the number of full-time Christian workers for the unevangelized and unreached, the bottom line is that we still see a huge discrepancy in the balance of labor. Incredible as it seems, statistics published *within* this decade indicate that about 94% of all full-time Christian workers minister in countries where at least 60% of the population already claims to be Christian.[8–9]

If these statistics are true, then it is obvious that the Christian nations are more than able to support people in full-time ministry. Yet among those who make "missionary decisions," only one percent actually makes it to the mission field. Ralph Winter attributes this low success rate to two factors: 1) few parents, pastors and friends encourage this type of commitment; and 2) few churches are eager to incur the additional financial costs of supporting a missionary.[10] I would like to add another factor in the low success rate and attrition in the mission field: the lack of intercultural training for leaders.

The Body of Christ should consider these statistics and purpose to intentionally train teams in intercultural leadership who can combine their gifts and express godly relationships for an effective witness to the targeted people as well as to the world.[11] Today Christian disciples, men and women, are sent out to do the work of world evangelism as Christ did while here on earth. Evangelism is not an option. It is a part of the Great Commission of the church. We were called to do our part to aid in the completion of this commission, not only as senders and goers but also as teachers. God has not changed his plan in the last 4,000 years. We cannot afford to try to change His plans by sending people without proper and extensive intercultural training. Jesus, as our example, spent three years with His disciples. True spiritual growth and fruitful training occur when spiritually minded, mature Christians concentrate on a small group of spiritual children, with whom they share their life and instruction until the children have become independent adults; themselves capable of taking on responsibility for others.[12]

Training Intercultural Leaders: Taking it to the Next Level

The last decade of the 20th century witnessed a systematic approach to cross-cultural training, particularly, as world-wide evangelization intensified. International movements such as AD2000 and Beyond and other worldwide movements created a remarkable mobilization of the global church towards the evangelization of the world at the end of the century. The Missions Commission of the World Evangelical Alliance has provided a systematic service on mission training, facilitating national, regional and global consultations and producing academic and training materials focused on cross-cultural evangelization. Its focus on trainers, as they become critical in properly equipping trainees, has been determinant in its agenda. Likewise, other major prayer movements are also operating across the world. These and other actions have kept Christians aware and intensely mobilized for world evangelization at the end of the 20th century.[13]

Summary

We are at a time in history when things are accelerating in the field of missions as well as evolving in reaching our destiny. We are currently undergoing a changing of the guards. We are no longer seeing only our western missionaries participating in intercultural missions or filling all of the leadership training positions. Now we are starting to see more ethnic and racial groups participating in the Great Commission. God's will be done on earth as it is in heaven. This is a welcome turn of the tide; these diverse people are a blessing and an asset to the body of Christ. Their diversity allows them the ability to enter those countries where entry has been prohibited to our Western missionaries. I am rejoicing with the Lord as I see His plan fall into place for His people.

Conclusion

I believe that the biblical basis for training intercultural leadership is grounded in the Word of God, and it is part of God's perfect plan for the completion of the Great Commission. If we hope to receive the promises God made to Abraham, we must walk in total obedience to His will and purpose. As Jesus was our perfect example, we need to take heed to His methodology of teaching, teaching, and even more teaching to those we intend to send out. He led His disciples by His example. He was all things to all men. In other words, He crossed cultural barriers and taught His disciples to do the same. The Bible has a lot to offer in the defense of cross-cultural training. The baton in the race that God has set before us has been passed from Abraham to Jesus and now it has been passed onto us, this next generation of global world changers for this end time harvest. God's plan has not been altered by time; therefore, His Word will not come back void. His charge is still the same as it was to the disciples 4,000 years ago. Dare to take Him at His word, and see the salvation of the Lord!

> "Go ye therefore, and teach all nations, baptizing them in the name of the Father, and of the Son, and of the Holy Ghost: Teaching them to

observe all things whatsoever I have commanded you: and, lo, I am with you always, even unto the end of the world. Amen."

Matthew 28:18–20 (*KJV*)

Christina Brooks is a graduate of Rhema Bible Training Center and Rhema School of World Missions. She is attending the School of Divinity at Regent University in Virginia Beach, Virginia, pursuing her masters degree in Practical Theology/Missiology. An itinerant speaker, Christina is associated with Accelerating International Missions Strategies (AIMS), one of the most effective mobilizing mission strategy teams in the United States. Christina is a modern day "Esther" ready and willing to share the uncompromising word of God in spirit and in truth.

NOTES

1 John 3:16. *The Holy Bible. Authorized King James Version.* Nashville, Tennessee: Holman Bible Publishers.

2 Luzbetak, Louis J. *The Church and Cultures.* (Techny, Illinois: Devine Word, 1963), pp 60–63.

3 Horne, Herman. *Jesus The Teacher: Examining His Expertise in Education* (Grand Rapids, Michigan: Kregel Publications, 1998).

4 Schirrmacher, Thomas. *Training for Cross-cultural Ministries*: Vol. 2000/2, "Jesus As Master Educator and Trainer." p 5.

5 Winters, Ralph D. and Steven C. Hawthorne. *Perspectives: On The World Christian Movements.* 3rd edition (Pasadena, California: William Carey Library, 1999). p. 103.

6 Foltz, Howard and Ruth Ford. *Healthy Churches in a Sick World* (Joplin, Missouri: Messenger Publishing House, 1998), p. 47.

7 Green, Keith. "Why Should You Go to the Mission Field?", 1982, 1984, *Last Days Ministries*, reprinted in OMS Outreach, July/Sept. 1996 pp. 4–5.

8 Foltz, and Ford.

9 Stewart, John A. and John A. Kenyon. *The Mission Handbook*, 15th ed. (Monrovia, California: MARC, 1993–95), p. 11, citing statistics from AD2000 Global Monitor, April 1991, and Zwemer Institute of Muslim Studies.

10 Winter, Ralph. "Kingdom Strikes Back: The Ten Epochs of Redemptive History"

11 Hoffman, Randy. "Removing Cultural Baggage," in *Training for Cross-Cultural Ministries*: Vol. 2001/1. p 4.

12 Schirrmacher, Thomas. "Paul and His Colleagues," in *Training for Cross-Cultural Ministries: An Occasional Bulletin of the International Ministry Training Fellowship*, Vol. 2000/3, Paul and His Colleagues, p 5.

13 Alvarez, Miguel. "Missionary Training, A Discipline," in *Journal of Asian Mission* 2:1 (March 2000).

4. Ecclesiological Basis for Training Intercultural Leadership

MICHAEL K. JEFFRIES

"Although the stage has changed dramatically since the first believers formed churches and commissioned field workers to establish additional churches, the players remain remarkably similar 2,000 years later."

Introduction

While most missions leaders would agree that the local church congregation is an essential dynamic in both sending and receiving missionaries, many would also readily acknowledge that the church is often an overlooked partner in the preparation and training of missionary candidates. In a time when the very concept of global missions is rapidly changing, an ecclesiology for missions training must urgently be addressed. Even when theoretical acquiescence would seem to signal the priority of the church's role in training of missionaries sent to the field and national leaders on the field, practical implementation is a more elusive achievement. The establishment of a meaningful ecclesiology for the training of multicultural leaders should include a review of the model provided by the earliest church and its first missionaries. Such study should encompass consideration of the mandate charged to the contemporary church, design of a method for comprehensive involvement, and posting of measures to determine the effectiveness of the church and its partners.

Although the stage has changed dramatically since the first believers formed churches and commissioned field workers to establish additional churches, the players remain remarkably similar 2,000 years later. The 1st century church at Jerusalem, often proposed as the initial model of cross-cultural ministry because of its impact among the Gentiles, provides insight into the preparation of Christianity's first missionaries. One missions leader suggests the impossibility of the first church's task in responding to Jesus' Great Commission:

> About 2,000 years ago, Jesus Christ commanded His disciples, "Go and make disciples of all nations" (Matthew 28:19). Given the realities of that time, the Great Commission was mission impossible." It was:
>
> - Physically impossible because there were no planes, cars, telephones, faxes, radios, or televisions.
> - Numerically impossible because there were only about 500 disciples.
> - Financially impossible because the total assets of the church was estimated at only $10,000.

- Sociologically impossible because most of the early converts came from the poor and outcasts and were not held in high esteem.
- Legally impossible because preaching the Gospel was considered a crime.[1]

Yet these undermanned, underfunded, undereducated, and misunderstood followers began a two-millennium missionary journey. Now, with more than 1.9 billion Christians in 237 nations, these first followers seem to have overcome the odds.[2] How, then, did Christ's initial adherents organize themselves and appoint and prepare ambassadors to extend communication of the Gospel's promise?

Paul, the Model Student in the Multicultural Missions School

The Book of Acts reveals the pattern of preparation in the church's tutelage of an enthusiastic convert, who through this training would come to be known as Paul the Apostle. Eugene Peterson, in his creative translation of the Bible, reminds us that Paul before his conversion unwittingly created the first missionaries. With the martyrdom of Stephen, all Jerusalem fell into fear. "And Saul just went wild, devastating the church, entering house after house after house, dragging men and women off to jail. Forced to leave home base, the Christians all became missionaries."[3] While the first Christians in crisis may not have seen the broader view that Peterson provides, these new missionaries had the benefit of only incidental training. By the time Saul experienced conversion on the road to Damascus, the church at Jerusalem was more fully prepared to act as a meaningful center for training and sending—and Paul was the model student in this school for multicultural missions. After a short time with some disciples in Damascus[4], Barnabas mentored the newly converted Paul.[5] Barnabas then supervised his on-the-job training at Antioch.[6] The church in Antioch, a mission point in itself, then commissioned the two[7] for continuing ministry in cities yet unreached with the Gospel message.

Although the biblical record offers few details of the extent of Paul's training, we know that it was both incidental and intentional. Incidental training occurred as Paul drew alongside his friend and mentor, Barnabas, who had walked longer in the ways of the Savior. The record in Acts clearly demonstrates that Barnabas ceded more and more responsibility to Paul as time continued. Intentional training, in the form of specific instruction by the leaders of the church in Jerusalem is also evident when Peter and James speak decisively concerning Gentile converts.[8] Even after Paul and Barnabas departed onto separate missionary journeys and the newer convert's ministry took on his own signature, Paul was careful to convey the tenets of the training he had received among the leaders in Jerusalem.[9]

Throughout Paul's extensive travels, his relationship to the church remained a foundational priority. Thomas Schirrmacher, writing in the International Missionary Training Fellowship's bulletin, adeptly contends that Paul's model is comprehensive in that it includes "life and instruction, teaching and counseling, pattern and imitation."[10] Timothy, Paul's protégé, received this training well, and extended it to those he trained. In 2 Timothy 2:2, Paul commands,

> "You have heard me teach many things that have been confirmed by many reliable witnesses. Teach these great truths to trustworthy people who are able to pass them on to others."[11]

The Example of the 1st Century Church

Given the example of the 1st century church and its apostle, Paul, how does the 21st century church approach preparation for its own "apostles"—those who are sent as ambassadors for the cause of Christ in contemporary, cross-cultural settings? Initially, this process requires an acknowledgement from leaders in missions and their counterparts in local churches that these two entities must coexist in partnership and cooperation. C. Douglas McConnell, International Director for Pioneers, cites this as the greatest difficulty facing those involved in world evangelization. Missions leaders must be prepared to meet the "challenge of including the local church in the partnership and not losing a clear focus on leadership from the field."[12] McConnell observes, "There is a critical need for frontier missionary types to develop an ecclesiology. We are church planters but in some cases do not understand what a church is, either theologically and even to a lesser extent in practice."[13] Yet, while McConnell's primary concern is the national (or receiving) church, the cause of his concern is the inadequate understanding of the role of the sending church exhibited by many field workers. These two expressions of the same church—the sending church and the receiving church—must be preeminently involved. "The church is both the goal and the agent of world evangelization," writes Frank Severn.[14]

For the missionary on the field to understand the importance of the local church, he or she must have been a church leader at home.

> "Paradoxically, one can do mission today without involvement with local churches. Many missionaries are sent out by parachurch organizations to

> translate the Bible into vernaculars, dispense aid to needy people, enhance the development of nations and train national church leaders in school settings without significantly relating to national churches or their leaders on the field. Christian missions is done without personal connection with local churches in either the sending or receptor nations."[15]

Potential missionaries, sensing the possibility of a call from God for international work, often bypass local church leaders at home, then fail to connect with national church leaders once they're on the field. If, as Emil Brunner is oft quoted, "the church exists by missions like fire exists by burning,"[16] then missions can properly exist only as an extension of the sending church. And the receiving church is then an expression of the mission of the sending church. This philosophy should be found foremost in the curriculum of training centers, Bible schools and other educational programs, which propose to teach biblical foundations. The purpose and place of the local church, as it sends and receives the workers who are expected to be its champion, must be among the highest priorities of those who carry the Gospel to and from the nations. In many cases, the model of Barnabas, Paul and the early church seems to have been forgotten, or misplaced in missions priorities.

> "At Antioch, the call to Paul and Barnabas came through the church. The church sent them. Sending missionaries is a call to the church and to the individual. Too often today, an individual feels called and then he or she seeks out a mission agency. Once the person is accepted, the next step

is gaining financial support from the churches. Where does the church fit into the decisions about who is sent and where they go? Our failure to follow the biblical pattern in too many cases is revealed in the lack of discipleship and training among missionaries sent to the field. The missionary comes to us, feeling that he or she would like to do evangelism and church planting in a different culture. But in some cases they have never done evangelism and discipleship in their own neighborhood and churches."[17]

Training for Missionary Candidates

Thankfully, some local church pastors from sending nations are realizing the importance of "in-the-church" training for potential missionary candidates. Their counterparts in missions agencies and other placement mechanisms are acknowledging the same need. Lois Fuller, in *Establishing Ministry Training*, observes: "The Great Commission was given to the church. The task of world evangelization belongs to the church. Training personnel for the task of world evangelization—missionary training—therefore, also belongs to the church."[18] In an advice to prospective missionaries, Bill Taylor and Steve Hoke counsel, "You want to be seriously involved in a church—worshipping, fellowshipping, learning and serving with a local church where you are."[19] This advised involvement includes not only active participation in worship and service, but recognition that the local sending church is a strong source for initial, purposeful pre-field training. "Increasingly, local churches are assuming greater responsibility in the training of their missionary candidates. This usually involves an intentional 'internship' or 'apprenticeship' in which specific character qualities and ministry skills are nurtured."[20] Indeed, the church's role in the candidate's decision-making process and personal spiritual preparation is significant:

> "Local churches play an enormous part in the life of each future missionary. They act as their spiritual midwife. They carry the responsibility for their initial discipling. They provide the initial context and the opportunities for them to develop their missionary skills. They assess the genuineness of their missionary call and evaluate their suitability for cross-cultural service. They can also be closely involved with the student during their period of formal preparation at a training centre, providing pastoral care, financial support and prayer backing."[21]

The Church Must Be Integrally Involved

Hoke and Taylor recognize as well that the church must be integrally involved in evaluation of the candidate: "It is also during such a trial period that a church decides whether or not to confirm and stand behind your future ministry."[22] Robert Ferris, in his "Ten Biblical/Education Commitments to Guide Missionary Training," asserts as well that "training is church-related; learning occurs best in the context of community."[23] Hoke and Taylor encourage candidates to conduct self-evaluation with the following interview approach:

- Describe your current involvement in a local church.
- How is the church benefiting from your investment in it?
- How are you presently investing your own finances in a local church ministry and its missions?
- What is your church's expectation for people who want to be missionaries?
- Is there a particular person in your church you would like to have as a mentor in the process of becoming a cross-cultural servant?
- With which of your church's missionaries could you discuss your aspirations?[24]

Most churches and agencies would agree that these are the right questions to ask. But how do the right answers lead to right practice? Once on the field, the importance of the local church (both at home and on the field) is often set aside. In *Kingdom Partnerships*, Jun Vencer contends, "Some missionaries by their actions do not seem to believe in the centrality and authority of the local church. They show little church loyalty, are free to attend any church, and give their tithes to other agencies but not to the church they are planting . . . There is no clear and common ecclesiology."[25]

When the field missionary abandons the Bride of Christ at the altar of expediency, the churches being birthed are left without nurture. This abandonment is especially profound when the field missionary is also responsible for the establishment and maintenance of training programs. Missiologist Lesslie Newbigin explains the paradox of this orphaning:

> "Just as we must insist that a church which has ceased to be a mission has lost the essential

character of a church, so we must also say that a mission which is not at the same time truly a church is not a true expression of the divine apostolate. An unchurchly mission is as much a monstrosity as an unmissionary church."[26]

Missionaries Should Be Both "Missionary" and "Churchly"

Missionaries and churches should both be "missionary" and "churchly," just as much as they must avoid being "unmissionary" or "unchurchly." Even as the field worker resolves to connect more intentionally to the work of the sending church and the receiving church, churches must fully take hold of their responsibilities as heirs to the heritage of Jerusalem and Antioch. While excellent independent training programs exist, the church must assert its involvement in the preparation of candidates, especially those from its own congregation. Opportunities are abundant for churches to be involved, as Bill Taylor observes in his concluding chapter for *Kingdom Partnerships for Synergy in Missions*, "Partners Into the Next Millennium." Taylor writes, "in every continent and in most countries, local churches in mission have a wealth of opportunities."[27] These opportunities, Taylor adds, are inclusive of the training modes. Of course, the opportunities can also become obstacles when meaningful attention is not given to appropriate practices in preparation.

"Every church is a training/sending base for global evangelism. Unfortunately, too many churches desire to go it alone in missions, even attempting to place long-term staff in restricted access nations. Part of the problem is a faulty

> understanding of the church at Antioch, simply seeing it as a classic sending church. Another difficulty is that these churches try to send their teams without serious commitment to three major dimensions: comprehensive pre-field training (including biblical and theological study); long-term language and culture learning; and on-field shepherding, strategizing and supervising. The best church partnerships that I know of accept the contributions that formal Bible/theology/missions schools can offer their missionaries, and they are actively partnering with an on-field mission agency with experience in that ministry."[28]

Paul Beals expands on these concepts, encouraging sending congregations, training programs and mission organizations to work as a "triad" for the purpose of "tackling the task of taking the Gospel to the ends of the earth."[29] Beals terms these three cooperative partners the assembly (the church), the academy (the training program), and the agency (the missions organization).

The Role of the Assembly

In response, Paul Borthwick, a missions pastor in a sending church, speaks from the assembly and embraces Beals' assertions while not always finding them to be consistent with practiced reality. Borthwick specifically encourages the church to become involved in the training of multicultural leaders and cross-cultural workers: "The local church can do the preliminary screening of its missionary candidates; we need to take more responsibility for our own people's preparation.... We definitely must take 'pastoral references' for church members more seriously."[30] He extends this commitment beyond normal screening activities to include psychological evaluations required by sending agencies and educational assessments to determine appropriate placement in ministry training. One writer, a Wycliffe missionary to Central America for 35 years, suggests further, "Churches would do well to consider designating some of their missions budget for helping candidates through cross-cultural training programs as well as encouraging advanced work during home stays."[31]

Communication Between Partners

Constant communication between the sending organization and the sending church, especially in regard to requisite continuing education, can enhance this opportunity for churches willing to receive that responsibility. Churches must also be more focused in their appreciation for the missionary's experiences and needs, establishing and continually enhancing ways for the missionary to report on progress and disappointments. Too often, the typical query from a congregation seems more like David Letterman's late-night talk show interview of *Survivor* castaways: "Did you see or touch any monkeys?"[32] Churches must be willing to dwell more deeply into an understanding of the on-the-field experiences of missionaries, so that church leaders can best equip the missionaries with greater training opportunities and best resource the receiving church by encouraging specific training objectives. Brian McLaren provides 21 reasons for difficulties in modern missions in his landmark book, *The Church on the Other Side*. He speaks from a pastor's perspective in bluntly acknowledging, "The home church is selfish. Even if we are not struggling as a church, we may still be self-preoccupied. We need another concert, another seminar, another Christian television station—quickly! Who was it who said, 'The greatest threat to world evangelization is the church preoccupied with her own existence'?"[33]

The Role of the Academy

Concurrently, missionary training centers ("the academy") must redouble efforts to acknowledge the importance of the church's role, not just in theology or theory, but in everyday practice. This includes the churches that send missions candidates to the training centers and the churches that will be served by the missionaries, once initial phases of training are complete. Ebbie Smith, in "Four Dimensions of Leadership Training," argues that the training program should "exist for the trainee and the churches they will serve rather than the trainers."[34] Smith, writing as Professor of missions and ethics at Southwestern Baptist Theological Seminary, critiques programs centered around the training center rather than the church: "Directors of training programs tend to build monuments to themselves and reproduce the programs from which they came. Classes are developed around the interests and the conveniences of the teachers."[35] Training centers should allow local churches to comment on curriculum, serve as board members, offer internships, sponsor funding, provide guest lectures and more. Again, this partnership should include sending churches and receiving churches and those receiving churches that will become sending churches.

The Role of the Mission Agency

Additionally, the mission agency or facilitating organization must be responsive to the churches that provide the "seedbed" for its workers.[36] Nearly every missionary candidate will be converted in a church, baptized in a church, discipled in a church—then too often disconnected from the church by a missions agency, which leads to the candidate being forgotten by the church. Borthwick recognizes the discordant relationship specifically between the church and agency: "Some agencies seem to see the local church only as a source of potential missionaries or money. A clear sense of partnership is usually missing (and this may be communicated to missionaries implicitly.)"[37] He says this is true because "many local churches have totally abdicated responsibility to the mission agencies for recruiting, training and sending missionaries."[38]

Partnership, from recruitment to training to commissioning to field evaluation, will ensure connection and affinity between the missionary, the missions agency, and the missions-sending church. McLaren illuminates the importance of this cooperation: "As a pastor who has served with a mission agency, I see the church from both sides now. To the local church, mission agencies can seem like vendors who keep calling, calling, calling, wanting, wanting, wanting. To the mission agencies, local churches can seem like selfish, inefficient, tradition-bound, politics-paralyzed ghettos of wasted Christian potential."[39] But, he insists, "we can't avoid the church. Lead some people to Christ, bring them together, and like it or not, you have one. That is why of all people, mission agencies should be reading about the church and caring about the revitalization and liberation of the church on the other side."[40] Thankfully, many agencies have been proactive in advancing these partnerships. Consider the transformation of the training and sending strategy of the largest denominational missions agency. Once shrouded in an agency-centered dogma, this agency now embraces a church-focused philosophy. "We believe the Great Commission was given not to the International Mission Board but to the churches and to Christians. We're an agency to help facilitate the churches and Christians carrying out the Great Commission, rather than being the owner and possessor of the missions."[41] This commitment on the part of the agency, which deploys more than 5,000 overseas workers, has accelerated the personalization of global outreach for the church and increased the local congregation's understanding of the training and equipping process.[42]

Each component of the preparation partnership—the sending church, the training center, the missions agency, and the receiving church—must understand and fulfill its role. The missionary must be purposeful and proactive in facilitating communication and cooperation among these four partners.

The Nicaraguan Model of Partnership

An excellent case study of this missions ecclesiology in action is that of Nour Sirker, a medical missionary in the Central American nation of Nicaragua. Following graduation from a New York medical school, Sirker and his registered nurse wife, Carolyn, returned to Nour's native Nicaragua to begin a practice among his own people. Forced into exile by the Sandinista Marxist revolution in 1979, Sirker returned to the U.S. and continued a career as an emergency room physician in South Florida. While in South Florida, Sirker became increasingly involved in the life of a local church, serving as deacon and being trained in specific methods of cross-cultural evangelism and Bible teaching. Given the opportunity to return by the newly elected democratic government of Violeta Barrios de Chamorro in 1992, Sirker was issued an invitation from a receiving church, the Amen Tabernacle in Managua. Immediately, Sirker sought the commissioning of his home church in Fort Lauderdale. Once assurance of this commissioning support was clear, Nour and Carolyn returned to the nation as medical missionaries under the auspices of a sending agency, Christian Relief Overseas.[43] This process included all four components: receiving church, sending church, missions agency, and training center.

After more than a decade in Nicaragua, Nour and Carolyn have duplicated this process and provided leadership for establishment of an elementary school, a hospital, a comprehensive evangelism training program for pastors and lay leaders, a ministry for men and, most recently, a seminary training program.[44]

The evangelism-training program is another example of Sirker's comprehensive approach to partnership: as the local missionary, Sirker enlisted six pastors to equip others in evangelism methods. He then sought funding from his home church in Fort Lauderdale for travel and tuition expenses. Because of Sirker's strong connections with both sending and receiving churches, these pastors were sent for training in a neighboring Central American nation. Soon, more advanced training for the lead pastor became appropriate. Sirker again drew upon the partnership between this receiving church and his original sending church to fund and facilitate the training, this time in the United States.

This model finds its extension in Sirker's newest project, the "Instituto Teológico Nicaragüense." The new training program is designed for pastors and missionaries to be sent into extended regions of Nicaragua, Central America's largest nation in size. Already, a new partnership has arisen between Sirker's sending church, his sending agency, his seminary-training program, and the original receiving church. Through these affiliations, that receiving church has become a sending church by commissioning a church-planting pastor/missionary for one of Nicaragua's poorest regions. [45] This pastor and the seminary in which he is being trained are emblems of Nour Sirker's prayerful faith that the work he and his colleagues initiated will continue as younger generations arise for the work in Managua and beyond. Like the apostle Paul, Sirker can know that the mission will advance: "In all my prayers for all of you, I always pray with joy because of your partnership in the Gospel from the first day until now, being confident of this, that he who began a good work in you will carry it on to completion until the day of Christ Jesus."[46]

Michael K. Jeffries is pastor for global missions mobilization at the 12,900-member First Baptist Church of Fort Lauderdale, Florida. With a passion for mobilizing believers for cross-cultural ministry, Michael has directed short-term missions projects to 21 different nations and oversees ongoing support for more than two dozen long-term missionaries. The Fort Lauderdale congregation includes members from nearly 70 nations and provides live translation and Internet streaming in Chinese, French, Portuguese, Romanian and Russian.

NOTES

1 Vencer, Jun. *Kingdom Partnerships for Synergy in Missions*, William D. Taylor, ed. (Pasadena, CA: William Carey Library, 1994), p. 101.

2 Johnstone, Patrick J. StG., Robyn Johnstone and Jason Mandryk. *Operation World: 21st Century Edition* (Carlisle, Cumbria, UK: Paternoster Lifestyle, 2001), 2.

3 Peterson, Eugene. *The Message* (Colorado Springs, CO: NavPress, 2002), Acts 8:3–4.

4 Acts 9:19.

5 Acts 9:27.

6 Acts 11:25.

7 Acts 13:2–5.

8 Acts 15:6–26.

9 Acts 16:4.

10 Schirrmacher, Thomas. "Paul and His Colleagues," in *Training for Cross-Cultural Ministry: An Occasional Bulletin of the International Ministry Training Fellowship* 100, no. 3 (2000): p. 4–5.

11 Tyndale House Publishers. "Holy Bible, New Living Translation," [online], 1996, cited 18 April 2003, available from <http://www.newlivingtranslation.com>.

12 McConnell, C. Douglas. "Looking Back . . . Looking Forward," in *Mission Frontiers: The Bulletin of the U.S. Center for World Mission*, June (2000).

13 Ibid.

14 Severn, Frank. "Missions Societies: Are They Biblical?," in *Evangelical Missions Quarterly* (July 2000): p. 321.

15 Van Rheenen, Gailyn. "Doing 'Missions' Without the Local Church," [online] missiology.org, 2000, cited 21 April 2003, available from <http://www.missiology.org/discussion/_disc1/0000000c.htm>.

16 Foster, Richard. "Growing Edges," in *Renovaré Perspectives*, July 1997, p. 1.

17 Niringiye, David Zac. "Jerusalem to Antioch to the World: A Biblical Missions Strategy," in *Evangelical Missions Quarterly* 26, no. 1 (January 1990).

18 Fuller, Lois. *Establishing Ministry Training: A Manual for Programme Developers*, ed. Robert W. Ferris (Pasadena, CA: William Carey Library, 1995), 122.

19 Hoke, Steve and Bill Taylor. *Send Me: Your Journey to the Nations* (Pasadena, CA: William Carey Library, 1999), p. 39.

20 Ibid., p. 40.

21 Harley, C. David. *Preparing to Serve: Training for Cross-Cultural Mission* (Pasadena, CA: William Carey Library, 1995), p. 45.

22 Hoke, and Taylor, p. 40.

23 Ferris, Robert. "Ten Biblical/Educational Commitments to Guide Missionary Training," in *Evangelical Missiological Society Bulletin* (Summer 1999).

24 Hoke and Taylor, p. 45.

25 Vencer, Jun. *Kingdom Partnerships for Synergy in Missions*, ed. William D. Taylor (Pasadena, CA: William Carey Library, 1994), p. 106.

26 Newbigin, J. E. Lesslie. *The Household of God: Lectures on the Nature of the Church* (London: SCM, 1953), p. 192.

27 Taylor, Bill. *Kingdom Partnerships for Synergy in Missions*, William D. Taylor, ed. (Pasadena, CA: William Carey Library, 1994), p. 239.

28 Ibid.

29 Beals, Paul A. "The Triad for Century 21," in *Evangelical Missiological Society Bulletin* (Spring 1999).

30 Borthwick, Paul. "A Love Affair That Must Be Cultivated Three Ways," in *Evangelical Missions Quarterly* 27, no. 1 (January 1991).

31 Oltrogge, David F. "Missionary Training: Two Important Components," in *Training for Cross-Cultural Ministry: An Occasional Bulletin of The International Ministry Training Fellowship* 95, no. 1 (1995): 6.

32 Birkitt, Stephanie. "Interview with Survivor loser Jake Billingsley. Monday, 9 December 2002 / Show #1917," [online] The Late Show with David Letterman, 2002, cited 21 April 2003, available from <http:/www.cbs.com/latenight/lateshow/exclusives/wahoo/archive/2002/12/archive09.shtml>.

33 McLaren, Brian D. *The Church on the Other Side: Doing Ministry in the Postmodern Matrix* (Grand Rapids, MI: Zondervan, 2000), 123.

34 Smith, Ebbie. "Four Dimensions of Leadership Training," *Evangelical Missiological Society Bulletin* (Summer 1999).

35 Ibid.

36 Taylor, Bill. "Why Do They Come Home?" in *Training for Cross-Cultural Ministry: An Occasional Bulletin of The International Ministry Training Fellowship* 95, no. 1 (1995): 8.

37 Borthwick.

38 Ibid.

39 McLaren, p. 140.

40 Ibid.

41 Rankin, Jerry, IMB President. "The Southern Baptists: A Glorious Transformation in Process," interview by Missions Frontiers Staff in *Missions Frontiers* (July–0ctober 1997).

42 Sharp, Terry, Director of state and associational relations for the International Mission Board, interview by author, 9 March 2003.

43 Poor, Wally and Betty Poor. "Global Priority Church Models 21st Century Missions: First Baptist Fort Lauderdale Finds a Multicultural Setting a Perfect Incubator for Missions Involvement," in *The Commission*, August 1999, pp. 41–42.

44 "Nice Foundation," [online] Nicaragua Christian Education Foundation, 2003, cited 24 April 2003, available from <http://www.nicefoundation.org/ourministries~ns4.html>.

45 Sirker, Nour, interview by author, 23 March 2003.

46 Philippians 1:5–6: International Bible Society, "Holy Bible, New International Version," [online] Bible Gateway, 1994, cited 24 April 2003, available from <http://bible.gospelcom.net/cgi-binbible?passage=PHIL+1&language=english&version=NIV&showfn=on&showxref=on>.

5. Hanging Out with the Almighty: Theological Basis for Training Intercultural Leadership

DERRICK LEE FRANK

"This remarkable human being envisioned to earthlings an example of a perfect relationship with God. No generation has enjoyed such a companionship since our founding parents' generation (Adam and Eve); nor has any subsequent generation seen such a harmonious bond with God since."

God is on a Mission

God Almighty is the same yesterday, today, and forever. The Father and Son are "Alpha and the Omega, the first and the last, the beginning and the end!"[1] His unshakable steadfastness is worth trusting in and patterning one's lifestyle after.

God is a God of mission and is determined to see Jesus' name glorified among all nations. For it is pronounced that, "'As surely as I live,' says the Lord, 'every knee *will* bow to me [Jesus] and every tongue *will* confess allegiance to God.'"[2] The Ultimate Judge can feel emotion. He experiences laughter[3], sorrow[4], jealousy[5], and wrath [anger][6]. Would we not be wise to obey and follow this example of resolve? In this chapter we will discuss how God's purpose behind His passion for every knee to bow willingly is revealed.

Hanging Out with the Almighty

At the end of the earth's creation, the Lord of Hosts asserted that all of the things that He created were, "very good."[7] Humanity was included in this affirmation. But, there was something that separated humans from the rest of the created order: We were made in God's image.[8] What did this distinction mean?

Ada and Ginny Lum suggest that this relationship was, "Not accidental or incidental but [rather] intentional."[9] God purposed it this way for three reasons. The first reason was so that He could have someone to bless. He gave all the "good" things that were created, both animal and vegetation for humankind to enjoy.[10] Secondly, the Divine One intended to have someone with whom He could freely communicate.[11] And finally, the Wise One desired that He would be able to walk in person with His objects of affection.[12] In summary, God made humans in His own image so that He would have an object with whom He could focus His immense love and with whom He could "hang out."

However, something horrible happened, humankind's freewill chose to disobey God's command and was dissatisfied with mirroring God's image. Instead, they desired to "be like God in knowing good and evil."[13] This act of treason caused shame on an otherwise pure creature and effected a chasm in this purposed relationship of interaction.

At this important juncture in history, God did not flinch. He must have cringed with the rejection, but nothing hindered Him from a stubborn resolve to again restore that right relationship. Furthermore, He prophesied to the enemy that the woman's seed [Jesus][14], "shall crush you on the head, and you shall bruise him on the heel."[15]

God's Heart for the Whole World

George W. Peters comments on the above promise that it, "was given to *the entire human race*."[16] From the beginning, there was no separation between White, Black, Asian, or Indian in the heart of God. All were included when this promise was given to Adam and Eve, the two roots of humankind.

Missionary Israel?

Was Israel different? Did they have a special favor from God that the rest of the peoples on earth did not? Or, were they themselves to be missionaries to the rest of the earth? The Hebrews were chosen because they were loved. For the Scriptures say, [17] "The LORD did not choose you [Israelites] and lavish His love on you because you were larger or greater than other nations, for you were the smallest of all nations! It was simply because the LORD loves you. . . ."[18] They were selected and loved because of love, period. It was nothing that they did to deserve it, or earn it, but simply because His love moved Him to choose the Israelites.

What was the Great Healer's purpose in this choice? It was so that they would, "give earnest heed to the voice of the Lord God, and do what is right in His sight, and give ear to His commandments, and keep all His statutes. . . ."[19] Do you see the connection between the creation story and God's heart to restore that perfect communion? In the beginning, God talked personally to humankind, and here, if the people obey Him, they will continue to hear His voice. He had it in mind that they would be a "kingdom of priests and a holy nation."[20] This was not a mandate for exclusiveness, but rather a calling for them to be God's ambassadors to other nations. For the priests' duties were not only to minister unto God but also "to make God's will known . . . to teach the Law . . . to conduct worship; including preparing what was brought by the people for their sacrifices."[21] A question might be raised as to how the *whole* nation of Israel was to fulfill this expression of the heartbeat of God? The answer is simple—by being missionaries to the other nations! They were to be missionaries!

Jonah

Were these specially chosen people successful in being an envoy to the world? No. They received the favor of God and selfishly hoarded it. The prophet Jonah illustrated the general feeling of his generation toward "outsiders." When God commanded him to preach in Nineveh (a heathen nation's capital), "Jonah rose up to flee to Tarshish from the presence of the Lord."[22] Only after being "caught" for his sin and swallowed by a whale, did he yield to be a missionary. But immediately after the heathen repented and divine mercy was granted, this representative of Yahweh became angry with God[23] and moaned, "Death is better to me than life."[24] Father God had "compassion"[25] on Nineveh and likewise yearns for the restoration of all humankind to its designed relationship. Today, the church has been given the reins of missionary duties, for the same pronouncement that was given to the Hebrews long ago has now been passed onto us. The Apostle Peter affirms this by teaching that, "For you are a chosen people. You are a kingdom of priests, God's holy nation, His very own possession. This is so you can **show** others the goodness of God . . ."[26]

Missionary Jesus

Unparalleled in all of history was the appearance of a man named Jesus, around 4BC–29AD. This remarkable human being demonstrated to earthlings an example of a perfect relationship with God. No generation has enjoyed such a companionship since our founding parents' generation (Adam and Eve); nor has any subsequent generation seen such a harmonious bond with God since.

Cross-cultural Jesus

Jesus was a missionary—God incarnate, the Word who had become flesh. He left His heavenly abode where He had existed before time was even created, for the purpose of repairing a broken bond. He is the one whom the Father God prophesied about in Genesis 3:15, who would crush the head of the deceiver. The New Testament states:

> "Though he was God, he did not demand and cling
> to his rights as God. He made himself nothing;
> he took the humble position of a slave and

> appeared in human form. And in human form he obediently humbled himself even further by dying a criminal's death on a cross. Because of this, God raised him up to the heights of heaven and gave him a name that is above every other name, so that at the name of Jesus every knee will bow, in heaven and on earth and under the earth, and every tongue will confess that Jesus Christ is Lord, to the glory of God the Father."[27]

What could be more cross-cultural than leaving a pure heaven (His home and habitat) to come to an earth filled with dirty and fault-filled people? Not only is it a fact that Jesus came into this world, but also that He *chose* to do so. He willingly left safety, a well-nourishing environment, praise, and the most intimate of families to be painfully humiliated, rejected, and killed by hypocrites.

Jesus' "Mission Policy"[28]

Jesus' "mission policy"[29] was evident in His lifestyle. It was much like an orange, it was a whole composed of separate yet essential parts. Therefore, the King's life example was complete and worth emulating. In the following paragraphs, a few different slices of the orange will be examined in the hope that we can follow His practices.

To begin with, the Restorer's motive for moving cross-culturally, as emphasized previously, was that of "*love*."[30] This impetus was behind everything else that occurred during Jesus' short stay on this planet. As Neil Anderson asserts, "God proved His love for us . . . by sending His Son. . . ."[31] Just as the old saying says, "As the Father does, so does the Son."[32]

Secondly, Jesus entered a *foreign culture*. As mentioned before, He came from the place of perfection and peace to an abode were rebellion is relished and practiced by all. Hebrews 4:15 says that Jesus, "*can* sympathize with our weaknesses, *and* was the One who has been tempted in all things as we are, yet without sin.[33] It could be suggested that He was also lured to respond negatively to culture shock, depression, and patriotism, which are all common temptations by missionaries, yet He was without misconduct.

Next, Jesus invested time in *growing* and in *adapting* to the 1st century Palestinian culture. The historian Luke upholds this fact reporting that, "The Child [Jesus] continued to grow and become strong, increasing in wisdom; and the grace of God was upon Him."[34] Our Example [Jesus] studied His culture, its laws, and observed its customs.[35] He wore their clothes, ate their food, drank their drinks, and surely sang their type of songs. But there was a limit to the Sacrificial Lamb's[36] flexibility, and this limit was that He would not sin.

Fourthly, the Rabbi[37] *contextualized* His message so that His audience could understand what He was trying to convey. The Son of God was such a genius that He knew perfectly how to not only adapt His divine message to the general culture, but also to communicate in varying situations to different relational spheres. The realms as they relate to Jesus are illustrated below in Figure 1.

Figure 1

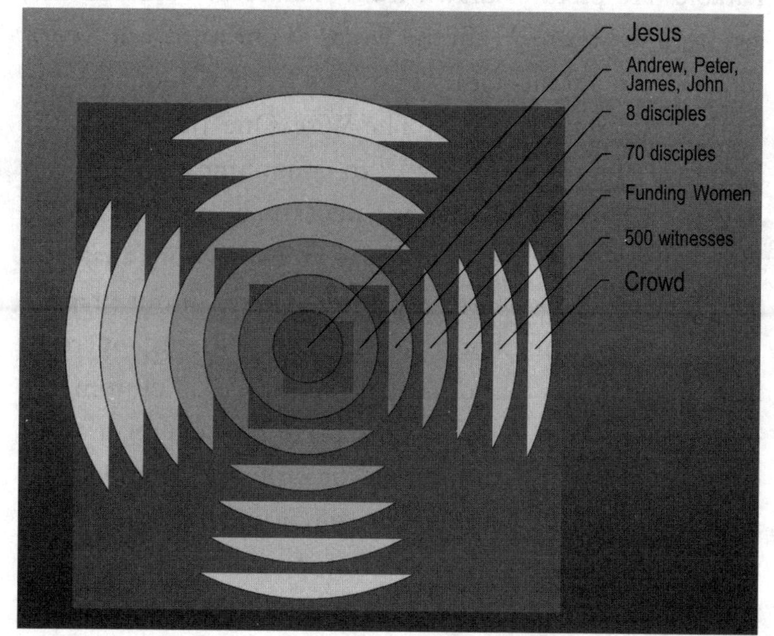

In light of these relational influences, Jesus interacted with each in alternative ways. He did so out of wisdom, knowing that He had only a short time on earth. The Father's Son only invested intimate time with a coalition of the willing. The more open and responsive the individuals, the more personal tutorage they received. Jesus knew that the only way He was going to make a true impact for missions was to pour His time, energy, knowledge, and being into a few divinely handpicked students. To each subsequent circle outwards on our chart, Jesus correspondingly invested less intimate mentoring. In parallel, once entering and personally orienting Himself to this foreign culture, the Ambassador [Jesus] was so entirely[38] integrated that He was able to utilize multiple methods to convey His message.

His most common technique was using *parables*. He used parables in at least one-third of His recorded messages.

Parables are pictures drawn from "nature or common life, arresting the hearer."[39] In the words of one saint, our Savior "turned His listeners' ears into eyes so they could see the truth and respond to it."[40] The Wise One [Jesus] had the "courage of a revolutionary" [41] to communicate to His followers in a way that was not necessarily comfortable to Him but was effective to the hearers. These word analogies were primarily spoken to the outer spheres in our graph.

The second method that the Servant [Jesus] operated in frequently was that of *teaching*. As was Jesus' custom, He often entered the host culture's place of worship, a synagogue, and taught with amazing authority and confidence.[42] Unlike parables however, instruction was primarily used for those who were more intimately associated with Jesus. The percentage of instruction became more frequent the closer one related to Jesus while the frequency of parables increased the more one was detached, as illustrated in Figure 2.

Figure 2

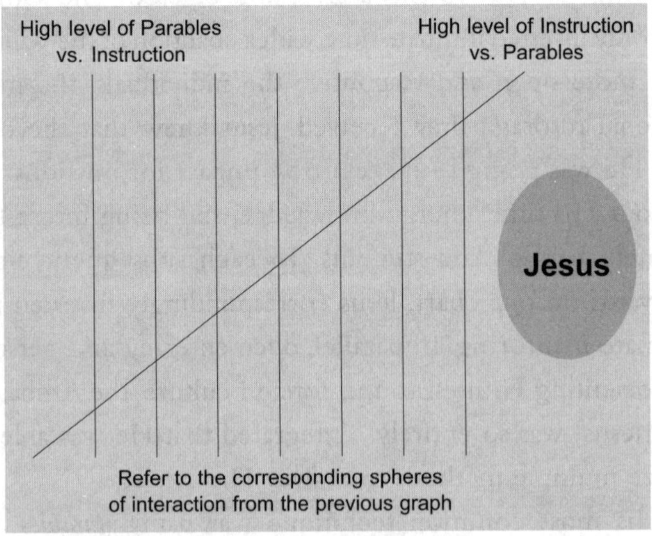

High level of Parables vs. Instruction

High level of Instruction vs. Parables

Jesus

Refer to the corresponding spheres of interaction from the previous graph

The third most common tool that Jesus used was *preaching*. This practice was often used with all of the other communication vehicles[43] both the ones already mentioned and those yet to come. Within the proclamations, He left no doubt that the Kingdom of God was at hand and the only way to receive eternal life was through repentance and trust in Him.

And finally, some of the other tools that the Rest Giver[44] [Jesus] made use of were those of *healing*,[45] *prophecy*, [46] *power illuminations*,[47] and at times, *discipline*.[48] But, what has not been mentioned yet was the oil that caused each of these parts to operate accurately at the appropriate time. This oil was Jesus' right relationship with the Father where He could "see" what the Father was doing and hence become a co-laborer with Him in His missionary business. For the Bible says that, "Jesus replied, "I assure you, the Son can do nothing by himself. He does only what He sees the Father doing. Whatever the Father does, the Son also does.[20] For the Father loves the Son and tells Him everything He is doing. . . ."[49] It was not merely enough for Jesus to leave His home habitat, become an accomplished cultural scholar, or become a cross-cultural communicator extraordinaire, but most importantly, He needed to be in the minute-by-minute will of the Father. Yet again, it was this loving obedience and sensitivity that made the heavenly message contextual, using a variety of means at the appropriate time in order to make converts.

A Whole God to the Whole Person: "Holistic Ministry"[50]

The next "mission policy" that the Heavenly Cross-Cultural Leadership Trainer [Jesus] exemplified to us is that of building a *mobilizing missionary school.* It was not enough for Jesus to preach, teach, tell parables, or do miracles, for these were only tools to help Him reach His goal. From the beginning, He was determined to have the work of the Lord continue long after His departure. Jesus sought to raise up and train national leaders who would spearhead a church planting movement for the purpose of birthing worshipers worldwide.

After 30 years of preparation for service in this unfamiliar country, Jesus finally surfaced out of the crowd to fulfill the Father's desire for His journey, which was three years of public ministry and His life's dramatic and triumphal exit. Immediately from the start of the Lamb's public witness, the Scriptures reveal that He thought it was important to gather a group of pupils.[51]

A rag tag of 12 individuals voluntarily signed up for this newly formed divine educational institute. While remembering that the Rabbi only accomplished what He heard from and saw in the Father, He demanded from them everything. They had to not only be willing to give up a night, a week for a two-hour class, but were also compelled to give up *everything* in order to enroll in Jesus' Holistic Educational Institute. This meant that they had to take a long sabbatical or quit their jobs, sell or at least abandon their homes, and become traveling students of their Professor [Jesus].

Jesus knew that in order for this church planting movement to explode rather than implode after He departed, it would need facilitators who not only had their heads filled with facts, but natives completely transformed in their soul, mind, and action. This meant that these future leaders would need to have their minds renewed with the truth, souls re-birthed and matured, and bodies mastered for acting on godliness. How did He meet this goal?

First, it was important for the Missionary [Jesus] to have the Father's handpicked disciples. John 17:6 testifies that Jesus was confident that He had these very special, personally chosen few, for it says, "I have manifested Your name to the men *whom You gave Me out of the world*; they were Yours and *You gave them to Me*. . ."

Second, once the whole class was gathered, lessons began immediately. Although some of the methods utilized included those mentioned above, a much more intense style was implemented. For they like no one else lived with their Teacher [Jesus]. It was only when that prerequisite was met that Jesus could employ the most effective of all the tools of communication and transformation. This was an experiential internship.

This training included the following:

- They ate together[52]
- The disciples received a special explanation of Jesus' parables and instructions and questions[53]
- They celebrated Jewish festivals together[54]
- The disciples witnessed and participated at times in Jesus' ministry to the crowds, etc.[55]
- The disciples slept at the same location as Jesus[56]
- The disciples were sent out on short-term mission trips so that they could begin to implement what they had been taught and seen Jesus do.[57]

The Sent One[58] [Jesus] gave to His disciples the most involved mentoring that could have been instituted. Consequently, He knew that for the nationals to be transformed enough, and to have a deep enough conviction in His message, a highly involved tutoring would be required for over a three-year period. In the Father's wisdom, Jesus knew that these 12 would not have been ready for empowering only after three years of Wednesday night Bible studies. They needed to witness Him in action and to receive the behind-the-scenes character teaching through watching and instruction. It was by this personal witnessing of the Rabbi in all the circumstances of life that effected the needed internal and external changes in the disciples. God instituted, and hence used, the rule that if a person is with a friend long enough, then they will naturally begin to think and behave like the other. Thus, by living with the Teacher, and by being involved with all that He did, the disciples had a significant body, mind, and soul understanding for their Missionary to leave and to be released into their own Kingdom building activities.

How successful was this divine mobilizing missionary school? What can be learned from its successes and failures? Well, 11 of the 12 passed, but special note needs to be taken that all 12 inadvertently served their purpose.[59] According to tradition, 11 of the 12 ended up amongst foreign peoples building the Kingdom of God. Although these are great statistics, Jesus did not send out perfect people but servants. Three examples of their immaturity can be found in that (1) all denied their Teacher at His arrest,[60] (2) Thomas's doubt,[61] (3) and Paul's later rebuke of Peter.[62] It is a humbling fact that no student in our mobilizing missionary schools will be perfect upon graduation, and unfortunately not everyone will pass. But, it must be remembered that God is in control, and is determined to accomplish the goal of global worship.

The "Mission Policy's" Final Goal

Jesus did not found the Missionary School merely to provide the native culture with well-developed and mature leadership, but rather He purposed to reproduce Himself in a cross-cultural setting. He had His face set like flint towards the goal to equip and mobilize more missionaries that would cross ethnic boundaries to be ignitions for worship worldwide. Jesus was also determined not to have these personally trained missionaries become stationary, but rather that they would themselves build missionary schools amongst those foreign peoples. In the process the multiplication would continue until all have heard the heavenly message.

In conclusion, the justice-giving God has exacted mercy on mankind through His Son Jesus. It is His resolute will that all have the opportunity to join in the mutually edifying worship of God. None are to be left out! Equally, Father God has through Jesus' death and resurrection, extended a hand towards us as an invitation to become like many saints of old in seeing that this goal be fulfilled. The fact is, in order for every people group to have a clear occasion when they have opportunity to join the worshiping throng, it will take more mobilizing missionary schools that are participated in and build across the globe. The question is not whether God is actively training cross-cultural leadership; the question is: Will we join Him in this kind of education?

Derrick Lee Frank was born and raised in Lancaster, PA. During his teen years he worked on the family pig farm and enjoyed it. After he completed high school he felt the Lord calling him to attend Elim Bible Institute in Lima, New York. He graduated with a Diploma in Biblical Studies in April of 2001. In August of that same year he married Kerri Lynne Wrisley whom he met at Bible school. They have a son named Joshua Paul. Derrick is presently pursuing an MBA and an M.Div. at Regent University in Virginia Beach, VA. Derrick and Kerri anticipate seeing what the Lord has in store for their family.

NOTES

1 The *New American Standard Bible* is the version used in this chapter, unless otherwise stated. The quote is taken from Revelation 22:13 with its parallel found in Isaiah 44:6, and 48:12.
2 Emphasis mine. Romans 14:11 and Isaiah 45:23. The concept is expounded in Philippians 2:9–11, where the passage reveals that Jesus is the name confessed.
3 Psalm 2:4.
4 Genesis 6:6.
5 Exodus 34:14.
6 Exodus 15:7.
7 Genesis 1:31.
8 Genesis 1:26, 27.
9 Lum, Ada and Ginny Lum. *World Mission: 12 Studies on the Biblical Basis*, (Illinois: InterVarsity Press, 1976), p. 11
10 Genesis 1:26–28, 2:15ff.
11 Genesis 2:16, 18, 3:9.
12 Genesis 3:8.
13 Genesis 3:5.
14 Romans 5:12ff clarifies the following passage that here God is referring to Jesus. Paul later also affirms that since we are now co-heirs with Christ that we also are co-seeds and that "God will soon crush Satan under our feet" (Romans 16:20).
15 Genesis 3:15.
16 Peters, George W. *A Biblical Theology of Missions*, (Chicago: Moody Press, 1972), p. 85.

17 This idea of Israel's chosenness is taken from an eulogy of Dr. Lyle Story at Regent University School of Divinity, February 26, 2003.

18 Parenthesis added, Deuteronomy 7:7–8, *New Living Translation*.

19 Exodus 15:26.

20 Exodus 19:6.

21 Miller, Madeleine S., and J. Lane Miller. *Harper's Bible Dictionary*, (New York: Harper & Row Publishers, 1973).

22 Jonah 1:3.

23 Jonah 4:1.

24 Jonah 4:8.

25 Jonah 4:11.

26 1 Peter 2:9 *New Living Translation*, emphasis added.

27 Philippians 2:6–11.

28 Crosby, Dan. "Untitled," in *Final Frontiers*, Fall/Winter 2001, 5.

29 Ibid.

30 Deuteronomy 7:7–8, emphasis added.

31 Anderson, Neil. *The Steps to Freedom in Christ*, (USA: Gospel Light Publishers, 1996), p. 7.

32 Unknown origin.

33 The words in italics were altered from the original text so that it would be more understandable; the meaning however, was not changed.

34 Luke 4:40, parenthesis added.

35 "Jesus was a Jew. He came from a Jewish family, He studied the Jewish law, He observed the Jewish religion." Shelly, Bruce L., *Church History in Plain Language*, (Dallas: Word Publishing, 1995), p. 3.

36 Jesus' example as a sacrificial lamb is also a picture of a true trainer of intercultural leadership. Trainers must be servants and willing to give of their whole selves.

37 In John 1:38, Jesus is addressed as Rabbi. This term means "teacher" and directly compliments our subject.

38 "entirely" can also be understood as "maturely."

39 Wiersbe, Warren W. *Preaching & Teaching with Imagination*, (Grand Rapids, Michigan: Baker Books, 1994), p. 164.

40 Ibid., p. 160.

41 Ibid.

42 Mark 1:21ff.

43 Matthew 4:23.

44 This name attributed to Jesus signifies that a trainer is not a slave driver, but rather one who leads people into that divine place where worry, anxiety, and fear is replaced by rest, peace, and joy. Its base text is Matthew 11:28–30.

45 Mark 2:1ff, 3:1ff.

46 Matthew 16:21.

47 Matthew 17:1ff, Mark 6:45.

48 Matthew 16:23, John 2:13ff.

49 John 5:19–20.

50 Lewis, Jonathan. "Holistic Missionary Training," TMs [photocopy], 2/20/03, courtesy of Regent University School of Divinity, Virginia Beach, VA, p. 2.

51 Luke 5:1ff, Matthew 4:18ff, Mark 1:16ff, John 1:40ff.

52 Mark 2:15–17.

53 Matthew 15:11f.

54 Matthew 26:17ff.

55 Mark 2:15–17.

56 Luke 21:37.

57 Matthew 10:1ff.

58 This title is based on Jesus' own testimony in Matthew 10:40 that He was sent for a purpose to this world by the Father.

59 John 17:12, "During my time here, I have kept them safe. I guarded them so that not one was lost, *except the one headed for destruction*, as the Scriptures foretold." (italics added)

60 John 18:25f.

61 John 20:24f.

62 Galatians 2:11ff.

Part Two

THE INDISPENSABILITY OF THE LOCAL CHURCH IN RECRUITMENT AND TRAINING

6. Missiological Training in the Local Church

TIMOTHY L. DILLMUTH

"The Great Commission was given to the Church! The task of world evangelization belongs to the Church! Training personnel for the task of world evangelization—missionary training—therefore, also belongs to the Church. While God may use an individual or a small group of individuals to excite others with a vision for missionary training, it is important to recognize that successful missionary training never can be a private project."[1]

Introduction

Before a local church can ever be a "missionary training church," it must first be involved in and excited about missions, but unfortunately for many churches this is not the case. There are many reasons given for a local church not to be involved with missions (time, finances, we've got enough problems of our own), but the Bible is filled with reasons to be involved. Interestingly enough, many missionary administrators are realizing that one of the most strategic avenues for missions is directly through the local church. The Body of Christ can no longer solely rely on parachurch organizations to support and finance the dedicated few who give up their lives to live in a foreign country. Missions needs the prayer and financial support, and the sending capabilities of local churches across the world. "This article assumes that local churches are already actively involved in fulfilling the Great Commission. The crucial question is, "Are churches seeking to be involved in the 'Missionary Training Process' itself?" Fuller sums up the need for the church to be involved in missionary training. He says: "The Great Commission was given to the Church. The task of world evangelization belongs to the Church. Training personnel for the task of world evangelization—missionary training—therefore, also belongs to the Church. While God may use an individual or a small group of individuals to excite others with a vision for missionary training, it is important to recognize that successful missionary training never can be a private project."[2]

As churches are becoming more involved in raising up and sending out the members of their own congregations as missionaries, it becomes important for the home church to have some part in the training of that individual. Phillips takes this thought a step further by saying,

> "It is the local church that must confirm the Holy Spirit's selection of candidates, equip them for service, and then send them out. Though important in the training process, preparing tomorrow's missionaries is not the primary responsibility of Bible colleges, mission agencies or furloughed missionaries."[3]

What many congregations don't realize is that effective missionary training begins with training the children of the church, which leads to a pre-candidate training program, and eventually a candidate training program.

Childhood Training and Education

A missions-minded church is a church that starts to teach the children about missions at a young age. Missions awareness should really begin as young as preschool and continue all the way through high school. Very few churches consider childhood training as a viable part of a missionary training program. Including this in the training plans can make a noticeable difference in the understanding of the participants. Consider the difference between two 18-year-old male Christians who both feel called to missions. One grew up in the church and heard about missions from time to time, but knows little about what is happening in the world, and missions in general. The other grew up in a church where he heard and learned about missions from a young age. This young man knows a general history of missions, and is familiar with the pioneers of the missions movement such as William Carey. He is also acquainted with the biblical basis of missions and aware that the Bible is basically a missions book. He has also been on a short-term missions trip, is vaguely familiar with the dangers and pitfalls involved with missionary service, and is aware that he needs much more training before actually going on the field full-time. The possibilities in this illustration are endless, but it is fairly easy to get the point. In both cases, God has truly called them, and God will use both of these prospective missionaries powerfully. But one of these males has a definite advantage in that he has been training his whole life for missionary service while the other is only beginning training. This missionary childhood training will not only have benefits for those children called to be missionaries, but also for all children who will eventually grow up and become active members of the Christian community. Can you imagine a Christian community where the lawyer, the banker, the stay-at-home mom, and the gas station attendant all have vibrant missions hearts? The first step in creating this community is missionary training with the children of the church.

Pre-candidate Training

The first thing that every church should do to prepare for the "pre-candidate" stage centers on appropriate missions awareness. A missions-focused prayer group is essential to every missionary training church. The church can never be an effective sending or training center unless missions is bathed in prayer by the congregation. In fact, the missions prayer group should precede any missions committees or conferences that convene. Ultimately, this is also an excellent way to foster an exhilarating cross-cultural environment where there has not been one in the past. As briefly mentioned above, another important element is a committed missions committee. Foltz says that "your missions committee is one of the primary bodies that will assume the task of mobilizing your local church."[4] It is important to remember that a missions committee is not an organization within itself that hibernates all year except at "missions conference time." Rather, this is to be an active committee that grows from the missions prayer group and fits within the existing structure of the church. The responsibility of this group is immense. Foltz says, "This group will carry the responsibility to orient every department and ministry of the local church toward its Great Commission goals."[5] In fact, it will be from this very missions committee that many of the missionary training decisions will be made. Lastly, at least an annual missions conference should be presented by the church to foster missions awareness and to help create an environment where people can be challenged to give and participate in missions. Fuller comments on similar programs when he says, "these programs enable people to pray and give to missions, and some trainees will be encourage to go further and to prepare for missionary service."[6]

These three elements are basic components of a successful missionary training program that all churches should develop regardless of the extent of their training goals. Without these foundational elements no more extensive or developed training can take place.

As a result of the missions prayer group, the missions committee, the missions conference, and the overall missions awareness in the church God will touch the hearts of individuals to answer the call to missions. This is where the "pre-candidate" stage, in the traditional sense, begins to take form. Different experts recommend different lengths of time for an individual to remain in the pre-candidate stage. Foltz describes the pre-candidate stage by breaking it up into two different stages. The first he calls the "missionary interest stage," which he describes as taking from two to six months to complete. The next stage he calls the "missionary discipleship stage" as taking ten to 12 months.[7] Using Foltz's method the pre-candidate stage could take as long as 18 months.

Regardless of the duration of the pre-candidate stage, it is essential that a number of things be accomplished during this stage. At the 1979 World Missions Conference, Rupert A. Eggert identified some qualifications that all missions pre-candidates must have in order to move to the candidate stage. He lists the following qualifications:

1 The applicant must have been genuinely converted and possess a vital religious experience. He should give evidence that his life is wholly consecrated to God.
2 He must be ready and willing to count the cost of service and be prepared for the hardships, both physical and emotional, which missionary service will require. He must have a firm trust in the Lord and believing that He will provide.
3 The applicant must be in fullest accord with the formal Statement of Faith.
4 He must posses knowledge of the Bible and, having a firm grasp of divine Truth, he must be able to impart it to others.
5 He must be familiar with the truth for which the sending body stands and for this reason it is desirable that he be a graduate from one of the groups recognized and approved schools of theology (graduates from other schools may be appointed if approved in all other respects). If the candidate is married, wherever possible, it is desired that the spouse have an academic degree or the equivalent of at least 30 hours of biblical or other mission related studies.
6 Each candidate should be a master workman in the divine art of soul-winning.
7 Normally a new missionary is not appointed to regular service overseas after he is 32 years old. If specialized work is required, appointments can be made up to 35.

Families should have no more than two children and if the wife should become pregnant between the appointment and the actual leaving on assignment it could be canceled.

8 Where language studies and proficiency is required, the appointment should not considered permanent until satisfactory knowledge and ability is demonstrated in the language.[8]

This list of qualifications are not meant to be blindly applied to every church situation, but is meant to be used as a guideline for local churches as they begin to form their own set of missionary qualifications. These guidelines are also not meant to restrict anyone from entering the pre-candidate stage, but rather they are markers to indicate when a prospective missionary is ready to become a full candidate.

Exactly what the pre-candidate does varies in each situation, but the pre-candidates task must be appropriate to the goals (helping the pre-candidate reach the candidate stage). Foltz identifies a few key activities that he has pre-candidates participate in. He requires a daily reading of *Operation World* along with a list of over 30 other books to read. He also allows the pre-candidates to get discipled further and to identify their spiritual gifts. Foltz requires that they take a missions perspective course, develop their five-year plan, and become involved in a local cross-cultural ministry.[9] These requirements seem to be a little too extensive for the average pre-candidate. It is important to remember that most pre-candidates will still have full-time jobs, and the point of the pre-candidate is to investigate their calling rather than smothering them with too much work. Again, the exact requirements are up to the individual churches.

Candidate Training Program

One common mistake in developing a missionary training program is developing one when one doesn't need to be developed. In other words, there is no reason to start a new work that ends up being almost exactly the same as another training center. The Body of Christ has a responsibility to work together when at all possible. If there are other organizations or churches whose belief system and goals match your own, then resources would be better utilized if both organizations joined together. Fuller says, "In the commercial world, when a company wants to launch a new product, they do market research to predict whether people will buy the product."[10] Fuller's illustration makes much sense when we consider that there is little need for a new training school to open if there are already similar training schools in existence. This information is not meant to dissuade any church from starting a training school, but rather to help each church determine the need and the direction to go once the need is determined.

Fuller offers thought provoking questions for a church to consider when starting a training school. He offers seven questions:

1 Who are the people to be trained? (What is their educational background, cultural background, economic background?)
2 What kind of co-workers will the trainees likely have? (They need skills in getting along with co-workers)
3 In what mission fields are the trainees likely to work? (The program needs to be tailored toward where the potential missionary will work)

4 What sending organizations will be served by the training? (Local congregations, church denominations, other independent missions organizations? Do they agree with the philosophy and curriculum of the program? Will they in the end be willing to employ our trainees?)
5 In what country is the training program located? (Are there legal and economic limitation on how the program can function? What about cultural expectations?)
6 Who will staff the training program? (You need qualified, full-time workers. Staff selection is the single most important factor in the effectiveness of any missionary program.)
7 What outside partners or sponsors will have an interest in the program? (Should foreign donors and staff be used for the program? If funding occurs from the church it exists to serve, natural accountability structures exist.)[11]

Ultimately, missionary training should have clear goals and objectives for it to be successful.The questions that Fuller raises are an excellent first step in researching the possibilities of starting a missionary training school in the local church. This will not only help you properly develop a training program, but it might help you identify another training program that already accomplishes your same goals. Or it might simply help you realize that you are not as close to developing a training program as you might have thought.

A missionary that has been through the pre-candidate stage successfully is qualified to begin actual training in the training program the local church has established. Taylor has identified three areas that are essential for a training program. He says that "character, skills, and knowledge" are integral to all missionary training programs.[12] All classes or activities for the trainee must fall into one of the three above categories. It is also important that each of these categories be properly represented in the curriculum, and that one item is not missed or ignored. A Bible school or a seminary will traditionally focus heavily on the "knowledge" category while not giving appropriate attention to the "character and skills" that need to be developed. On the other hand, church training programs tend to focus on the "character and skills" while being weak in the knowledge category. The key is to cover all bases, but the method in which the bases are covered can be done through various methods. A church is free to send a trainee to Bible school for the "knowledge," and focus on the "character and skills" themselves. Ultimately, the possibilities are endless.

Phillips describes his training goals in a different fashion, but they are still able to fit into those same three categories. Phillips says that all trainees need these elements:

1. Disciple: taught the spiritual disciplines, candidate discipling others, using spiritual gifts
2. Educate: work with Bible schools and seminaries, reading list, mission conferences, coordinate classes with neighboring local churches, look into mission agencies
3. Counsel: many candidates do not know what to do next, help candidates have a road map for direction
4. Assign: get candidates assigned or involved in ministry now, accountability, internship with home church
5. Evaluate: evaluate how they are doing at home, this will often reflect how they will do on the field

6 Send: when the candidate is ready, and the Holy Spirit has confirmed the call, the church should send him or her out. [13]

It is important to note that the above goals are general. To make a training school practical, some goals may need to be personalized to meet the needs of different students. A good example of this is when the training school determines whether it will specialize its training or not; if so, it will then determine how it will be done, depending on where the candidates are planning to serve. The length of this stage is also something to be determined, and will be dependent on the methods one chooses to use. If a Bible school or seminary format is required, this stage could last as long as three to five years, but if a church-based missionary training program is applied it might only last one year.

One successful training school, in existence since 1995, is the Asian Center for Missions. They require each candidate to complete 18 modules with a total of 630 hours of training time. The classes they require are:

> World Missions Course, Theology of Leadership, Spiritual Gifts, Missionary Life, Inductive Bible Study, Personal Discipline in Ministry, Cultural Anthropology, Language Acquisition Made Practical, Spiritual Warfare and Deliverance, Cell Church Dynamics, Money Matters, Cross Cultural Evangelism, Cross Cultural Church Planting, History of Missions, Christian Counseling, Introduction to Eastern Religions, Basic First Aid/Holistic Evangelism, and Field Research. [14]

The Asian Center for Missions primarily trains non-Western missionaries for service, and they work extremely close with each applicant's home church. So this is an example of a para-church organization working closely with the local churches in sending out missionaries. Another example is the Mountainside Missionary Center located near Libby, Montana. Their training program takes place from January through May (five months), with module style classes running from five to eight days each. They also incorporate scheduled mission outreach projects that help to enhance the personal character development, relationship building, and practical application of each candidate.[15] Some of the classes that they offer in their curriculum are:

> Integration of the Old Testament, World Missions, Acts, Defending of the Faith, Spiritual Warfare, Prayer and Fasting, The Pauline Epistles, Ministry Priorities and Personal Management, Understanding God's Will and Ways, Practical Theology, Evangelism and Discipleship, Biblical Counseling, Bible Study Methods and Interpretation, World Religions and Cults, Cross-Cultural Ministry, Teaching English as a Second Language, Preaching and Teaching, I and II Corinthians, Ministry in the Local Church, Team Building, Leadership Development, Church Planting, Missionary Preparation, Children's Ministry, and Youth Ministry.[16]

Both ACM and Mountainside offer different models from which to pattern a program. When developing a new training center, one can take pieces of each method to accomplish the goals that need to be accomplished; however, one piece that must be incorporated is an internship program.

An internship program can mean many things to many people, but Cunningham adequately describes what an intern is: "A person working under supervision to serve and develop skills in ministry."[17] An internship is a vital part of every missionary training program, because it develops the skills of the candidate more than sitting in a classroom would. 2 Timothy 2 is one portion of Scripture that is a good foundation for an internship program. Verse 15 (Updated *NASB*) says, "Be diligent to present yourself approved to God as a workman who does not need to be ashamed, handling accurately the word of truth." In today's society an excellent way to "present yourself approved" is to work alongside proven men, where one's character and skills can be evaluated. Following up with this is 2 Timothy 3:10 which says, "But you followed my teaching, conduct, purpose, faith, patience, love, perseverance." Basically, Timothy was Paul's intern, because he worked alongside of Paul for a period of time, and then he was sent without Paul to do the work of the Gospel.

Cunningham describes some particulars of an internship program for churches doing this on their own. He emphasizes the importance of a job description that has "general, broad expectations for the intern, purpose of the internship, and intern's relationship to church, and becomes more specific as the church learns more about the intern and his specific gifts."[18] He also goes on to describe the internship's two-fold ministry: "The intern is to work towards the development of lay people in that area of ministry" and "the intern's acquisition of new skills and abilities. Not only do we want the intern to equip lay people, we want the internship to equip the intern."[19] In the missionary candidates situation the church has a unique responsibility to provide an internship that would directly benefit the prospective missionary in his future endeavors. If the local church is not able to provide such an internship, then the local church should be the active agent in finding an internship suitable for the candidate. Ultimately this part of the missionary training can vary in length, but six to nine months is probably an adequate period of time. During this period, it would be helpful if the church would support the missionary with a stipend. Also the candidate could begin raising support, which could carry over into his or her real missionary appointment.

Conclusion

Finally, it takes all three phases of missionary training to produce a church culture in which missionary training is feasible. Childhood training is often seen as an expendable training component; on the contrary, it is a necessary ingredient for producing a successful training program the whole church supports wholeheartedly.

Pre-candidate training is also an area that is not often thought of as true missionary training, but it is an integral part of raising up men and women to be future missionaries. The candidate training session is the heart and soul of the missionary training program, and requires a major commitment by any local church. It is important for each church to remember that in most cases it makes more sense to join together with other churches or para-church organizations to meet the needs of a missionary training program. Resources and time are generally better spent when those of a like mind are working together towards a similar goal.

But if through extensive research a church finds that there are no adequate regional missionary programs meeting its specific need, then a missionary training program through that local church may be appropriate. Ultimately, it is important that all training and internship programs work towards the goals set by the church and agreed upon by the candidate.

Timothy L. Dillmuth is a graduate of Regent University with a Master of Divinity in Missiology. Tim has a heart for the nations, and is currently a staff member of China Outreach Ministries (COM). As part of COM, Tim ministers to Chinese university students in the Boston area alongside local churches who have a similar passion. Tim resides in Massachusetts with his wife and child.

NOTES

1 Fuller, Lois. "Starting a Missionary Training Programme," in *Establishing Ministry Training: A Manual for Programme Developers*. Robert W. Ferris, ed. (Pasadena: William Carey Library, 1995), pp. 121–138.
2 Ibid.
3 Phillips Jr., Woodrow. "Growing Missionaries in Your Church," in *The Role of the Local Church in World Missions: Sending*. John C. Bennett. ed. (Wheaton: ACMC, 1982), p. 36.
4 Foltz, Howard L. *Triumph: Missions Renewal for the Local Church*. (Joplin: Messenger Publishing House, 2000), p. 79.
5 Ibid.
6 Fuller, Lois. "Starting a Missionary Training Programme," *Establishing Ministry Training: A Manual for Programme Developers*. Robert W. Ferris, ed. (Pasadena: William Carey Library, 1995), p. 124.
7 Foltz, Howard L. *Missionary Preparation Proudly Presented by the Local Church*.
8 Eggert, Rupert A. "A Comparison of Methods Used to Identify and Select Missionaries." Found at: http://www.wls.wels.net/library/Essays/Authors/E/Eggert Methods/EggertMethods.rtf. 4.
9 Foltz, pp. 12–13.
10 Fuller, p. 123.
11 Fuller, pp. 127–130.
12 Taylor, Bill. "Principles for Pre-Field Missionary Training." Found at: http://www.urbana.org/_articles.cfm?re Corinthiansdid=265.

13 Phillips, pp. 36–43.

14 Asian Center for Missions curriculum guide.

15 Mountainside Missionary Training Program. Found at: http://www.internationalmessengers.org/Pages/mmt.html.

16 Ibid., http://www.internationalmessengers.org/Pages/mmt.html.

17 Cunningham, William. "Training Workers through Church Internship Programs," *The Role of the Local Church in World Missions: Sending.* John C. Bennett, ed. (Wheaton, IL: ACMC, 1982), p. 54.

18 Ibid., p. 58.

19 Ibid., p. 61.

7. Methods of Training Intercultural Leaders

AIMEE ELIZABETH DINWIDDIE

"Effective missionaries have been recognized as the people best able to identify the qualifications necessary for missionary service."[1]

Introduction

There are various directions when looking into the separate types of methods for training cross-cultural leaders. It is the challenge of this chapter to evaluate the current methods by exploring the benefits of each type in the hope of finding a solid answer to the question: What is the most effective method of training leaders? We go back in time and search for biblical and missiological methods for training leaders. As our search continues through the current spectrum of training methods, the solution is found through an analysis of modern methods and a study of the rate at which seminaries and other educational institutions are accomplishing their purposes.

In this chapter, it is important to emphasize that the most viable factor and focus of training is to promote indigenous church planting, thereby allowing a newly planted church to thrive and act as a sending agency for missions solely within its own means. Church planting is an extension of the existing church body, therefore it is viewed as a part of a "wider stream of worldwide revival and evangelism."[2] Church planting is also a partnership between indigenous churches and sending churches, committing to the same purpose of church growth.

Missiological History of the Methods of Training

Today, we look into the advancement of training for missionaries, whether it is long-term or short-term service. It is difficult for a modern, educated society to experience a methodology of historic missionary training, for there were no extensive, historical methods in the days of William Carey and other first generation missionaries. William Carey's view was not shared by the clergymen in his time when he said,

> "A Christian minister is a person who in a peculiar sense is not his own; he is the servant of God. . . . He engages to go where God pleases, and to do, or endure what he sees fit to command, or call him to in the exercise of his function. . . . I question whether all are justified in staying here, while so many are perishing without means of grace in other lands."[3]

Many missionaries were from the working class during that age. They used their expertise in serving overseas as missionaries. The modern missionary movement emerged mainly from Western Europe and the eastern shores of North America.

Clergymen were settled in their occupation, and therefore did not desire to leave their parishes. They were generally educated people so missionary service was left to those that had little education. "Among early writers on missions with this background, it is remarkable to find that few seem to expect much response from ordained and beneficed clergymen as missionary recruits."[4] There was little effort by clergy in identifying the need in other parts of the world. They saw the immediate need for security within their class, their financial standing, and their ranks among the church. But the missionary heart was found in the working class, because they little to relinquish financially or socially.

Qualities that a Missionary Candidate Should Possess

So what were the requirements of the 18th century missionary? Andrew Walls defines the necessary qualities that a missionary candidate should possess before accepting the sacrificial identity: "The missionary needs spiritual qualifications, knowledge of the Bible, and common sense. Competence with a mallet or a saw is all to the good, but formal education in not necessary—which is all well, for educated people are most unlikely to offer."[5] Since the mainstream missionaries in that day were uneducated, how were they then trained to face the difficulties of the missionary life? There were no past publications listing the virtues of

African, Asian, or Hispanic cultures, thousands of miles from their own familiar surroundings. How could they possibly go without knowledge of what they might face as they pursued God's will for all people? Their occupation and adventuresome spirit gave them the freedom to experience a new dimension of Christianity. Some acknowledge John Wesley's heart as the initiator of a generative revival for spreading the Gospel, simply because he noted that it was commanded in the Bible.

The Church of England allowed no one who was not an ordained minister to have the status of an Anglican missionary. The "present improved state of this island (United Kingdom),"[6] required such education prior to missionary ordination. There was, however, an allowance for the missionary "dwelling among savages rude and illiterate," which released him from the requirement of education in a place where there was no need of such. The first missionary voyage consisted of 30 participants, all qualified by the standards of the London Missionary Society. Their trip sent them to the Pacific Islands in 1796, and their occupations ranged from dissenting ministers to blacksmiths. Their strategy for the people of the Pacific Islands was to teach European trades, an assumed asset among the natives. Of the 30 original missionaries, only a handful of them were successful in full-time missionary service in the Pacific Islands.

The Experience in the Pacific Islands

This "trial and error" missionary attempt demonstrated the need for some kind of training or missiological education. Such training stressed the importance of intellectual standards in a candidate; otherwise, the candidate would have difficulty in learning a new language and adjusting to a new culture. The experience in the Pacific Islands also proved the success of tradesmen and their ability to help in practical ways the receiving culture through humanitarian aid and basic acquisition of biblical truth. For more than half a century, the missionary consensus continued with little training. The methods of training have been revisited, revised, and improved as the need has increased substantially over the years. By trial and error throughout many centuries of missionary attempts, we have collected numerous and valuable methods of preparation from past missionaries for the missionaries of our future.

The Student Movements

In the last two decades of the 19th century recruitment enabled eager young men from the universities and public schools, as well as the uneducated, to strongly pursue "the new faith missions."[7] This revival of missions created the need for formalized training, and although it came into creation at a slow pace, formal training would eventually be incorporated. Publications of missionary accounts were now serving as a popular literary deposit in missionary training. John William's *Narratives and Missionary Enterprises in the South Seas* (1839), Robert Moffat's *Missionary Labours and Scenes in Southern Africa* (1837), and perhaps the best-known account of missionary experience, Livingstone's *Missionary Travels and Researches in South Africa* (1857), gave insightful information and allowed a swelling of knowledge to transform missionary training and education. These publications and many others also changed the past stigma of missionaries from being uneducated clergy to scholastic men and women.

Although success on the mission field is not defined by the amount of education a missionary gains in life, past experiences have proven that missiological education and preparation, especially through the study of past publications, serves as important equipping tools. Today, most missionaries are required to experience some sort of training. Most full-time overseas missionaries today are educated within the university setting or have experienced some sort of continued education in a Bible school setting. We will continue this modern training methods journey in the coming sections.

Individuality of Training

While serving as a physical therapy assistant, I saw patients who had day-to-day goals that were expected to be accomplished. The only sufficient means of knowing what the patient could handle on the first day of therapy was through a series of initial examinations that concluded in a baseline of physical abilities. Therefore, a patient who has suffered from a car accident and has minimal mobility in his legs is not going to be expected to run the first day of therapy because a solid baseline has been formed of what he can and cannot do. Methods of training are also dependent on the individual who has been called to serve on the mission field. In any field of expertise, there is a value in determining a baseline as a standard for goals to be set. Before a protocol can be set for training, it is important to have an understanding of the spiritual, physical, mental, financial, and emotional history of the particular candidate. For example, a spiritual gifting test will direct the team leader in knowing how the individual might best be used in the team. Preliminary testing should cover all five areas mentioned above, and it can also be used as a baseline for determining the trainee's needs (strengths and weaknesses). Additional testing may be used after the candidate has been accepted and approved by the mission agency, but it is helpful to use the information gained from the initial application and interview process as a baseline. Overall, training should be catered to the individual's growth areas. The candidates should experience, through the power of the Holy Spirit, a change in their life in all areas: spiritual life (growth of heart-knowledge) and gaining progress in knowing the heart of God for all people, educational life (growth of head-knowledge), and experiential life (experiencing the head and heart-knowledge as one and practically applying these combined truths to everyday missionary life).

Missionary training today requires a well-rounded curriculum. Just as theological and missiological education play an important role in training, spiritual formation and leadership growth before and during service on the mission field should be equally pursued in training. Many missionary agencies and churches provide a variety of training methods, and most emphasize individual growth as a part of their training program. The next generation of missionaries face the greatest battle: To overcome life obstacles they have faced throughout the years. This is a task that can only be accomplished through their devotion to their own spiritual growth and their readiness for the field.

Contextualizing Individuality

Individuality is also contained within the context of the receiving culture. Contextualization, as defined by *Webster's Dictionary*, means "to place (a word, event, etc.) into a particular or appropriate context for the purpose of interpretation or analysis."[8] Therefore, as a method of missiology, contextualization adheres to the concept of transforming the message of the Bible into a culturally understandable form.

Secular thought may view contextualization as Eliza Doolittle's interpretation of "when in Rome, do as the Romans do."[9] But Christian contextualization refers to the application of biblical Truth, not transformation for the sake of "fitting in." Biblical Truth is constant, while the application is altered into an understandable cultural meaning. This was consistently exemplified in the New Testament as Jesus continually spoke Truth to many different cultures in parables that could be related to the audience listening. He spoke of the Kingdom of God in agricultural and farming terms because it applied to the crowd at hand. Similarly, we are to exemplify Christ in reaching the lost within the context of their own cultural values, characteristics, and history.

Cultural Awareness is Part of Contextualization

Worldview is expressed in different forms in different cultures. For instance, Americans' assumptions about the world stem from the cultural thought patterns prevalent in America. "The worldview is a gestalt within which all understanding of the world takes place. The result is a self-sustaining, mutually reinforcing system of beliefs and perspectives that give meaning to almost all of life."[10] True knowledge of a culture is derived from the understanding of cultural, religious, historical, and social values because it is in these concepts where perspective is altered. There are various types of worldview: upward look, inward look, outward look, downward look, and backward-forward look. Which if these do you think American worldview tends to fall into? The United States tends to be a mesh of many cultures, so the worldview is a direct representation of the numerous sub-cultures that exist.[11]

Methodology of Training

When seeking any form of training, there are three areas defined by Bill Taylor in *Send Me! Your Journey to the Nations:* character, skills, and knowledge.

Character formation refers to a person's own spiritual journey as a source for growth. This might include growth in spiritual maturity, spiritual gifts, moral purity, and discipline in spiritual quality time. The skills area of growth might be experiential learning; which include language acquisition, communication techniques, professional development, and relational abilities. The last area of growth recommended by Bill Taylor was the area of knowledge, which encourages growth in "biblical and theological truth, language learning principles, ministry and missions foundations, leadership, fellowship development, and understanding of global partnership, a basic grasp of human personality and health issues, professional/occupational training, and bivocational issues."[12]

Educational Training

The goal of educational training is to allow the trainee to grow in an area of knowledge that he or she has never experienced before. Missionary training is a new experience to anyone who has recently been called into full-time missionary service. A missionary might enter into training as a veteran pastor, but the perspective of that pastor is now altered as the calling of missions has entered into the future vision of his ministry. Although the pastor may possess biblical knowledge, there are other key concepts that have never been presented in his past educational experience. Therefore, biblical and missiological education continues to be a vital stage of readiness.

In educational training, various skills essential to missionary life should be taught. Group dynamics in a cross-cultural situation needs to be addressed. When a norm in a culture becomes formalized, it becomes a law or rule in that particular context. With that dynamic, there can be miscomprehension when entering into a new environment. In training intercultural leaders, there needs to be a consideration of laws and rules that might not be evident in your home culture, but might be a standard for the culture to which you are being exposed.

Once in England, a country that is most similar to the United States, I found myself in more than one embarrassing situation. Tradition envelops English culture and terminology tends to be very different than in United States. Something as simple as the word, "pants" was understood to be the word for "underwear" in England. Understanding cultural differences and studying the variations between the exiting and entering culture will help relieve some of the possible difficulties that might come up in a culturally mixed group.

Types of Educational Training

There are three types of educational training available: formal, informal, and non-formal training. Formal training usually consists of an accredited graduate level missiological education. "Formal education means relocation to a training institution."[13] It is generally high on the academic scale but can offer little life experience opportunities. It generally emphasizes missiological and biblical knowledge. A good academic program will also include a nurturing spiritual formation program. "Formal education is planned, supervised, primarily theoretical, classroom oriented, graded by examinations and graduations and degrees."[14] It is generally a Western form of education and can be helpful for those who are interested in developing leaders overseas.

Informal education refers to learning received from your environment. It comes about from observing group and individual interactions, living and learning from the mistakes and successes of those around you. Much of this type of learning is caught, not taught in a classroom setting. This knowledge comes mainly from situations unintentionally experienced but this knowledge is impressionable.

Non-formal education is the middle ground between formal and informal. It is not designed for the classroom but it is intentional, planned, and purposeful. It can include internships, a mentoring/discipling relationship, and supervised field trips. This is a form of intentional equipping, but it can also serve as a "caught" method. Most Bible schools and training institutes provide these types of learning opportunities.

Indigenous training centers are beneficial for training because they can be a source of continued education and training for the newly planted missionary or the veteran missionary wishing to update his skills. Biblical, theological and missiological training can take place generally in a formalized Bible school or university graduate level studies. It is in the areas of cultural adaptation; language acquisition; contextualization; cultural and religious studies and experiential, non-formal education where training centers can play a vital part. "Missionaries need to be trained within their particular settings."[15] It is recommended that the trainee spend adequate time in the receiving nation in continued training to avoid missionary burnout and attrition.[16]

Below is a chart of educational opportunities for various levels of missionary interest:

Levels of Training for Missionary Apprentices

Training and Experience Levels	Type of Preparation		
	Classroom	Field Training	Experience
Level I– Pre Missions four to five years of undergraduate work	College undergraduate, Bible, anthropology, language	One year formal education in another culture and language	Four summers with two different agencies
Level II- Mission Training three to four years of graduate work	University graduate study: theology, biblical studies	One to two years of field work in area near experienced service	Field work done in cooperation with selected agency
Level III- Intern Acquisition and people study	Two years of language	None. Coaching by senior missionary	Assignment to specific people group. Language study

Training and Experience Levels	Type of Preparation		
	Classroom	Field Training	Experience
Level IV- Associate Missionary Two to six years of work on field	Nine months of work at school, at end of field work	Supervision by senior missionary	Work with mission team to evangelize group
Level V- Missionary Two to six years on field	None	Supervision of associate missionaries	Decision to go to new field or stay at present field
Level VI- Senior Missionary Four to eight years of field work and teaching	Two years of graduate study	Teaching of trainees and interns. Field evaluations	Decision to return to a people or field teaching situation

Chart taken from *Missions and Theological Education in World Perspective*, p. 338.

Experiential Training

Mentoring as a Tool for Personal and Spiritual Growth

I once heard a story of a man who was a marathon runner. He was living out the last lap of his fully lived out life. He came upon some old running shoes, those that had lasted through many experiences and adventures.

As he looked at his old shoes, he was reminded of where they had taken him. As a young teenager, this man came to know the Lord. His future was given to him in the shape of a promise for his family's business. But as God got a hold of him, he announced to his family that his passion would not result in the family business, but in Jesus alone. It was then that those old shoes carried him to a marathon where he soon met and married his wife, and thus began a fulfilling, God-driven life. His ministry would take him many places around the world, and his experience as a missionary was marked by strong leadership, and more importantly, by servanthood. He continued to mentor many young, Spanish-speaking men into ministry. As he looked ahead to the future missionary movement, he passed on the old pair of shoes to a younger missionary friend, saying, "Finish well."[17]

Can you imagine the impact this man's testimony will have on the future leaders of tomorrow? A vital step in experiential learning is a coaching or mentoring relationship. It is in that environment where information is passed on, where growth increases dramatically, and where lives are changed.

The principles of Transformation Leadership Coaching or TLC can be utilized in training leaders overseas and promoting authentic Christian values in relationships among the Body of Christ. Similar to the marathon runner's shoes, mentoring begins with one experienced missionary investing in the lives of those with a passion to minister among unreached people groups and among their own society. It is a deposit of knowledge in the growth of a believer, and the joy in witnessing God's movement in and through a person's life.

Transformational Leadership Coaching is taught in three separate tracks, each lasting for 13 weeks. An individual has the option of completing all three tracks in order to receive Christian Coaching Certification, also called TLC Certification. This enables people to be specifically trained to mentor or coach others in the three tracks and/or in "as-needed" coaching. The "as-needed" coaching in this case would be in the area of missionary preparation.

TLC consists of 15% of actual exercises and class work. The remaining 85% is spent in "doing exercises," or experiential learning. The following are some of the teaching values you will receive through the application classroom information:[18] "Being with Jesus had a transforming effect on the disciples' heart, character and identity. They became changed men. That's called leadership formation. Leadership Coaches model and impart from a changed and changing life. Experiencing up close and personal a life that God has deeply processed inspires, challenges, and changes us in ways that are 'caught, not taught'."[19] The model of Jesus as a teacher among His disciples is the forward thrust of the Christian coaching movement. The coaching movement has been popular in the secular business world of today, but Christian coaching is stepping up on the values-driven leadership aspect of mentoring. Below are just some of the values that Christian coaching embraces in encouraging change and maturity in future leaders[20]:

- Transformation is primarily experiential, not informational.
- God initiates transformation through real, everyday life experiences.
- Ministry flows out of being.
- Each person is a uniquely-designed individual whom God has entrusted with stewardship of his life.
- Kingdom success is defined by growth and change.

- We will invest strategically in leaders in a way that calls and teaches them to impact others.

Mentoring is also emphasized in training materials for World Evangelical Fellowship as it illustrates the three kinds of mentoring: upward mentoring, co-mentoring (internal and external), and disciple mentoring. Upward mentoring "pushes leaders forward to expand their potential."[21] It supplies an experienced mentor with an inexperienced future leader and maximizes personal growth through teaching. Co-mentoring is utilizing a peer mentor as a source of growth through day-to-day interaction and accountability. Disciple mentoring means "empowering younger or less experienced leaders.[22]

One-on-one interaction with your coach and peer mentor

- Applying what you are learning to your own life
- Watching your coach model something, then doing it yourself
- Testing your skills on others in group sessions
- Journaling, discussion and reflection to help you integrate your learning
- Practice in using coaching techniques and exercises with your spouse or a friend
- Timely specific feedback and focused debriefing

Below is a model of mentoring by WEA Missions Commission missionary training track:[23]

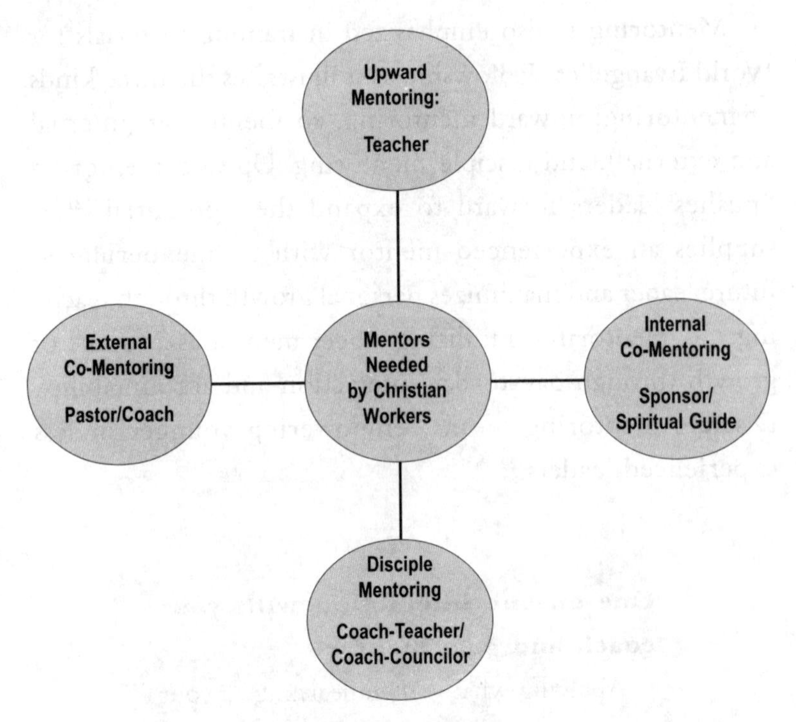

Diagram taken from Steve Hoke and Terry Walling's *Send Me! Your Journey to the Nations* (WEF: Pasadena, CA, 1999), p. 111.

Robert Clinton and Paul Stanley in *Connecting* provide a similar model which presents the idea of vertical mentoring (mentors), horizontal mentoring (peers and co-mentors), and downward mentoring (discipleship). Clinton says, "A growing leader needs a relational network that embraces mentors, peers, and emerging leaders, in order to ensure development and a healthy perspective on his or her life ministry."[24] The book says that this constellation model is not an option, but it is imperative to human growth.

Missionary training needs to incorporate all three aspects of the constellation model. Having peers that you can relate to on a regular basis, whether it be from a spouse or a friend, is just as important as an upward and downward mentoring relationship. All three are functional and life-changing when they are utilized as one.

Practical Application as a Learning Tool

The educational foundation that was formed in previous training can be applied practically through leading community outreach as a team. Emphasizing hands-on training will maximize growth as the trainee experiences the concepts that were previously learned in the classroom firsthand. It is also important that an experienced leader guides them in their experience since mirroring serves as one of the most significant learning tools. It is in practical application where ideas and concepts can be solidified in the hearts of future missionaries. "Knowing as the basis of doing"[25] is an example of experiential learning. In the teachings of Christ, it is not the "knowing" that is emphasized, but the actual "doing." Furthermore, the book of James raises the concern that the emphasis on doing was "in danger of being lost." The world slipped into an opposite viewpoint when it took a more Hellenistic view where knowing was valued more than doing. But as Christ's model emphasizes, it is in the "doing" where "knowing" is accomplished. Learning that is comprehensible and retainable is gained from experiencing life in all its positive and negative aspects. Values are founded in the experiences of our life, and in the lessons we choose to accept as a part of God's overall plan.

Spiritual Training Methods: Preparing the Way of the Lord

In the disciplines of spiritual formation, developmental progression is one aspect of training that is personalized and self-motivated. Accountability can occur through outside relationships, but it solely depends on the trainee whether he will pursue spiritual formation for missionary growth goals. "Every surge of missionary activity in history has grown out of revitalized personal prayer and personal renewal."[26] Revival, church renewal, healing, and other miracles in the mission field are attributed to prayer and the overwhelming power of the Holy Spirit in their own life. Testimony is the greatest asset in reaching people and can only be strengthened if the trainee allows time to understand how God crafted the events in their life. "Ministry flows out of being."[27] The success of your ministry and the rate at which change occurs among the receiving culture is influenced by the decisions the trainees will make concerning their spiritual discipline.

In his book, *Streams of Living Water,* Richard Foster encourages a move from the Holy Spirit in the lives of his readers. He describes various traditions in the spiritual journey; traditions such as the Spirit-empowered life, the prayer-filled life, the Word-centered life, the compassionate life, and the sacramental life. The different traditions are noted throughout the Bible, and serve as the stages of spiritual formation that a trainee should experience.[28] The purpose of spiritual formation in the training process is to find a discipline and focus that is dependent on the Lord and the power of the Holy Spirit. This dependency is vital to everyday life on the mission field.

Spiritual Preparation Evaluation Questions

Simple questions that serve as a baseline for spiritual growth[29]:

1 Are you learning to pray?
2 Are you studying God's Word?
3 What is your sense of God's "call" on your life?
4 Are you telling the story of the reality of Christ in your own life?
5 Is there a fragrance in your life, an unmistakable evidence of the presence of God?

Lastly, God provided the discipline of spiritual growth to serve as a witness of His grace in our lives. Prayer and devotion to the Lord fights the battles that the physical body is incapable of fighting. It begins a process of preparation, heralding the victory in spiritually oppressive situations that all missionaries experience at many points in their overseas career. God's provision is evident in those that find focus and centeredness in their lives on God before, during, and after their missionary service.

Conclusion

Accurate training methods will help depreciate the attrition rate among upcoming missionaries and leaders. It is in the methods of training where foundation is set for future missiological service. The purpose of education and accurate training methods is to educate and train church leaders and pastors for planting viable and self-sustaining churches in their own community, and beyond the 10/40 Window. Future missionaries need to be prepared and fully capable of defeating strongholds in foreign soil and in places where the Gospel has never been spoken. Through educational, experiential, and spiritual progression in our lives, the Lord is preparing the next generation for revival and a new missions movement in the years ahead. The heart of the next generation of missionaries will thrive on raising up indigenous leaders to go beyond the walls of missionary training. It will support and encourage native people groups to reach an unfamiliar culture for Christ, allowing a movement within Second and Third World nations to reach the unreached for the glory of the Lord.

In training, the most important aspect is deepening our knowledge of the world around us, finding the most effective solutions in reaching the lost in other nations, and raising up a new generation of missionaries through creative ways of learning. For the veteran missionary, it is now important that you not only reflect on your experiences, but make yourself available for the opportunities the Lord gives you to pass on the knowledge and wisdom that you have been blessed with through the years. And for those who are experiencing missions for the first time, whether it be a new revelation of God's missions calling on your life or just entering into a training program, it is important for you to remain in a receiving spirit, discerning what is Truth and seeing how God has revealed such Truth through your own life experiences. While receiving Truth and knowledge, ask God to reveal how they can transform your own life as well as how they might be actively transmitted to a new generation for Christ.

Aimee Elizabeth Dinwiddie received her Bachelor of Arts degree from Ouachita Baptist University in 1999. Upon graduation, she worked at Baylor Healthcare Systems of Dallas in the Rehabilitative Medicine arena as a Speech Therapy Assistant. Aimee is now a missionary serving with AIMS as a Humanitarian Aid Representative. She also travels to various missions organizations to promote a partnership in recruiting, training, and sending humanitarian aid and relief and workers to the field. She currently resides in Virginia Beach, Virginia, where she is employed with New Life Christian Fellowship as Assistant to the Director of the Equipping Department, while pursuing an M.A. in Missiology as a full-time student at Regent University. Aimee has served within non-denominational churches as a youth and young singles leader, where she coaches and mentors young people as they pursue what God has called them to be.

NOTES

1 Hoke, Steve and Bill Taylor. *Send Me! Your Journey to the Nations*. (Pasadena, CA: World Evangelical Fellowship, 1999), p. 24.

2 McClung, Grant. "Globalbeliever.com: Connecting to God's Work in Your World." (Cleveland, Tennessee: Pathway Press, 2000), p. 184.

3 Carey, William. *Enquiry into the Obligations of Christians to Use Means for the Conversion of the Heathens* (Leicester, 1792), p. 71ff.

4 Walls, Andrew. *The Missionary Movement in Christian History: Studies in the Transmission of Faith*. (Maryknoll, NY: Orbis Books, 1996), p. 161.

5 Ibid., p. 163.

6 Ibid., p. 164.

7 Ibid., p. 188.

8 Agnes, Michael. *Webster's New World College Dictionary Fourth Edition*. (New York, NY: McMillan, 1997). p. 315.

9 Lerner, Alan. *Pygmalion and My Fair Lady*. (New York: Signet Penguin Group, 1956), p. 157.

10 Fraser, David. *Planning Strategies for World Evangelization*. (Grand Rapids, MI: William D. Eerdmans Publishing, 1990), p. 109.

11 AIMS. *Short-Term Missions Training: Key to Success*. (Orchard Park, NY: Buffalo School of the Bible, 1989), pp. 20–21.

12 Hoke, Steve and Bill Taylor. *Send Me! Your Journey to the Nations*. (Pasadena: CA: World Evangelical Fellowship, 1999), p. 29.

13 Clinton, Dr. Robert. *The Making of a Leader* (Colorado Springs, CO: NavPress, 1998), p. 91.

14 Taylor, Bill and Terry Walling. *Send Me! Your Journey to the Nations.* (Pasadena, CA: World Evangelical Fellowship, 1999), p. 30.
15 Woodberry, J. Dudley. *Missiological Education for the 21st Century.* (Maryknoll, NY: Orbis Books, 1996), p. 116.
16 Taylor, William. *Too Valuable to Lose: Exploring the Causes and Cures of Missionary Attrition.* (Pasadena, Ca: William Carey Library, 1997), p. 207.
17 Taylor, Bill. *Send Me! Your Journey to the Nations.* (Pasadena, CA: World Evangelical Fellowship, 1999), p. 100.
18 More information at http://www.transformationalcoaching.com/.
19 http://www.transformationalcoaching.com/approach.htm, April 20, 2003.
20 More information at http://www.transformationalcoaching.com/.
21 Hoke, Steve, and Terry Walling. *Send Me! Your Journey to the Nations.* (Pasadena, CA: World Evangelical Fellowship, 1999), p. 111.
22 Ibid, p. 111.
23 Ibid.
24 Clinton, Robert. *Connecting: The Mentoring Relationships You Need to Succeed in Life.* (Colorado Springs, CO: NavPress, 1992), p. 159.
25 Conn, Harvie. *Missions & Theological Education in World Perspective.* (Farmington, MI: Associates of Urbanus, 1984), p. 38.
26 Hoke, p. 34.
27 Stoltzfus, Tony. *TLC Training Manual.* (Virginia Beach, VA: TLC, 2003), p. 1.
28 Foster, Richard. *Streams of Living Water.* (New York, NY: Harper Collins, 1998), p. xvi.
29 Hoke and Walling, p. 35.

8. Missionary Selection

JOHN CARLOCK

"To speak of mission in any sense, then, is to speak first of all, of God and His divine prerogative to sovereignly choose laborers for His harvest . . .
The Church has the responsibility to insure that those sent out for missionary service are called, qualified and equipped for the challenge."

Introduction

The enormity and the seriousness of the task of world evangelization make the selection of missionary candidates of critical importance. The selection must be carefully thought out and implemented by local churches, missionary agencies and training institutions. Strategic planning and ample resources will be of little help when placed in the hands of individuals who are unqualified and ill-equipped for cross-cultural ministry. Governments insure that only their best and brightest are dispatched to foreign lands as ambassadors who will represent their countries. Businesses competing today in the global marketplace and sending personnel for foreign assignments are aware of the risks involved and are discovering the need for careful selection of staff to avoid substantial financial loss. If dollars and diplomacy motivate businesses and governments to carefully select their representatives and workers, the Church should do no less, especially in light of the eternal consequences of the missionary enterprise and the building of Christ's church worldwide.

Consider also the tragic consequences of countless individuals and families who leave for the field with all the enthusiasm and zeal for their new assignments only to return home shortly afterward devastated and disillusioned by their experience. The financial cost pales in comparison to the cost in human lives. The church has the responsibility to insure that those sent out for missionary service are called, qualified and equipped for the challenge. Sending out lambs to a den of wolves is both unethical and irresponsible.

Having spent 27 years in Peru with Wycliffe Bible Translators and having assisted in the assessment and selection of over 800 missionary candidates, Larry and Lois Dodds share their thoughts and insights on this issue:

> "Ethical issues for missions begin immediately, right up front in the recruitment, assessment and selection of missionaries. We believe that inadequate assessment and casual selection is a violation of ethics, for we have an ethical, moral and spiritual responsibility to select people suited for the complex and heavily stressful cross-cultural experience. Choosing and sending out those who lack the personal resources of spiritual maturity, resiliency, hardiness, solid ego-strength and relational skills is to set people up for failure and loss."[1]

The extensive study on missionary attrition conducted by the World Evangelical Alliance Missions Commission in 1996 provided an invaluable resource for those involved in sending cross-cultural workers. In the prologue, William Taylor explains the primary motivation behind the study:

> "The causes and solutions of undesirable attrition are complex; personal, family, and institutional cultures are difficult to change; the spiritual warfare is nothing to laugh about; and the long-term cross-cultural ministry is frankly tough. But ultimately we are talking about people, real-life individuals—children, youth, and adults. And that's what drives our study."[2]

Proper assessment and screening will by no means resolve every issue related to missionary attrition, nor will it guarantee success for every candidate approved. It will, however, insure that the proper steps have been taken to minimize the risk and tragic consequences of sending overseas those who are neither called nor qualified. Out of pastoral concern for individuals and families, those responsible for appointing and sending candidates for missionary assignment can do no less.

It is important to avoid from the onset the wrong assumption that missionary selection is primarily a human prerogative or initiative, for it is not, anymore than the missionary work of the Church is primarily a human activity. The foundation of all that is done in every aspect of the Church's mission is the missionary nature of God and His plans and purposes for the nations as revealed in the Scriptures.

"The missionary purpose of the church rests firmly on the missionary nature of God . . . To speak of mission in any sense, then, is to speak first of all of God. He is the rock-solid foundation of the church's missionary endeavor. Its calling and responsibility to do mission come from the God who is in His nature missionary. Our missionary purpose flows from God and His eternal purpose with regards to humankind."[3]

To speak then of missionary selection is to speak first of all, of God and His divine prerogative to sovereignly choose laborers for His harvest. Jesus stated in John 15:16 (*NIV*), "You did not choose Me, but I chose you, and appointed you to go and bear fruit." Consequently, the church does not choose candidates for missionary service; God does. The role of the church is secondary and serves to confirm the call of God through a systematic and biblically based screening process. Missionary "screening" perhaps better defines this process than missionary "selection." For the purposes of this discussion, however, the two words will be used interchangeably.

Biblical Basis for Selection

The Old Testament provides numerous examples of God's people ministering in cross-cultural settings and the divine desire to reach all nations. Individuals such as Abraham, Joseph, Moses, Esther and Nehemiah, and a number of prophets including Elisha, Daniel and Jonah were called by God to leave their cultural context or were strategically placed in foreign lands for divine purposes. In these instances, selection was based upon divine prerogative with little or no information given on the criteria used. It is evident, though, that these men and women were of sound character and were willing to obey the voice of the Lord as His will for their lives and ministry was progressively revealed. It is also evident that the testimony of their lives and ministry clearly demonstrates the hand of God at work and His divine favor resting upon them.

In the New Testament we see Jesus selecting His 12 disciples after a night spent in prayer, though on what basis He chose them from others is not known. Clearly, divine guidance is implied and the fact that they had already committed to following Him is evident. It is significant to consider that each one of the 12, apart from Judas, would one day be involved in cross-cultural ministry. Acts 1:14–26 shows how prayer played significantly in choosing a replacement for Judas. The selection of the new apostle was based upon a primary requirement: The candidate must have been with Jesus from the time of His baptism until His ascension into heaven.

Deacons were chosen in Acts 6 and qualifications were again clearly stated: candidates were required to be honest men of good reputation, full of the Holy Spirit and wisdom. Again, prayer preceded the appointment of these men. It is not surprising then that when the church in Antioch sent out Paul and Barnabas on their first missionary journey, prayer was a part of the selection and appointment process. In the account given in Acts 13:1–4, the believers were both praying and fasting when the Holy Spirit directed this local church to send out these two men. As churches were established, elders and deacons were chosen based upon the qualifications stated by Paul in his letters to Timothy and

Titus. These included issues involving doctrinal beliefs, character, and family life.

We can see from these New Testament examples the importance of prayer in the selection process for church leadership and service. Central also in this process are the role of the local church and the progressive establishment of clear and verifiable criteria for determining a person's qualification for a particular ministry. Evidence of strong Christian character and spiritual maturity are the most important considerations to be taken into account when selecting candidates for ministry. Though only one of these examples deals specifically with missionary selection, that of Paul and Barnabas in Acts 13, there is clearly biblical precedent for the establishment of guidelines and the necessity for screening individuals for leadership and ministry, in whatever capacity.

Missiological Foundations

Those involved in the selection process of missionary candidates must have a clear understanding of missiology with all its theological, historical, and philosophical implications. The purpose of missions, the unique challenges that cross-cultural workers face, and the current trends and strategies in world evangelization are essential components to be considered and understood by church leaders responsible for the selection of missionary candidates. In an article dealing with missionary selection and the local church, Dr. Gailyn Van Rheenen states that the first vital and preparatory step in the selection process is that "church leaders must become learners who seek to understand the basics of missions and understand the process of missions."[4] Without such learning and a clear understanding of missions and the unique challenges involved in cross-cultural ministry, the selection process is seriously flawed from the onset.

The spiritual nature of the missionary task necessitates more, however, than just a clear understanding of missiological principles. The importance of prayer has already been demonstrated in the biblical examples given and must not be underestimated or overlooked by those involved in the selection process. In his article "Missionary Training: A Discipline," Miguel Alvarez begins his discussion of the selection process with these five words: "The candidate is prayerfully chosen . . ."[5] Roland Allen, writing about the spiritual nature of the missionary task states, "The end is spiritual, the means also must be spiritual."[6] Decisions based upon missiological principles and depending on measurable criteria in the candidate without recognizing the need to earnestly discern the Lord's will through prayer, and perhaps fasting, will certainly not meet success.

Gerald Wright, in his article "The Purpose of Missions," uses the biblical imagery of light and darkness to outline the missionary task. He includes proclamation through word and deed, emphasizing a holistic approach to ministry, the necessity for spiritual warfare and divine empowerment, transformation of culture as the kingdom of light confronts the kingdom of darkness, and the gathering of believers into communities of faith. Though all Christians are called to be light, "the calling to be light has special relevance for the missionary and for the mission of the church to a lost world." Wright goes on to state:

> "Missionaries [are] to cross the barriers that separate people from the Gospel and present them

> with the knowledge, claims, and character of God. It requires special gifting from God that enable them to become bicultural, to be severed from kin and country, and to recognize avenues of proclamation and ministry in settings different from their own."[7]

With this imagery of light and darkness in mind, the selection process of missionary candidates and those responsible for determining the qualifications for cross-cultural ministry must consider two important questions: (1) Are they walking in the light? This would include evidence of conversion, calling, Christian development and obedience, character, and beliefs; and (2) Are they able to manifest this light in a different culture? This would include personality traits, physical and emotional health and well being, unique gifting, spiritual empowerment, maturity, and ministry experience.

Selection Criteria

Conversion, Calling, Commitment and Character

Because of the spiritual nature of the missionary task, the selection process should emphasize the spiritual characteristics of the candidate. Missionary candidates must first of all demonstrate clear evidence of a salvation experience and a clear biblical understanding of conversion. Most agencies obviously begin here, but many fail to take into account the pre-conversion experiences and background of those seeking appointment. Examining the family history, upbringing, experiences and religious beliefs prior to conversion is an important element in understanding the candidate and may bring to light both strengths and weaknesses that could help or hinder ministry in the field.

It is God who calls and raises up laborers for the harvest, and individuals need to know that they have been divinely called and be able to clearly articulate this calling. The missionary call, according to Robert Speer, "involves, for one thing, God's will; and, for another, man's discovery of that will.[8]

> "Any vocation, or call, involves two separate choices: God's choice of the person and the person's choice to accept what is perceived as God's call. Those who respond to the call are willing to sacrifice their own desires for the greater good of humankind."[9]

It is this sense of divine calling that will anchor the individual to a specific course in life and help them persevere through the difficult process and preparation for appointment that will enable them to endure the hardships and trials of overseas ministry. Evidence of the calling should not only be articulated by the candidate but also demonstrated by the preparation involved. "Certainty about God's call is usually demonstrated in some measurable ways, such as having already served within the church or para-church organizations."[10] When God calls an individual to a specific ministry, He gives ample time for preparation, and this should be evident in the candidate's life.

A commitment to Christ involves a commitment to His Church, and candidates need to be able to demonstrate their faithfulness to a local church, the discipleship process they were involved in, and their relationship to the leadership and membership of their home fellowship. It is important that confirmation of the call and spiritual counsel and training are provided by those closest to the candidate, and the local church and its leadership must be an integral part of the selection process. Those who have witnessed the candidate's life over a period of time best determine personal character and issues such as interpersonal skills, sociability, family life and willingness to serve. Biblical teaching and missiological studies both emphasize the importance of Christian character in the selection process. Loren Cunningham, the founder of YWAM, made this observation:

> "The basic element required for effective Christian missionary service is a Christlike character expressed in daily life. Missiological studies of the time were beginning to prove something which was obvious to most foreign missionaries: namely that character faults and interpersonal relationship problems were the primary cause of missionaries leaving the mission field after the first term of service."[11]

Studies on attrition conducted by the World Evangelical Alliance Missions Commission also highlight the importance of character and interpersonal skills. "The prime causes of preventable early return of missionaries cluster in areas of character and spirituality, relationships and interpersonal conflict."[12] The primary conclusion reached to remedy this problem was to "focus more attention on the local church"[13] in the selection and training process.

Financial difficulties overseas are another primary cause of missionary attrition. A candidate's stewardship of personal finances ought to be closely examined. Tithing and giving are matters of character and obedience to God's Word and demonstrate faithful stewardship. Missionaries are required to raise financial support and will have a difficult time doing so if they haven't first been faithful givers themselves. "Give and it shall be given unto you," according to Luke 6:38. Personal debt and financial obligations at home will only add to the stress of adjustment to ministry overseas and may hinder longevity in the field. The inability to live within one's means and improper money management are often indications of a more serious underlying problem that needs to be dealt with. A simple lifestyle demonstrated by sacrifice and frugality is essential on a missionary budget and ought to be evidenced in the candidate's life at home.

Physical and Mental Health, Personality, Spiritual Gifts, Education and Ministry Experience

The physical and emotional demands of living in and adjusting to a foreign culture necessitate that the candidate be of sound body and mind. An increasing number of mission agencies and denominations are using personality profiles and psychological testing to determine a candidate's ability to make the necessary cultural adjustments and carry on effective ministry overseas. Agencies and denominations responsible for sending out over half of the North American missionary force "engage professional Christian psychologists for screening, orientation and counseling of missionary candidates."[14] Though some argue against the use of such testing, Stanley Lindquist, founder of the Link Care Center in Fresno, California, "considers it a matter of stewardship of both human and material resources and believes that to withhold such services would be an abrogation of personal responsibility."[15] Paul Goring in his book, *The Effective Missionary Communicator*, concludes that "adequate research is not available to indicate whether psychological screening actually contributes significantly to more effective missionary personnel selection."[16] Issues related to the physical well being of the candidate are obviously easier to assess, but both physical and emotional health need to be considered.

Various tests should be administered to determine the candidate's spiritual gifts, biblical knowledge and language aptitude. The candidate should have some formal education in theology and missiology and have some prior experience in personal evangelism and discipleship. Ministry experience should demonstrate a willingness to serve and submit to those in authority, and should include some exposure to a cross-cultural setting. Opportunities abound in our day for cross-cultural ministry right at home or on short-term mission trips and there ought to be evidence that the candidate has taken advantage of these opportunities. Joshua Massey relates his experience of feeling called to reach Muslims in South Asia and yet overlooking the many opportunities to minister to Muslims in his college campus.

> "I believe my blindness to the incredible opportunities all around me was related to the erroneous idea that "missions" is something that occurs overseas, not in my home town. Church and mission leaders all want to see some "ministry experience" from missionary applicants before going overseas, but few expect significant pre-field, local, cross-cultural experience."[17]

The ability to adapt and make the necessary cultural adjustments overseas will be greatly enhanced by a candidate's willingness to experience cross-cultural ministry while at home.

Selection Model

Core Requirements for Selection:

- Conversion and Calling
- Spiritual Maturity
- Physical and Mental Health
- Ministry Experience (including some cross-cultural)
- Doctrinal Beliefs
- Interpersonal Skills
- Theological and Missiological Training
- Financial History

Variables for Consideration:

- Age
- Language Aptitude
- Marital Status
- Specialized Skills

(a) Application

This will include general information about the candidate and the candidate's family: education, employment history with references, medical history, financial situation, home church, ministry and cross-cultural experience. The candidate will submit with the application a personal and family history paper which will include upbringing, pre-conversion experiences and religious beliefs, conversion experience, doctrinal beliefs, when and how they received a call for missionary service, and what steps have been taken in response to that call. Two references of the candidate's spiritual leadership will be required, as well as two general references. Those responsible for the selection of candidates will prayerfully consider the application, contact the various references and determine whether or not to continue the process.

(b) Interview

Interviews will be conducted with the candidate and spouse, both separately and together. Issues such as devotional life, marriage and family, sources of stress and methods of coping, relationships with peers, church family and spiritual leadership, attitudes toward different denominations and willingness for cooperation, accountability, and any other areas deemed necessary after reviewing the application and personal history paper will be discussed. The candidate will also be asked to state his or her philosophy of ministry, conviction of calling, and desired field of ministry.

Those conducting the interviews should be spiritually prepared and ask the Lord for guidance and discernment throughout this process. To avoid general answers, some questions need to be direct and specific. Statistics show that over 35% of ministers in the U.S. consider Internet pornography to be a temptation. The Assemblies of God have recognized this as an area of concern for their missionary family and have devoted time during their annual School of Missions to deal with this issue. "Has the candidate been exposed to pornography in the past year? What is being done to avoid this temptation?" would be examples of direct questions. Other questions suggested by this model include: "Are there any life-controlling problems or addictions that the candidate is still dealing with? How many times has the candidate shared his or her faith in the past two months? Has the candidate spoken negatively about church leadership with another Christian? Are there areas of unforgiveness that have not been dealt with? Does the candidate struggle with anger, depression, anxiety or fear, and what has been done to deal with these issues?" It goes without saying that information shared in the interview is held in the strictest of confidence and such specific questions should only be asked in a one-on-one situation.

Interviews will also be conducted with the candidate and his or her spiritual leadership regarding doctrinal beliefs, willingness to serve, submission to authority, interpersonal skills, faithfulness and dependability, consistent character, and evidence of spiritual gifts. Determination will be made with the candidate's spiritual leadership on whether the individual is ready for missionary service or requires more training and/or formal education.

(c) Testing

Tests will be administered to determine the candidate's personality profile, spiritual gifts, biblical knowledge, and language aptitude. Upon completion of these tests and upon consensus reached with the candidate's spiritual leaders, the candidate will enter a probationary period before final appointment is made. This will include raising funds and serving one year overseas under the direction of a veteran missionary. The candidate's ability to culturally adapt, cooperate with other missionaries in the field, build meaningful relationships with nationals, maintain spiritual and physical health, and endure the hardships and difficulties faced will be evaluated and a final decision for full appointment will be made.

Conclusion

Throughout this chapter I have highlighted the enormity of both the task at hand and the serious nature of world evangelization. In this light, the selection process of missionary candidates is of critical importance.

Given the profound historical and philosophical implications of missions, I proposed a selection criteria that explores the spiritual characteristics of candidates, including their conversion, calling, commitment, and character. In this respect, missionary churches and agencies are using a battery of tests to determine the applicant's physical, mental, and spiritual fitness for cultural adaptation and cross-cultural ministry. The selection process, comprised of application, interview, and testing stages, would help recruiters ascertain the existent personal, family, and church support to the candidates' goal.

I have also discussed that proper assessment and screening will by no means solve every issue related to missionary attrition, nor will it guarantee success for every candidate approved. It will, however, insure that the proper steps have been taken to minimize the risk and the tragic consequences of sending overseas those who are neither called nor qualified.

And finally, it is important to avoid from the onset the wrong assumption that missionary selection is primarily a human prerogative or initiative. The foundation of all that is done in every aspect of the Church's mission is the missionary nature of God and His plans and purposes for the nations as revealed in the Scriptures.

John Carlock has an M.A. in Practical Theology from Regent University. He is serving in the Middle East and is involved in holistic ministry, training, and Christian education. He is an ordained minister with the Assemblies of God. He and his wife have three children.

NOTES

1 Dodds, Larry and Lois Dodds. "Selection, Training, Member Care and Professional Ethics: Choosing The Right People and Caring for Them with Integrity," Online: http://www-students.biola. edu/~jay/ethical care.html.

2 Taylor, William, ed. *Too Valuable to Lose: Exploring the Causes and Cures of Missionary Attrition* (Pasadena, CA: William Carey Library, 1997), xiv.

3 Rogers, Ron. "The Missionary Purpose of God's People," in *Missiology: An Introduction to The Foundations, History, and Strategies of World Missions*, J. Terry, E. Smith and J. Anderson, eds. (Nashville, TN: Broadman & Holman Publishers, 1998), pp. 119–120.

4 Van Rheenan, Gaily. "Can Local Churches Effectively Select and Care for Missionaries?" Online: http://www.missiology.org/MMR/mmr9.htm.

5 Alvarez, Miguel. "Missionary Training: A Discipline," in *Journal of Asian Mission* 2:1 (March 2000), p. 101.

6 Allen, Ronald. *Missionary Methods: St. Paul's or Ours?* (London: World Dominion Press, 1962), p. 103.

7 Wright, Gerald. "The Purpose of Missions," in *Missiology: An Introduction to The Foundations, History, and Strategies of World Missions*, J. Terry, E. Smith and J. Anderson, eds. (Nashville, TN: Broadman & Holman Publishers, 1998), p. 28.

8 Speer, Robert. "What Essentially Constitutes a Missionary Call?" *The Call, Qualifications and Preparation of Candidates for Foreign Missionary Service: Papers by Missionaries and Other Authorities*, Fennell Turner, ed. (NY: Student Volunteer Movement, 1906), p. 3.

9 Jones, Marge and E. Grant Jones. *Psychology of Missionary Adjustment*, (Springfield, MO: Logion Press, 1995), p. 18.

10 Dodds.

11 Rickard, Peri. "Youth With A Mission Training: From the Nations to the Nations," in *Internationalising Missionary Training*, William Taylor, ed. (Grand Rapids, MI: Baker Book House, 1991), p. 164.

12 Taylor., p. 351.

13 Ibid., p. 154.

14 Goring, Paul, *The Effective Missionary Communicator: A Field Study of the Missionary Personality*, (Wheaton, IL: Billy Graham Center, 1991), p. 4.

15 Ibid.

16 Ibid, p. 3.

17 Massey, Joshua, "Hometown Ministry as Pre-Field Preparation," in *Evangelical Missions Quarterly*, Vol. 38, No. 2, April 2002), p. 197.

9. Organization and Planning: Maximizing Missionary Training

JASON L. DEVERNA

"Strategies force Christians to both seek the mind of God and the will of the Holy Spirit; looking for answers to questions like what God desires and how can we conform to the future of His desires?"[1]

Welcome to a new era in missionary training. This chapter will examine the need for organization and planning within the missionary training enterprise. As society advances, so too must the discipline of missionary training. It is time for the church to craft proper training systems for effective preparation of missionaries. Systematized order and intent are needed in missionary training. Often, churches have been reactive rather than proactive in dealing with missionary training. There is a new day in missions, one that calls for resources to be directed strategically to produce effective results. The new day in missions requires more planning and a highly effective integration of all the tools and resources the Lord has given us. We must reach the peoples of the world carrying the cry of παντα τα εθνη (all people groups)"[2]

Missionary preparation must be rethought and re-planned with a new thrust. It is essential that the strategies and plans be developed with an understanding of those they seek to reach.[3] Al Ries explains the power of focused energy:

> The sun is a powerful source of energy. Every hour the sun washes the Earth with billions of kilowatts of energy. Yet with a hat and some sunscreen, you can bathe in the light of the sun for hours at a time with few ill effects.
>
> A laser is a weak source of energy. A laser takes a few watts of energy and focuses them in a coherent stream of light. But with a laser you can drill a hole in a diamond or wipe out cancer.[4]

Like the focused energy of a laser, the church must now move into a new phase of strategic development in missionary training. Strategic planning and organization are needed to harness the resources, knowledge, and skills available. This is an "Esther" moment in our generation "for such a time as this."

Organization and Planning: Establishing Its Relevance

The first part of this chapter will identify the biblical pattern for planning and organization. We define missions planning as "partnering with God to build His kingdom." Some general issues in attrition will be addressed. The chapter will also present several trends in the world, in missions, and in education. A compilation of all pertinent information will reveal the need and relevance for strategic planning and organization in a missionary training context.

A Biblical Basis for Planning and Organization

The Bible is full of stories of men and women who have partnered with God to build His kingdom on Earth. Both the Old and New Testaments have illustrations of men who planned to accomplish a specific task. There is perhaps no greater example than Nehemiah. He was filled with grief and compassion for Jerusalem. He lamented the condition of the land, praying that God will hear his prayer on behalf of God's children. Nehemiah received an assignment and burden from God to see the walls of Jerusalem rebuilt and the city restored.

Nehemiah was the cupbearer to the king and was shown to have planned his actions (Nehemiah 2). First, Nehemiah came before the king (vs. 2–8). When the king noticed that Nehemiah was sad, the king asked Nehemiah what he would like. Nehemiah knew exactly what he wanted, needed, and the amount of time necessary to complete the task.

> "The king said to me, 'What would you request?' So I prayed to the God of heaven. I said to the king, 'If it pleases the king, and if your servant has found favor before you, send me to Judah, to the city of my fathers' tombs, that I may rebuild it.' Then the king said to me, the queen sitting beside him, 'How long will your journey be, and when will you return?' So it pleased the king to send me, and I gave him a definite time.

> And I said to the king, 'If it pleases the king, let letters be given me for the governors of the provinces beyond the River, that they may allow me to pass through until I come to Judah, and a letter to Asaph the keeper of the king's forest, that he may give me timber to make beams for the gates of the fortress which is by the temple, for the wall of the city and for the house to which I will go.' And the king granted them to me because the good hand of my God was on me."
>
> Nehemiah 2:4–8 (*Updated NASB*)

Nehemiah planned. He calculated time, material, and costs. When he had his opportunity before the king he seized the moment. Because of his effort in planning and the favor of God, Nehemiah received all he requested. The king not only gave him the time off but papers for materials and protection for the journey.

The second instance in which Nehemiah is a model planner is in Nehemiah 2:11–20. Nehemiah arrived in Jerusalem and examined its condition. He made an astute assessment and proceeded with implementing a plan.

> "So I came to Jerusalem and was there three days, and I arose in the night, I and a few men with me. I did not tell anyone what my God was putting in my mind to do for Jerusalem and there was no animal with me except the animal on which I was riding. So I went out at night by the Valley Gate in the direction of the Dragon's well and on to the Refuse Gate, inspecting the walls of Jerusalem which were broken down and its gates

> which were consumed by fire. Then I passed on to the Fountain Gate and the King's pool, but there was no place for my mount to pass. So I went up at night by the ravine and inspected the wall. Then I entered the Valley Gate again and returned. The officials did not know where I had gone or what I had done; nor had I as yet told the Jews, the priests, the nobles, the officials or the rest who did the work. Then I said to them, 'You see the bad situation we are in, that Jerusalem is desolate and its gates burned by fire. Come, let us rebuild the wall of Jerusalem so that we will no longer be a reproach.' I told them how the hand of my God has been favorable to me and also about the king's words which he had spoken to me. Then they said 'Let us arise and build.' So they put their hands to the good work."
>
> Nehemiah 2:11–20 (*Updated NASB*)

Nehemiah demonstrated the wisdom of assessing the situation and developing a plan. He understood the state of affairs and gave vision and leadership to those around him. Nehemiah motivated others to share his burden for rebuilding the wall. Together they accomplished the task in less than two months. Through planning, organizing and partnering together they completed the task. While the church's job today is much greater, the lessons Nehemiah teaches are timeless. Missionary trainers have a responsibility to motivate and equip others to reach the nations.

Another great motivator and equipper was the Apostle Paul, a New Testament model for planning. While his plans may not have been detailed, Paul had a definite strategy.

Paul's strategy included cities of major importance—centers of Roman administration, Greek civilization, Jewish influence and commerce. From these beachheads, the message was able to spread more quickly into surrounding areas. One of the factors that greatly assisted the spread of the Gospel was the advancement of the Roman Empire. Information flowed more freely in the empire because there was a common *lingua franca* and travel as fairly easy.

Another of Paul's strategies was to convert people of influence and who occupied positions of leadership. Paul understood that winning an influential member of society would have a greater impact culturally. If the leaders were converted, the message would be widely disseminated.[5] This strategy was principally the same for both geography and social class. Paul went to places where people would be able to spread the message more freely and quickly.

There are numerous other examples in scripture:

- *Habakkuk 2:2–3:* God instructed the prophet Habakkuk to write down the vision for it was not yet the appointed time.
- *Luke 14:25–33:* Jesus warns of the costs of following Him by using the analogy of a builder.
- *Proverbs 20:5:* A plan in the heart of a man is like deep water, but a man of understanding draws it out.
- *Proverbs 20:18:* Prepare plans by consultation and wage war with wise guidance.
- *Proverbs 24:6:* Wage war; wise guidance in abundance of counselors, there is victory.

It is essential to understand that planning without God's guidance is merely an act of man. It is essential to define planning from a faith-filled perspective.

What is Planning for Missions?

Planning is faith-filled and spirit-led preparation. It is partnering with God to know His mind and will. In his article "On the Cutting Edge of Mission Strategy," C. Peter Wagner agrees with Dayton and Frasers's assessment that strategies force Christians to both seek the mind of God and the will of the Holy Spirit; looking for answers to questions like what God desires and how we can conform to the future God desires.[6] Strategic planning should not be viewed as something separated from the mind of God. Rather, it is as Nehemiah stated (2:12), "I did not tell anyone what my God was putting in my mind to do for Jerusalem." For Christians planning is something that is God-breathed and inspired. Since it is impossible to please God without faith (Hebrews 11:6), Wagner says that planning strategy according to the will of God is pleasing to Him.[7]

At times, planning has been viewed as acting against the Holy Spirit. Dayton and Fraser call this the "In the Way" strategy which expects the Holy Spirit to give guidance once action is undertaken. The result is God's responsibility and anything that happens is God's will.[8] However, planning is not a substitute for the work of the Holy Spirit. Jesus invites each of us to join Him in the worldwide task of building His church.[9] Planning is not a faithless activity. It is neither rigid nor bureaucratic, but flexible.

Acts 15–16 demonstrates man's engagement and flexibility in working with God. The Apostle Paul begins his missionary journey with set intentions but on several occasions he is redirected by the Spirit of God. Paul's illustration is an example of what planning can look like. Planning is spirit-led when God redirects one's actions to follow the Spirit's movement and direction. Planning is an act of engaging God. It is directed towards His Lordship over the Church and the world. No man's ingenuity and genius could come up with "the plan" that can save the world. God has already done that. Planning is about mankind seeking to know God and fulfill the role God has set for each individual to play. Planning can be a paradox. That is, we plan as much as possible, and yet at the same time we believe that God is at work in everything. Plans are made as though the future is our responsibility, while believing God is the one who makes it happen.

Factors in Missionary Training

How does planning relate to missionary training? The connection can be made when one examines the factors in attrition, missions mishaps, emergency responses, and global trends. Many developments in the world today have greatly affected missions: ease of travel, more access to information, more Two-Thirds missionaries, and more prepared and capable missionaries. Yet why is planning still necessary in missionary training? Planning is necessary because it is stewardship. As C. Peter Wagner states:

> "The foundational principle of New Testament stewardship is that the steward takes the resources given by the Master, uses them for the Master's purpose, and returns to give the benefits and the honor to the Master. This has direct application to mission strategy. Since we know that the Master's will is to make disciples of all nations, we are responsible, as good stewards, to use what resources He has given us to accomplish

> that task. . . . If we are investing resources of time, personnel and money in programs which are supposed to make disciples but are not, we need to reconsider them and be willing to change the program as needed."[10]

Missionary training is not a game of chance. There are many precious resources that are in danger of being wasted. Viewing the missionary movement and training through 1900s lenses will not produce the type of missionaries needed to complete the Master's commission.

Veteran missionaries and writers Kath Donovan and Ruth Myors looked into the generational differences between missionaries. The article is profoundly enlightening and has potential to bring significant discovery into the development of a missionary training program. Understanding the differences across the generations is key to moving missionary training to the next level. In their article they identified missionary attrition as a fairly recent trend. In their experience in 1966, the only cause for leaving the field was retirement or death. Missionaries faced similar challenges then as they do now, but they did not leave.[11]

Emphasis will be given to the attributes of the "busters," the generation currently producing the next line of missionary workers. "Out of this generation comes missionary applicants from broken homes, who often have a great deal of pain in their lives to work through. They may be particularly vulnerable to emotional problems in the field. Because of their group orientation, busters work best in teams and cannot be expected to cope with isolated places without adequate support from their peers."[12] Due to the many issues that are facing busters, they should be adequately screened and counseled before departure. They also need ongoing pastoral care and support in the field while being a part of a team community.

A missionary training organization must be aware of the characteristics of their missionaries' generation. "In the past traditional denominational leaders treated missionary training as merely emergency events. If one decides to go, then some kind of training was to be provided, but there was not much consistent strategic planning for it."[13] A review of the history of the western missionary movement indicates that there was no deliberate efforts to establish effective missionary training programs.[14] Crisis intervention and the emergency response syndrome that has often been used by denominations is simply an old wine skin approach that is no longer applicable. Strategic proactive planning and organizing is essential to the development of missionary training programs.

"By missionary training we understand the ability to provide instruction in the cross-cultural discipline. Such an instruction includes spiritual foundations or practices designed to impart proficiency to undergo the missiological task. This training is driven to form proper missionary skills, as behavior, spiritual habits and mental attitude."[15] The individual missionary is now the single most important aspect of attrition. What could not move missionaries from the field 40 years ago moves this generation into attrition. The chief problem today is lack of qualified personnel for cross-cultural service. Hence the expressed need to develop creative missionary training programs.[16]

Miguel Alvarez, an experienced missionary trainer, asserts that there is no significant correlation between formal schooling and attrition. However, there is a considerable relation between specific missionary training and field retention of missionaries.[17] Specific training should be strategically planned to address the needs of missionaries as they prepare for a life devoted to building the kingdom in a cross-cultural context.

It is an exciting time to be engaged in missionary work. While the times are uncertain, the mandate has not changed. The church must continue to pursue its call to all people. By planning and organizing effective missionary training schools, the church will continue to press toward the mark of its high calling.

Global Trends Affecting Missionary Training

Adequate planning and organization will also be able to help stave off future missions mishaps like post WWII Japan and post Iron Wall Russia. Currently, of grave concern are issues that may surface in the Middle East with the opening of Afghanistan and Iraq. Will the global church be ready? As geo-political changes shape the world, the missionary movement will also need to adjust and change with it—change in methodology but not theology. It is the church's job to be ready with missionaries trained for effective ministry in such an environment.

As anti-American/Western sentiments increase across the globe, the world has become a more dangerous place for western missionaries. However, even with the risks, the usefulness of the western missionary is not in question. There are places in the world where Two-Thirds missionaries may have easier access. The number of Two-Thirds World missionaries has continued to rise. The church across the world is actively engaged in mission activity. Organizations like Accelerating International Missions Strategies (AIMS) and the Caleb Project are actively engaged in helping connect missionaries to mission needs and unreached people groups. They function not from a strictly Western perspective, but with a global church perspective connecting resources from all over the world.

Urbanization is another global trend in modern society. In 1800, only 2% of the Earth's population was located in the city. By 1900, the percentage had risen to 8%. However, by the year 2000 the percentage of urban dwellers rose to 50% of the world's population.[18] The enormous increase in the urbanized world presents both challenges and opportunities for the advancement of the Gospel message. As a result of a ripe field for harvest in the cities, increased attention to the needs of urban cross-cultural work must be addressed. These missionaries must be equipped for success.

Without doubt one of the major trends in modern society is the quick access to information. We now live in the "information age." The Internet has revolutionized the way information is relayed and retrieved. Lack of information is no longer a problem. However, knowing how to find and assess good information is crucial. The church should not fear information overload. The business world is amazingly adept at adjusting to rapid change. For businesses, it is simple: Change or be changed. The market will determine their relevance. In the article "Surviving Information Overload," Tony Vinas gives several business strategies used to assess information. "Information . . . is what fire was to prehistoric cavemen. Properly controlled and applied, it sustains life and perpetuates evolution. But mishandle or neglect it, and it can quickly destroy."[19] David Allen, a productivity consultant, states: "Our schools and our culture have yet to provide effective training for the decision-making needed for managing input. . . . The implications of this information explosion are clear. People could read 24 hours per day, 365 days per year, and never catch up with what is written. The world's corpus of knowledge is growing much faster than any person can keep up with."[20]

Missionary training programs need to equip missionaries with the skills to sift through large amounts of information, and quickly. Missionaries must be able to recognize what information they need to know and can use. Information savvy societies need information savvy ministries to be focused and effective. The ability to handle information and address change is crucial for the church as it moves into the next century. The Body of Christ should be a leader in innovation and technology not lagging decades behind the modern workplace. God has called us to be the head and not the tail.

There are also major trends in global education. The advent of the Internet and increased communication capacities allow for a new global classroom. With the momentum towards globalization, four significant trends are capturing the attention of international educators. These trends include increased flexibility, degrees without borders, one language, and a less certain world.[21] Increased ability for a global classroom and a broader student base should be considered when planning and organizing a missionary training program. As these trends are true for secular education, they also apply to missionary training.

The need for new strategies and systems is clear. The old patterns of neglect and sparse training are simply no longer sufficient. Thankfully many organizations have heeded the call to sharpen the focus of missionary training. Today more than ever there is a push towards a clear discipline integrating systematic approaches and techniques. The need for planning and organizing is apparent and so are their advantages.

Planning and Organization: Establishing the Benefits

Networking Resources

One of the buzzwords in leadership is "networking." One might ask, what relevance does the concept of networking have in the context of missionary training? It is quite simple, it is developing synergy. *Webster* defines synergy as "working together better than working separately." Synergy is a rather simple concept but often untapped in the Body of Christ. Planning and organization facilitate networking, which leads to synergy that produces greater results. Planning and organizing do the following:

- Diffuse the "personal kingdom" mentality
- Encourage partnerships rather than recreating the wheel
- Inform organizations of resources and potential partners
- Generate a more focused effort

Dayton and Fraser define planning and organization:

> "Planning is setting a desirable objective imagining many of the different ways of reaching that objective then laying out step, by step programs for reaching those objectives. Planning not only includes the means and methods for reaching goals, it also considers who will do the task, how much will it cost and when will it be done.
>
> Organization is arranging the work in a way that is most likely to bring about the desired result. Organizing looks at the plans and asks

> questions like, "What would be the most effective way to relate people one to another to carry out the task?" Organizing deals with relationships between individuals (or organizations). It is a picture of the Body of Christ as described by Paul."[22]

We are called by God to be good stewards and to organize the Body of Christ in a way that will bring maximum return on investment.[23] Strategic planning and organizing facilitate what God has commanded us to be and do. In the appendix to this chapter on page 201, *The Power of Separate and Networked Relationships* shows the benefits of relationships that work together and the synergy they create. The first diagram depicts ten organizations that are seeking to make an impact using their own resources. The concentric circle is the degree of influence the organizations have. While each organization is effective individually, none of them impact the entire box nor does all of their influence combined. However, in diagram two the ten organizations network their resources to generate synergy. The circle at the center represents the pooled resource of the organizations. Each organization grew in its ability to influence, and as a whole they influenced the entire area designated by the outer circle. Everyone increased in effectiveness and impact. That is the power of synergy and the benefit of effective planning and organizing.

Organization and Planning Strategies

This section will focus on the practical implementation of planning strategies in the context of missionary training. Leadership guru Steven Covey states, "Successful people make a habit of beginning with the end in mind."[24] The same principle applies for organizations. It is important to have a strategy in place because "all things have two beginnings, a mental or first creation and a physical or second creation."[25] Developing missions training programs that are affective and fruitful is a God-given purpose. As stewards of God's vision to reach all the people of the Earth, those seeking to develop a program must be both systematic and faith-filled.

The first step in developing a missions training program is to determine what that program will look like. There must be answers to questions like: Who? How? When? Where? What? How Much? How long? Who are the stakeholders? Will this be a cooperative effort with a local church in the model of Modality/Sodality?[26], Or will it be a singular entity with a broad-based connection with many local churches? Who is going to be trained? What type of curriculum will be used? Who will teach?

The book *Establishing Ministry Training* is an excellent resource for developing a training program. The first chapter is primarily devoted to the concept of developing a consensus within a development team.

There are six commitments essential to the process that need to be in agreement:

- Specific goals of the Missionary Training Program (MTP)
- Context of the MTP
- Structure of the MTP
- The learner and strategies of the MTP
- Types of learning and strategies of the MTP
- The ultimate goal of the MTP

"End in mind," thinking is key to building consensus on strengthening commitments within the training staff.[27]

What type of missionary does the organization want to produce? Taking the training team through the commitment process may be the critical role of the program developer. Having deliberately chosen commitments before beginning the development process is integral for the success.[28] *Establishing Ministry Training* also suggests guidelines for consensus building. A shortened version follows:

- Believe consensus is attainable
- Respect participants, their values, and opinions
- Identify common ground and work forward
- Listen to values and feelings rather than words
- Constantly verify your understanding
- Gently test feelings, assumptions, and values—biblically and empirically
- Explore alternative means to guard appropriate values
- Elicit and record mutual confirmation or intermediate agreements
- Be patient and persistent

Training program administrators must organize resources accordingly and have a clear view of what they want to achieve through their training.[29]

As this chapter has shown, specific planning is not faithless but rather faith-filled. As good stewards it is important to do excellent research with good information. Many God-given dreams have fallen short of the original expectations of the dreamer. With the stakes so high it is imperative that the next generation of missionary trainers get it right. Developing a business plan that is thorough and detailed will be a tremendous asset. As dreams are broken down into goals and action steps, they move from the realm of the abstract to the concrete. Developing a business plan will address many of the necessary questions and issues, since it will help practioners in understanding available resources and honing the training programs' specific niches.

Missionary training is a discipline that requires a systematic, well planned, well organized, and intentional approach. This focus is essential as the church moves into the next century. Today the only constant is change. If the missionary movement is to maintain momentum in our ever-changing world then those who prepare missionaries will also need to change—in their methods and approaches. Fortunately, the shift is being made and missionary training as a well thought out, deliberate discipline is taking place. May God help us reach all people groups (παντα τα εθνη)!

Jason DeVerna is a Master of Divinity student at Regent University in Virginia Beach, Virginia.

Appendix

The Power of Separate and Networked Relationships

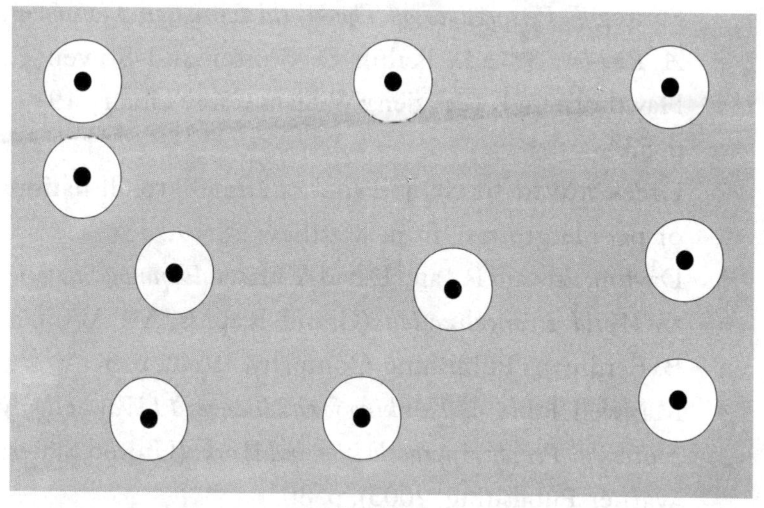

Diagram 1

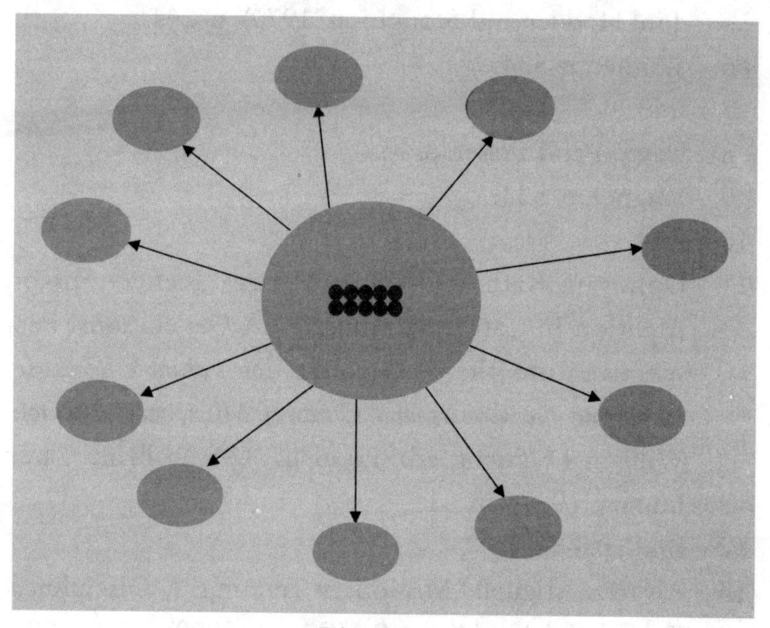

Diagram 2

NOTES

1 Wagner, C. Peter. "On the Cutting Edge of Mission Strategy," *Perspectives on The World Christian Movement: A Reader*, 3rd ed., Ralph D. Winter and Steven C. Hawthorne, eds. (Pasadena: William Carey Library, 1999), p. 534.
2 Greek παντα τα εθνη "Panta ta ethne" (to all nations or people groups), from Matthew 28:19.
3 Dayton, Edward R., and David A. Fraser. *Planning Strategies for World Evangelization* (Grand Rapids, MI: William B. Eerdmans Publishing Company, 1990), p. 5.
4 Maxwell, John C. *Thinking for a Change: 11 Ways Highly Successful People Approach Life and Work*. (United States: Warner Publishing, 2003), p. 80.
5 Green, Michael. *Evangelism in the Early Church*, (London: Hodder and Stoughton, 1970), p. 261.
6 Wagner, p. 534.
7 Ibid.
8 Dayton and Fraser, p. 15.
9 Wagner, p. 534.
10 Ibid.
11 Donovan, Kath, and Ruth Myors. "Reflections on Attrition In Career Missionaries: A Generational Perspective Into the Future," in *Too Valuable To Lose: Exploring the Causes and Cures of Missionary Attrition*, William D. Taylor, ed. (Pasadena, CA: William Carey Library, 1997.), p. 41.
12 Ibid., p. 45.
13 Alvarez, Miguel. "Missionary Training: A Discipline," *Journal of Asian Mission* 2:1 (March 2000), p. 91–102.

14 Ibid., p. 94.
15 Ibid., p. 95.
16 Ibid., p. 97.
17 Alvarez, Miguel, class lecture, "Training Intercultural Leadership," Regent University, Virginia Beach, Virginia 2003.
18 Bakke, Dr. Ray, class lecture, "Urban Ministry Conference," Regent University, Virginia Beach, Virginia 2003.
19 Vinas, Tony. "Surviving Information Overload," *Industry Week*, (April 2003), p. 25.
20 Ibid, p. 29.
21 Bisoux, Tricia. "Smarter, Faster, Better," in *BizEd*, (January/February 2003), pp. 34–36.
22 Dayton and Fraser. p. 19.
23 Ibid., p. 31.
24 Covey, Stephen. *The Seven Habits of Highly Effective People* (New York: Simon & Schuster, 1989), p. 98.
25 Ibid., p. 99.
26 "Organized versus unorganized missiology," as described by Ralph Winters in *World Christian Perspectives.*
27 Ferris, Robert W. "Building Consensus on Training Commitments," *Establishing Ministry Training: A Manual for Programme Developers*, Robert W. Ferris, ed. (Pasadena, CA: William Carey Library, 1995), pp. 6–15.
28 Ibid., pp. 6–15.
29 Ibid., p. 23.

Part Three

STRATEGIC INITIATIVES AND NEEDED COMPONENTS FOR INTERCULTURAL TRAINING

10. Funding Missions in the 21st Century

CHRISTOPHER D. JONES

"The business of missions is large and complicated. But if we intend to evangelize the world we are going to have to face our fears and change our paradigms. Statistics show that we will never evangelize the world with our current ministry model! We need to continue to evaluate the effectiveness of our ministry dollars and begin to understand that the ministry of fundraising is a critical part of the process of world evangelization."

Introduction

In this 21st century it is important to view the world missionary movement through a new set of lenses. Today we see a postmodern church, which is more Asian, Latin, and African than Western. As the developing world begins to cut the apron strings from her Western parents, new paradigms are emerging for "doing" the work of ministry in these contexts. Missiology and theology are changing, but the ties that bind are often strongly monetary. Can the churches of the developing world become totally non-dependent on their Western missionary partners? Should they?

One area in which the developing world is beginning to become independent is the area of funding their missionaries.The long-time missions receiving countries are becoming mission-sending countries. Latin Americans, Asians, and Africans are beginning to send out their own missionaries into the 10/40 Window totally funded by their home currencies. Many suppose that this shift towards sending developing world missionaries is the added push required to fulfill the Great Commission. Toward a proper view of this paradigm, this chapter will address the funding of missionaries in two areas: the cost and process of world evangelization; and new paradigms for the stewardship of world evangelization funds.

The Cost and Process of World Evangelization

Calculating the Cost of World Evangelization

A young lady is raised in a non-Christian home where the name of Jesus is never mentioned. Her grandmother, however, prays for her daily and takes her to church on the few weekends out of the year when she comes to visit. She grows up to experience the hard effects of the life of sin that was modeled by her parents. But one day things begin to change when a female coworker befriends her. The newfound friend is a breath of fresh air for the young lady. She has never known anyone quite like her before. In a way her friend reminds her of her grandmother. As the relationship grows, the young lady begins to spend more time with her new friend, sharing meals and conversation. It seems so natural when she starts attending church with her friend. At the church, the preaching ministry is passionate and the young lady actually feels comforted by the pastor's words and presence. He is kind of like the father she never really had. In a matter of months the young lady commits her life to the Lord. The pastor and the girl's new friends are there to encourage her through the process of believer's baptism. Within one year this young lady's life has been completely changed. She immediately goes out and begins to tell her experience to others. She has become a disciple of Christ.

The purpose of this illustration is two-fold. First, we must never forget that the process of world evangelization involves the lives of real people. People who are hurting will gladly welcome the warmth and newness of Christian fellowship. Throughout this chapter I will be equating souls with dollars in a rather mechanical manner, but this is not to demonstrate that the task of evangelism is completely mechanical. It is, however, because the task is so important to me. If we can become more efficient at what we do, then more people will be able to experience the life-changing grace of our Lord and Savior Jesus Christ.

The second purpose of this illustration is to demonstrate the costs associated with the conversion of one soul. Although it looks like there were no significant costs associated with this particular conversion, the factors are actually three-fold:

1 The first cost we must recognize is the cost of the prayers of her grandmother. We cannot overlook the hours that are spent in intercession for the lost.
2 Secondly, the valuable time and energy of her new friend must be considered. Without the presence of

a contextual witness, the Gospel message available all around us goes undiscovered.

3 Finally, we must include the cost of the professional pastor. His ministry played an influential role in the young lady's salvation. Also, since he is paid a salary, his cost is most easily tracked.

From the previous example we can develop a simple formula for the cost of world evangelization:

$ Professional Christian Ministry
+ $ Lay Christian Ministry
= $ Total Cost of Ministry

From this equation we see that the total cost of evangelistic ministry is equal to the sum of professional ministry and lay ministry. Another interesting concept is that the financial cost of lay ministry is directly related to the total cost of professional ministry.

This is because the only cost to the church for lay ministry is the amount of professional Christian ministry that the laity consumes (the cost of the professional Christian ministry directed toward the laity). Therefore, in order to calculate the cost of evangelizing one soul we must include the cost of the professional ministry directed toward both the unbeliever and the laity.

This amount is represented by the total dollars given to all church and para-church ministries throughout the world. Without the services of Christian radio, television, conferences, literature, and churches directed toward the believers, the believer would be less effective and world evangelism would be effectively reduced. Ephesians 4:11–15 explains that the professional ministers (apostles, prophets, evangelists, pastors, and teachers) are given to the world in order to equip the saints for the work of the ministry. Therefore we must equate all dollars spent on Christian ministry with evangelism and not just the small percentages spent on "international missions" or "evangelism."

Once again, the cost of our seemingly free witnessing opportunities is the combination of all the professional Christian resources we have consumed: Christian literature, media, and church services. Everything is intricately intertwined. It is the net effect of all Christian ministries, which produces the evangelistic harvest of souls each year. Although not all ministries are efficient or effective, they each play a role in the cost of evangelizing the world. Therefore in order to examine the cost of world evangelism we must examine the total cost of worldwide Christian ministry.

What is the Cost of World Evangelization?

Following the proposed formula we can calculate the cost of world evangelism with our present model of ministry. This model for world evangelism is simply the combination of every church and para-church Christian ministry in the world.

David Barrett effectively demonstrates that the combined income of all church and para-church ministries in the world today is $270 billion dollars annually.[1] He also shows that the result of these ministry dollars is approximately 45 million souls baptized per year. This yields an average cost per baptism of $6,000. Therefore with our present model for world evangelism we can expect that for every $6,000 given to a church or para-church ministry that one new person will be birthed into the kingdom of God.

Of course the process is more complicated than this, not all ministries operate efficiently, and therefore all ministries do not bring the same return for your kingdom dollar. In spite of this reality, old paradigms for ministry teach us that all ministries are needed and equally valuable. We would never close a church because it is failing to make an impact on the world around it. As long as there is funding available then the church or ministry will continue. But this is *not* a biblical paradigm.

The parable of the talents demonstrates that anyone not bringing forth fruit will be stripped of their funding and that this funding should be given to someone who will produce fruit.

> "You wicked, lazy slave . . . you ought to have put my money in the bank, and on my arrival I would have received my money back with interest. Therefore take away the talent from him and give it to the one who has ten talents . . . and cast out the worthless slave into the outer darkness."[2]

This description of financial stewardship more closely resembles a modern business than a ministry. Jesus appears to be a harsh manager of resources. Our churches and parachurch ministries must be equally harsh. However, the decisions made regarding ministry effectiveness cannot be made haphazardly. Before we begin the deconstruction of our present ministry models we need to look closely at the data concerning the results of ministry. The following data demonstrates some of the current trends within our worldwide ministry model, answering the questions: Where are the funds going? And what impact are these funds having on the world?

Current Trends for World Evangelization Resources

- In nations where the percentage of "Great Commission Christians" has approached 50% of the total population the cost for one baptism is approximately $23,000. However in the real mission fields where less than 10% are Christian the cost to baptize one individual is only $3,000.[3]

% Great Commision Christians	$ per Baptism
44.2%	$ 23,019
34.9%	$ 23,293
23.8%	$ 9,126
14.7%	$ 5,352
4.4%	$ 3,349

- Whenever the percentage of GCCs increases within a country, the number of baptisms per full-time Gospel worker decreases. This means that more of the ministry dollars are spent on flock maintenance than expansion.[4]

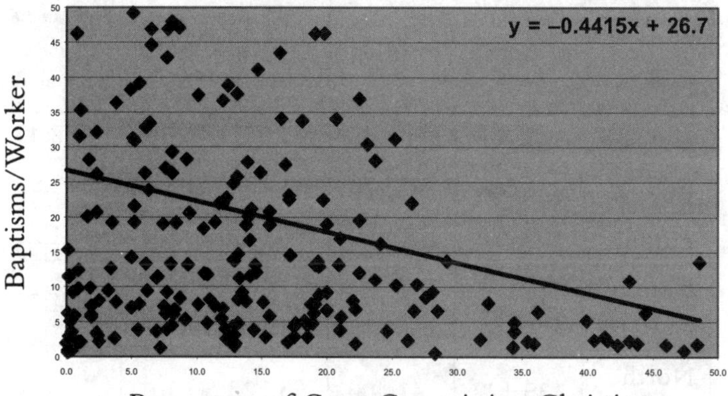

- The following chart breaks down the same information by continent. In Africa the cost per baptism is only $250 each, but in North America the cost is $27,025.[5]

Continent	$ received by churches and para-church ministries (billions)	Baptisms/year	Citizen Christian Workers	$/baptism	Baptism/ Christian worker
Africa	3.6	14,373,418	708,330	$250	20.29
Asia	10.5	9,630,494	623,470	$1,090	15.45
Europe	124.2	7,023,145	1,703,840	$17,685	4.12
Latin America	28	10,864,866	354,280	$2,577	30.66
North America	99.1	3,667,019	1,630,365	$27,025	2.25
Total	265.4	45,558,942	5,020,285	$5,826	9.08

- Although they baptize fewer souls within their own context, the following chart demonstrates that the western churches of Europe and North America are the *only* net missionary sending continents in the world.[6]

Continent	Missionaries Sent	Missionaries Received	Net Missionary Receiver or Sender	Sent Missionaries as % of Christian Workers
Africa	17,406	90,463	-73,057 (receiver)	2.45
Asia	24,504	57,970	-33,466 (receiver)	3.93
Europe	192,351	105,699	86,652 (sender)	11.28
Latin America	41,544	108,121	-66,577 (receiver)	11.73
North America	135,122	41,400	93,722 (sender)	8.28

Data Analysis

Data analysis demonstrates that as a nation becomes more "Christianized," the ministry within that nation begins to change from an evangelistic mission to an equipping and sending ministry. This is largely due to the phenomenon of saturation and can be illustrated with the following example.

My engineering background helped me to understand that a towel drying in the sun loses moisture quickly as the first 10–20% of the water evaporates. However, as the towel becomes drier it also becomes harder for the surrounding air to remove water from the towel. By the time you are drying the final 10–20% of the moisture from the towel, the time required must be multiplied exponentially. In fact there is a certain point, which is the relative humidity of the surrounding air, beyond which the towel will never dry without external means, such as your electric clothes drier. This is why, in humid conditions, a towel may still feel damp when removed from the clothesline.

The church of the largely Christian world is operating in the same conditions as the mostly dried towel. It requires more energy and time to create a change in this context and therefore evangelism is more expensive. However, man did not allow himself to be satisfied with damp clothes on a clothesline; in fact, some creative individual designed a way to convert electric energy into hot air and effectively reduce the drying time of a towel to less than one hour. The church in the West must do the same thing. You cannot force the towel to become drier faster, but through the power of creativity you can become more efficient and dry your towel in less than an hour.

This is currently happening through the creation of new and more effective methods of ministry. The local church alone is no longer the only model for ministry today. Television and radio are spreading the Gospel and encouraging Christians in more effective means than ever before. The Body of Christ is also finding more effective ways to organize itself. This is demonstrated by the fact that in the year 1900 approximately 90% of all ministry dollars were funneled through the local church or denomination. Today only 40% of all ministry dollars go through the regular channels of the local church or denomination.[7] *Christianity Today,* in a recent article titled, "Up and Comers: 50 Evangelical Leaders 40 and Under," shows that only two of the 50 leaders named as the most influential Christian leaders in the Christian world were head pastors of a church. Another six leaders were church staff members, but the remaining 42 were associated with activities other than the leadership of a local church.[8] The models for Christian ministry are changing, para-church ministries are here to stay, but is the church as a whole truly becoming more effective?

Statistics show that with all of our efforts, strategies, and funding the world is actually becoming less Christian. "Global Christianity which numbered 34% of the globe's population in AD1900, numbers 33% in AD2000."[9] The methods for world evangelism are becoming more effective, but we are not seeing more fruit. I believe that the main reason for this is the failure to kill old ineffective programs fast enough. In a recent business conference I heard one speaker state, "With enough time and enough money any business idea can be successful, but in business we do not have that luxury." We can no longer rely upon old ministry models and funding paradigms. False ideas about ministry funding, which are non-biblical and actually hinder church growth and world evangelization, must be replaced with biblical standards of excellence.

New Paradigms for Ministry and Financial Stewardship

The cost of one baptism with our current ministry model is $6,000. This number extrapolated to the least evangelized areas of the world and multiplied by the populations of those areas returns a figure of $10.7 trillion required to bring the entire world population to the 50% Christian mark. As a point of reference the entire combined Gross National Product of the world today is $15 trillion.[10] The plain reality is that we cannot accomplish our task with our present model. (Even if the whole world tithed!) Let's vow together to dismantle any and every ineffective paradigm for ministry that we have learned and begin once again to build a biblical basis for world evangelism. The following is a list of six paradigms that I believe will propel world evangelization and the sending of developing world missionaries in the third millennium.

1 The churches of the "Christianized World" must embrace their role as equippers and missionary senders

Due to saturation, the churches of the Christianized world become less effective as evangelists in their own context, but more effective as equippers and missionary senders. Therefore, they must embrace their role as missionary senders. This new paradigm will replace the current measures of church success, baptisms and attendance, with a more effective one—ministers equipped and sent.

Businesses see this same pattern whenever markets become saturated. This is one of the reasons for globalization and new product development in Fortune 500 companies.

In the real world, whenever domestic markets become saturated, companies seek export opportunities or attempt to develop new technologies to leverage their market advantage. One example is Coca-Cola, which derives 76% of its sales from international markets.[11] Due to saturated domestic markets they have taken their product into the most remote areas of the world. Within the context of rural India, Coca-Cola marketers have encountered great obstacles, "most rural Indians are too poor to buy appliances like refrigerators; the average income is $42 a month . . . but the sales teams have found plenty of rural locations worth exploiting."[12]

Latin American, Asian, and African missionaries equipped and mobilized by the western church could also be viewed as new "products" in the business of world evangelism. Products that in many ways may be more contextual to the markets they address. But this does not eliminate the need for Western missionaries. People and funds raised from the western church play a crucial role in world evangelization by planting churches among the unreached or training leaders from the developing world.

If a church is having a hard time finding new converts in a saturated area, then why not branch out? Change the focus from evangelism to leadership development and new life will flow into a dead church. Become a sending church! There are plenty of unreached people groups out there that do not yet have a witness.

2 Dependency hinders the work of God

Dependency is the act of supporting with outside funds a non-indigenous ministry, which could not support itself. Although in a zeal for missions the Western church is often tempted to step in and help support a developing world ministry, this practice has actually been found to be counter productive. We need to release national ministries to support themselves and disciple them to give and support their own missionaries. See Appendix 1 (page 229) for a model of Latin American missionaries sent to the 10/40 Window and funded from their own Latin American church structures.

Glenn Schwartz has written an excellent article which details the problems associated with financial dependency. Among the issues he discussed are: "How to destroy local initiative," "If it is not reproducible forget it," "How to keep a church poor." His article demonstrates that enabling poverty through unwise giving only enables poverty and is in no way effective. One national who was victimized by a paternalistic Western dependency model stated, "The missionaries did not teach us to tithe because they thought we were too poor. They did not know that we were poor because we did not tithe."[13] Giving is one facet of the biblical stewardship mandate and must be taught.

We will only stop creating dependency when we recognize that the outside funds are actually hindering evangelism and ministry. This is both biblical and practical. In our own lives we often see how well intentioned parents often create dependency in their children and this becomes one of the barriers to maturity. The same principle applies to young churches. Money spent on dependency (financing non-indigenous work) is not only a wasted resource it is also destructive. In fact the Southern Baptist Convention (SBC) manual for Church Planting Movements (CPM) states that one of the major hurdles to the self-replication of churches in a CPM is an atmosphere of dependency. "When well intentioned outsiders prop up growth by purchasing buildings or subsidizing pastors salaries, they limit the capacity of the movement to reproduce itself spontaneously and indigenously."[14] Missionaries must avoid dependency in their models and instruct short-term teams and volunteers of the dangers and reasons for these decisions.

3 Giving is a discipline which must be taught

We must learn to view fundraising as a ministry. Jesus commanded us to go into the entire world and teach every creature to obey His commandments. This includes, being baptized, loving others, wholeheartedly worshiping God, and giving to others. As missions fundraisers we are inviting Christians to develop in an important area of their Christianity: Giving! Pastors need to teach this through demonstration and practice. New converts should shortly be discipled in the area of giving. Every missionary must learn to disciple pastors, churches, and individuals in the area of being financially accountable to world missions. Statistics show that only about 6% of the $270 billion given to churches are used for missions.[15] The church must be trained to give. But for this to happen a lot of energy will need to be spent in developing the discipline of "giving" among Christians.

The necessity of the fundraising ministry can be seen through the comparison of two evangelical denominations: the Southern Baptists and the Assemblies of God (AOG). These two denominations both have mission agencies, are both evangelical, and both send missionaries. The International Missions Board (IMB) of the Southern Baptist Convention fully funds through its cooperative program 5,441 international missionaries of various statuses.[16] The Assemblies of God, however, sends out 1,841 international missionaries who are all required to raise their own support.[17]

Although the IMB has well trained missionaries who need not be concerned about where their funds are coming from, the agency has begun to notice a disconnection developing between the missionaries and the sending churches. Since the IMB missionaries are not required to raise their funds the churches have lost personal communication with their missionaries and to a large degree are not aware of what the missionaries are doing. This is becoming a major problem. Missionary stewardship and vision are not being developed in the local church.

The evidence is more accurately reflected in the following statistics: The 5,441 IMB missionaries are sent out by 20 million SBC affiliates. The 1,841 AOG missionaries are sent out by 2.6 million AOG affiliates. [18] This means that the ratio of missionaries to church members in the SBC is 1:3,675. The ratio for the AOG is 1:1,412. This is a 2.6 times difference. Although there could be many contributing factors to this huge difference, both the author and the IMB realize that the lack of "face time" with real missionaries leads to a lack of missions giving. There is no shortcut. Pastors, churches, and individuals must be discipled as missions givers and this process requires a fundraising ministry.

4 Fundraising is biblical, not just a Western model

Many individuals believe that the concept of approaching individuals for funding is not spiritual. More importantly, missionaries from the "developing world" may also think that this is merely a Western paradigm. Clearly from examples in the Bible we can see that ministries should be funded; Levites (Numbers 18:24), Jesus (Luke 8:2–3), and Paul (Acts 18:4–5). Jesus states, "The workman is worthy of his hire" (Matthew 10:10). However, the problem arises whenever individuals actually solicit the funds for their ministry. At this point, the most obvious question becomes, is asking for money biblical?

This question is most appropriate for missionaries, because they lack the weekly opportunity to collect an offering from their church. Also, churches do not automatically seek out missionaries and offer to fund them. Therefore, if the funds are going to come in, missionaries are going to have to ask. One of the most effective ways to ask for funds is to discuss your ministry "in person" with individuals or churches who may be interested in assisting and then asking them directly for the resources to do the ministry. See Appendix 3 (page 240) for a list of the most effective communication methods.[19]

One excellent biblical example of this style of fundraising ministry is found in the book of Nehemiah. Here we find that Nehemiah receives a burden for the ministry of rebuilding the walls of Jerusalem while he is in Babylonian exile (1:1). Having received information concerning the status of the city (vs. 2–3), he commits himself to prayer seeking God for how he can be a part of this ministry (vs.4–10). Finally after much prayer he approaches the king for the funding to complete his task. (2:4–9) When the time comes Nehemiah actually asks the King for the materials required to complete his task! The verses outlining the actual conversation follow.

> "The king said to me, 'What is it you want?' Then I prayed to the God of heaven, and I answered the king, 'If it pleases the king and if your servant has found favor in his sight, let him send me to the city in Judah where my fathers are buried so that I can rebuild it.'

> I also said to him, 'If it pleases the king, may I have letters to the governors of Trans-Euphrates, so that they will provide me safe-conduct until I arrive in Judah? And may I have a letter to Asaph, keeper of the king's forest, so he will give me timber to make beams for the gates of the citadel by the temple and for the city wall and for the residence I will occupy?' And because the gracious hand of my God was upon me, the king granted my requests."
>
> Nehemiah 2:4–9 (*NIV*)

Some believe that it is unspiritual to tell anyone but God about our financial need. This mindset must be addressed, for without the discipline of missions fundraising the average potential giver will never know your need or have the opportunity to participate. We have already demonstrated what potential this ministry of fundraising has for developing mission vision. There is no way around it, we must simply give people the opportunity to participate in the work of ministry that we do.

5 Implementing "best practices" is not secularizing ministry; it is good stewardship

Manage wisely. Currently around the world, the study of the field of funding and development for non-profit organizations has become popular among secular MBA schools. But many in the Christian world are afraid to tap into these resources for fear that they will be secularizing their ministry. This mindset cannot continue. Christian leaders must become involved in this area of ministry and begin to create and employ biblically sound methods for fundraising.

In an article entitled, "The Business of Missions: What is the Bottom Line?" John Orme states, "We need to be good managers and stewards of those moneys which are called missionary support."[20] However, throughout the article he develops a huge dichotomy between modern business practices and biblical stewardship. How can this be? Everyone believes that we should manage wisely, but without standards and benchmarks to compare ourselves, then we have no idea whether or not we are being good stewards? Statements such as "we need to be good managers" are merely wishful thinking, unless we are willing to adapt best practices. Failure to benchmark and analyze is irresponsible management. Responsible management requires us to submit our ministries to the eyes of accountability. The ECFA has developed standards for financial accountability with regards to accounting and fundraising, but these do not go far enough.[21] We must also employ management accounting.

In Peter F. Drucker's article "Managing for Business Effectiveness," he shows that businesses should constantly re-evaluate their practices. "Every product, every operation, and every activity in a business should, therefore, be put on trial for its life every two or three years. Each should be considered the way we consider a proposal to go into a new product, a new operation or activity."[22] By properly studying the results of our fundraising and ministry techniques and holding these results to standards of biblical accountability we can release our creative energy to do more with less.

However, far too often, ineffective ministries use the catch phrase, "If we can just win one soul, then it is all worth it." As if to imply that we are not judged by our performance. However, in reality Jesus was a much shrewder manager than this; He cursed the fig tree for having no fruit. Dayton states, "Bad management is very noticeable. Some indicators are low organizational morale, financial shortages, ineffective efforts, and a general feeling of confusion."[23] Although the line between difficult harvest fields and ineffective methods can be thin, we must learn to tell the difference. How do we do this? In business each process is benchmarked and studied extensively to ensure maximum efficiency. We must begin to do the same things.

6 Missions fundraising is more than raising money; it is developing people

Whenever missionaries wear their "fundraiser's hat" they also have a responsibility to participate in the process of rightly outfitting Christian soldiers for their place in the battle. The greatest resource we have in this battle for souls is the rightly equipped and mobilized Christian soldier. The power of the human mind has converted useless sand into useful silicon computer chips. How much more can a rightly outfitted and spiritually equipped Christian contribute to the cause of world evangelization and kingdom growth? But before we can do this work we must understand that all ministries do not look the same. Although millions of believers congregate into churches to be edified by worship and the hearing of God's Word, these are not the only ways a Christian can serve the Kingdom of God. Many believers are trapped with a feeling of meaningless existence because they have no idea what their unique significance is to the

Kingdom of God. We can't just ask these Christians for their money. We have to get them involved in the fight. But in order to equip and release this vast army of untapped potential we have to expand our definitions of ministry.

As we are raising funds we will have plenty of opportunities to explain to others how they can get involved in the process of world evangelization. Selfishly, it would be easy to explain to them that the best thing they could do is to giving us their money! Ignorantly, we could tell them to drop what they are doing and become a missionary like ourselves. But effectively we have to be wise counselors. Listening to where they are and how they could best be used in the battle. The following examples are given to illustrate the different approaches to "counseling" givers.

Secular Vocation	Selfish Paradigm	Traditional Ministry Calling	New Paradigm Expanded Ministry Calling
Medical doctor: "I want to be more involved!"	"Give me your money!"	Quit your secular job and go to seminary to become either a traditional pastor or a missionary who plants a church or a medical clinic.	Remain at your job and become a witness to those around you, a missions giver, and assist in medical outreaches throughout the world. OR Leave your vocation and become a full-time missionary who equips and releases others to do practical health outreach; training thousands of

Secular Vocation	Selfish Paradigm	Traditional Ministry Calling	New Paradigm Expanded Ministry Calling
			indigenous healthcare workers to be "medical evangelists."
Accountant: "I want to be more involved!"	"Give me money and do my books."	Quit your job and become a traditional pastor or a tentmaking church planter.	Develop a ministry to assist individuals, churches, and mission agencies with their financial stewardship and accountability; partnering to create computer technology, which could benefit mission agencies and reduce ecclesiastical crime ($16 billion dollars lost each year![1]).

Conclusion

The business of missions is large and complicated. But if we intend to evangelize the world then we are going to have to face our fears and change our paradigms. We will never evangelize the world with our current model! Successful businesses regularly evaluate the status and effectiveness of each business unit. We need to continue to evaluate the effectiveness of our ministry dollars and how we can do a better job with them. The ministry of fundraising is more than a necessary evil. It is a critical part of the process of world evangelization to mobilize the Body of Christ to reach every nation for His glory.

Christ Jones is a graduate of Regent University. He is currently working as the International Strategy Coordinator for AIMS (Accelerating International Mission Strategies, PO Box 64534 Virginia Beach, VA 23467). He and his wife Lynne have three children: Kristin, Sarah, and Michael. His ministry focus is unreached people group consultation and he has a strong desire to see the Body of Christ mobilized to complete the Great Commission.

APPENDIX 1

Case Study for Developing World Missionaries

One example of the power shift in missions thinking is the development of the "back to Jerusalem" project which plans to send 100,000 Chinese missionaries into the 10/40 Window. There is also a similar plan to send 100,000 Latin American missionaries into the 10/40 Window. However, as previously stated we must not oversimplify this process. It takes a lot of church energy to develop a missions candidate to the point where he is capable of entering missions training. And it takes resources to train and send these individuals, but it is happening. Many individuals are responding to the call and their home churches are sending them out. The following survey response will serve as a case study to demonstrate how this may work.

Apartado Postal 1247-1000, San José, Costa Rica
Tel: (506) 221-5522 • **Fax:** (506) 233-4389
E-mail: fedemec@racsa.co.cr
Website: www.fedemec.org
Executive Director: Cristian Castro Hernández
Year Founded: 1986
Theological Posture: Inter-denominational

Description of Ministry:

- **Motto:** Serving the church by sending workers
- **Primary Goal:** Training, informing/mobilizing, evangelization, church planting
- **Target Group:** Indigenous peoples (tribes), unchurched cities, unreached peoples
- **Activities:** Lectures, seminars, films, publications, courses, personal contact.

Survey Response from Cristian Castro Hernandez of FEDEMEC[25]

1 *How many of your missionaries are serving outside of Latin America and North America?*

Of the 70 missionaries working under FEDEMEC, 60 are serving outside of Latin America and North America.

2 *Do you have missionaries inside of the 10/40 Window?*

Some 40 missionaries.

3 *How much does it cost to send a missionary to the 10/40 Window? (Annual budget of an individual missionary.)*

These amounts are average, according to our experience. The cost depends on the city, country, or ethnic group to which the missionary is sent. Every country is a different reality; for instance, the budget for single people working in Mali is different from that of missionaries serving in Qatar. The average support budget is $500 to $700 per month, plus expenses for airfare and settlement.

Average Expenses		
First Month	Expense	One year
$ 600	Support	$ 7,200
1,900	Airfare	1,900
1,000	Settlement	1,000
$ 3,500		$10,100

4 *For which countries or regions are these budgets appropriate?*

I think these amounts apply to most areas of the world but not to the Arabian Peninsula and Europe, where living costs are much higher.

5 *Do your missionaries receive money from tentmaking? If so, what percentage of the budget?*

No. The majority of our missionaries receive 98% of their funding from churches, donors, supporters, etc. However, a few receive a little help from other sources such as own business in native country, home rental income, or interest on savings.

6 *Do your missionaries receive money from Central American churches? If so, what percentage of the budget?*

Yes. The majority of our missionaries receive between 30% to 50% of their support from their own churches, while the rest of their funding comes from other regional churches, denominations, friends and supporters. In a few cases, a single church supports its own worker 100%.

7 *Do your missionaries receive money from U.S. or European sources? If so, what percentage of the budget?*

Few of our workers actually receive funds from foreign donors. These contributions are less than 10% of the total funding; however, we also have two laborers who receive more than 50% of their support from foreign sources.

8 *Do your missionaries receive money from Central American individuals? If so, what percentage of the budget?*

Three of our missionaries receive 10% or less from Central American sources.

Funding Sources		
Source of Funding	**Number of Missionaries**	**Percentage from Source**
Personal	Majority	2%
Own church	Majority	30–50%
Regional or Denominational church and agencies; personal supporters	Majority	60–40%
Central American churches and agencies	3	10%
Foreign churches and agencies	Few	<10%

9 *Feel free to comment on any other sources your missionaries may use to fund their ministries.*

Basically, I believe our missionaries use two funding sources: support from their church, other churches, and individual supporters and personal income—savings, rental income. (These amounts are small.) In order to raise funds for development projects, FEDEMEC introduces proposals to foundations, ONGs, churches, and business people.

10 *Please comment on any techniques, books, stories, testimonies, or unique ideas that you have found helpful in the funding process.*

First, during our 16 years of service we have learned how to raise funds, create a budget, and write and submit project proposals. We have been both practical and empirical, to the point of applying both simple and unusual techniques. What is good is that all these techniques have worked.

Second, we have benefited very much from the experience of ministries such as COMIBAM, YWAM, Campus Crusade, and others. These organizations have developed materials, seminars, and workshops about how to raise funds and other topics. We try to take advantage of all the available resources at this time.

Third, I believe we have learned some lessons from the world of business, ONGs, and other secular institutions on how to raise funds for projects and workers. We would be blind to not extract some learning from this secular schools.

In general terms, I believe the following:

- Every country and organization has a different reality. The fulfillment of needs and the raising of funds must be executed according to that reality. Our reality will indicate how we should finance our missionary task. We cannot expect more than what our church can give.
- On the other hand, we must always be learners. We need to keep seeking materials, workshops, seminars, and the experience of others and their situation. We need to ask: How did they do it? Could it work here? I am trying to say that the money is there, we just need to ask for it or seek it. But we also need to learn how to procure funds strategically and orderly.
- We also need to learn to be ready. What does this mean? Our needs, budgets and projects must be documented, current, written down and printed. Sometimes it is hard for us to press what we think or feel into paper. Many foundations and churches look for recipients for their donations and ask for specific projects; however, we discover that we do not have our project on paper. It is only in our hearts and minds. We must be ready. Let us put our needs and projects on paper.
- The last, and most important aspect, is to ask our Lord and Father to help us. We need to ask Him to give us His wisdom, His strategies to look for funds —*without manipulation*. May He also place the right donors before us! Without God this cannot be done; it is impossible.

Appendix 2

Evangelical Council for Financial Accountability (ECFA) Standards of Financial Accountability[26]

Standard #1: Doctrinal Statement

Every member organization shall subscribe to a written statement of faith clearly affirming its commitment to the evangelical Christian faith and shall conduct its financial and other operations in a manner which reflects those generally accepted biblical truths and practices.

Standard #2: Board of Directors and Audit Review Function

Every member organization shall be governed by a responsible board of not less than five individuals, a majority of whom shall be other than employees/staff and/or those related by blood or marriage, which shall meet at least semiannually to establish policy and review its accomplishments. The board or a committee consisting of a majority of independent members shall review the annual audit and maintain direct communication between the board and the independent certified public accountants.

Standard #3: Audited Financial Statements

Every member organization shall obtain an annual audit performed by an independent certified public accounting firm in accordance with Generally Accepted Auditing

Standards (GAAS) with financial statements prepared in accordance with Generally Accepted Accounting Principles (GAAP).

Standard #4: Use of Resources

Every member organization shall exercise management and financial controls necessary to provide reasonable assurance that all resources are used (nationally and internationally) to accomplish the exempt purposes for which they are intended.

Standard #5: Financial Disclosure

Every member organization shall provide a copy of its current audited financial statements upon written request.

Standard #6: Conflicts of Interest

Every member organization shall avoid conflicts of interest. Transactions with related parties may be undertaken only if all of the following are observed: 1) a material transaction is fully disclosed in the audited financial statements of the organization; 2) the related party is excluded from the discussion and approval of such transaction; 3) a competitive bid or comparable valuation exists; and 4) the organization's board has acted upon and demonstrated that the transaction is in the best interest of the member organization.

Standard #7: Fundraising

Every member organization shall comply with each of the ECFA Standards for Fundraising:

7.1 *Truthfulness in Communication*

All representations of fact, description of financial condition of the organization, or narrative about events must be current, complete and accurate. References to past activities or events must be appropriately dated. There must be no material omissions or exaggerations of fact or use of misleading photographs or any other communication which would tend to create a false impression or misunderstanding.

7.2 *Communication and Donor Expectations*

Fundraising appeals must not create unrealistic donor expectations of what a donor's gift will actually accomplish within the limits of the organization's ministry.

7.3 *Communication and Donor Intent*

All statements made by the organization in its fundraising appeals about the use of the gift must be honored by the organization. The donor's intent is related to both what was communicated in the appeal and to any donor instructions accompanying the gift. The organization should be aware that communications made in fundraising appeals may create a legally binding restriction.

7.4 *Projects Unrelated to a Ministry's Primary Purpose*

An organization raising or receiving funds for programs that are not part of its present or prospective ministry, but are proper in accordance with its exempt purpose, must either treat them as restricted funds and channel them through an organization that can carry out the donor's intent, or return the funds to the donor.

7.5 *Incentives and Premiums*

Organizations making fundraising appeals which, in exchange for a contribution, offer premiums or incentives (the value of which is not insubstantial, but which is significant in relation to the amount of the donation) must advise the donor of the fair market value of the premium or incentive and that the value is not deductible for tax purposes.

7.6 *Reporting*

On request, an organization must provide a report, including financial information, on the project for which it is soliciting gifts.

7.7 *Percentage Compensation for Fundraisers*

Compensation of outside fundraising consultants or an organization's own employees based directly or indirectly on a percentage of charitable contributions raised is not allowed.

7.8 *Tax Deductible Gifts for a Named Recipient's Personal Benefit*

Tax deductible gifts may not be used to pass money or benefits to any named individual for personal use.

7.9 *Conflict of Interest on Royalties*

An officer, director, or other principal of the organization must not receive royalties for any product that is used for fundraising or promotional purposes by his or her own organization.

7.10 *Acknowledgement of Gifts-in-Kind*

Property or gifts-in-kind received by an organization should be acknowledged describing the property or gift accurately without a statement of the gift's market value. It is the responsibility of the donor to determine the fair market value of the property for tax purposes. The organization should inform the donor of IRS reporting requirements for all gifts in excess of $5,000.

7.11 *Acting in the Interest of the Donor*

An organization must make every effort to avoid accepting a gift from or entering into a contract with a prospective donor which would knowingly place a hardship on the donor, or place the donor's future well-being in jeopardy.

7.12 *Financial Advice*

The representative of the organization, when dealing with persons regarding commitments on major estate assets, must seek to guide and advise donors so they have adequately considered the broad interests of the family and the various ministries they are currently supporting before they make a final decision. Donors should be encouraged to use the services of their attorneys, accountants, or other professional advisors.

APPENDIX 3

Ladder of Communication Effectiveness[27]

Most Effective

One-to-one conversation
Small-group discussion

Large-group discussion
Telephone conversation

Handwritten letter
Typewritten letter

Mass produced letter
Newsletter

Brochure
News item

Advertisement
Handout

Least Effective

Results From Study Of 7,401 Appeals From 100 Navigators Staff

Number Appealed To	Appeal method	Yes, Monthly	Yes, Annual	Yes, Cash	Undecided	No
3,263	Face-to-face	46%	4%	10%	13%	27%
1,882	Telephone/letter	27%	4%	14%	15%	39%
839	Personal letter	14%	2%	16%	12%	56%
736	Group meeting	9%	2%	9%	4%	76%

NOTES

1 Barrett, David B. and Todd M. Johnson. *World Christian Trends AD 30—AD2200: Interpreting the Annual Christian Megacensus*, (Pasadena, CA: William Carey Library, 2001), p. 661.

2 Matthew 25:14–30 *NASB*.

3 This information was estimated by the author using data from Barrett and Johnson (p. 662). $270 billion divided by 45 million baptisms yields an average of $6,000 per baptism. Using numbers for the baptisms per Christian worker and GNP of the population we can estimate the cost per baptism in each country.

4 These numbers were plotted from data found in Barrett, *World Christian Trends AD 30—AD2200* Companion CD, (Pasadena CA: William Carey Library, 2001).

5 Barrett, p. 661.

6 Barrett, "Companion CD."

7 Barrett, p. 656.

8 Carla Barnhill. "Up and Comers: 50 Evangelical Leaders 40 and Under." *Christianity Today*, (Nov, 11, 1996, Vol 40. No. 13), p. 20.

9 Barrett, p. 656.

10 Ibid.

11 Coca-Cola, "2001 Annual Report," available online at www2.coca-cola.com.

12 Kriplalani, Manjeet. Business Week Online: "Rural India, Have a Coke; Multinationals target the villages." May 27, 2002, available online at www.businessweek.com.

13 Schwartz, Glenn. "Dependency," *Perspectives on the World Christian Movement*, Hawthorne and Winter, eds., (Pasadena, CA: William Carey Library, 1999), p. 592–594.

14 Garrison, David. *Church Planting Movements*, available online at www.IMB.org/cpm/chapter7.htm.

15 Barrett, p. 661.

16 IMB, "Fast Facts," available online at www.IMB.org.

17 AOG Foreign Mission Board, "AOG World Missions 2002 Annual Stats," (May, 2002).

18 Johnstone, Patrick and Jason Mandryk. *Operation World*, (Waynesboro, GA: Paternoster Publishing, 2001). Total numbers of affiliates for both denominations were taken from Operation World.

19 Morton, Scott. *Funding Your Ministry: Whether You're Gifted or Not*, (Colorado Springs, CO: Dawson Media, 1999).

20 Orme, John. "This Business of Missions—What is the Bottom Line?" IFMA News, (Volume 51, Winter 2000, Number 4), available online at www.ifmamissions.org.

21 See Appendix 2 (page 233) for a complete list of financial accounting standards from the ECFA.

22 Drucker, Peter F. "Managing for Business Effectiveness," *Harvard Business Review* (May–June 1963), p. 33.

23 Dayton, Edward R., and David A. Fraser. *Planning Strategies for World Evangelization*, (Grand Rapids, Michigan: Eerdmans Publishing Company, 1990), p. 20.

24 Barrett, p. 656.

25 Castro Hernandez, Cristian. "personal communication survey response", (March 29, 2003).

26 ECFA. "ECFA Standards of Financial Accountability," available online at www.ecfa.org.

27 Morton, p. 76.

11. Understanding Partnerships Through the Eyes of a Native

RENÉ A. GALLO GONZALES

"In real partnership, there must be mutual agreement. We serve the same Lord with the same goals and destination. We are members of the same body, so mission societies should recognize their partners in the work of evangelization. We need to contribute ourselves and share our gifts with each other, towards the completion of world evangelization in our generation."[1]

Introduction

As the American missionaries arrived in the city of Tegucigalpa, Honduras, they expressed their excitement for the great work of God they were about to accomplish. They set their feet to travel to the mountains of La Esperanza, Intibucá, where they would minister to the native Indians through medical brigades and educational workshops. They were met at the airport by a group of young native people from the Association of Christian Ministries of Honduras (Asociación de Ministerios Cristianos—ADEMIC) and a long-term American missionary.

During the trip to the mountains, they discussed their missionary strategies on how to win the native Honduran Indians for Christ. Everything sounded great, until one of the natives asked the big questions: "So how do you plan to retain the harvest of souls after you leave this country? After your eight days are over, and America smiles at you again, who will care for the souls that will be saved during the medical brigade and evangelistic services? Who will build and pastor the church among the Yamaranguila people of Intibucá? From where will the finances come to plant a church among this people group? How many of you speak Spanish and are willing to minister in Honduras on a long-term basis?"

They all looked at the young man asking those questions as if he was pouring a bucket of cold water over their heads. He awoke them to the sad reality that missions cannot be done without the natives playing their role in the missionary endeavor. As missionaries, our role should be one of coming alongside instead of neglecting their cultural background and inserting our Western mindset.

In this chapter I will present some simple and practical ways to provide a better understanding of partnership and the missiological ramifications of practicing good and healthy partnerships. This chapter will provide a definition of partnership, its biblical foundations, missiological implications, its inter- and cross-cultural necessity and a practical model. We will try to see partnership through the eyes of the Two-Third World natives.

Definition of Partnership

There are so many words that relate to "partnership" that a clear definition of the term is needed to fully comprehend the intent of this document. The *American Heritage Dictionary of the English Language, 4th edition*, defines it as "A relationship between individuals or groups that is characterized by mutual cooperation and responsibility, as for the achievement of a specified goal."[2]

There has been a major misconception in the West that partnership is mainly the sharing of financial resources for world evangelism or informational networking. We tend to measure success based on how much we spend, instead of on how much development has occurred in people. Let us understand that partnership is more than sharing finances and resources. For Interdev, "partnership is an active step beyond networking. The primary focus of a network is to share information. The focus of a partnership is to take joint action—to do something, and to do it better by working together. Partners need not give up their organizational identity to work together."[3]

Taylor believes that terms such as "cooperation, teamwork, networking, joint ventures, and strategic alliances" are all part of the partnering process, but cannot fully express its meaning; this can be simply defined as "using mutual means to accomplish a task."[4]

For Daniel Rickett, partnership is "a complementary relationship driven by a common purpose and sustained by a willingness to learn and grow together in obedience to God." He furthermore introduces the concept of developmental partnership as "a cooperative relationship between two autonomous bodies whereby each enables the other to grow in its capacity to initiate and carry out change for the sake of the Gospel."[5]

Let's point out that none of the above definitions provide a comprehensive description of what real biblical partnership is, for, it goes beyond mutual cooperation and sharing into mutual loving. Luis Bush offers what we consider one of the best definitions of Christian partnership, "an association of two or more autonomous bodies who have formed a trusting relationship, and fulfill agreed upon expectations by sharing complementary strengths and resources, to reach their mutual goal."[6]

Thus, from the above definitions, we can present the basic components of a healthy Christian partnership:

1. *Relationship* — Partnership is based on a solid Christ-centered, not a self-centered, relationship between two or more Christian organizations that share a burden for world evangelization. This relationship must include "compatibility in doctrinal beliefs and ministry values."[7]
2. *Association* — Once the relating entities reach a healthy level of trust they can enter into covenantal associations or alliances.
3. *Mutual cooperation* — To achieve expectations, all the participating parties will share and fulfill the same duties and responsibilities.
4. *Sharing complementary resources* — Spiritual and physical resources will be shared unselfishly. Neither entity will expect the other to fully subsidize the missionary endeavor. Each ministry or missionary agency must be financially independent of the other partners. Therefore, they are independent as a ministry, but interdependent in the fulfillment of the Great Commission.

5 *Enabling each other* — Each partner involved seeks to empower the others so that they will develop their full potential.
6 *Sharing joy in the results* — The ultimate purpose of Christian partnership is the end result—reaping the harvest of souls. God is the "Lord of the Harvest" (Matthew 9:38). Our duty is to sow the seed, He produces growth and we reap the harvest. If your partnership is not producing results, it is not effective.

After examining the above definitions and components I would like to offer a definition of Christian partnership:

> Christian partnership is a Christ-centered, relational covenantal association or alliance between two or more Christian ministries/agencies; it is based on mutual trust and cooperation by sharing complementary spiritual and physical resources in order to develop each other's capacities, producing the end result of the fulfillment of the Great Commission.

The Biblical Foundations of Partnership

All throughout the Bible we see the importance of unity. Psalm 133:1, states: "Behold, how good and how pleasant it is for brothers to dwell together in unity."[8] Furthermore, Ecclesiastes uses the metaphorical illustration of "a cord of three strands is not quickly torn apart"(4:12). We sing about unity, and preach about it, but live lives of individualism and we even neglect it within the Body of Christ. The New Testament presents us with a clear paradigm of unity in Jesus.

As Jesus began His earthly ministry, He made a decision that forever changed the relationship between God and man. He called 12 common people to join Him in the Great Commission task. Yes, this was, and still is, the greatest biblical example of partnership. The Almighty God joined efforts with man to deliver the message of salvation to the world. He could have done evangelization on His own, but rather, He did it, and continues to do it, in partnership with man.

In John 17:20–23, Jesus presents the plea for unity before His father on behalf of His disciples and for the ones who would believe in Him through them (v. 20). In verse 21, He prays, "That they may all be one . . . so that the world may believe that . . ." Jesus was sent from the Father. In verse 22, Jesus declares that the same glory He received from the Father, He also gave to the disciples so "that they may be one." In verse 23, we find the climax of Jesus' prayer, "That they may be perfected in unity . . ." God's desire is that His disciples practice perfect unity with the purpose of showing the world the reality of Jesus' Sonship and the love of the Father. Butler observes that we can see how Scripture "calls for believers to work together in unity. . . . Except for the Great Commission itself, this is one of the strongest comments Jesus made on missions. He hinged the credibility of our mission message on our oneness in Him."[9]

Howard Foltz sees partnerships as an urgent need in the Body of Christ. He states, "we must move from local church/para-church competition to holistic cooperation."[10] In his exposition on 1 Corinthians 3:9, Foltz notes that Paul uses "we" to show that there is no competition among himself, Apollos, and Cephas, rather there is cooperation because they are workers together in the cause of Christ. He points us to the theological application of the concept of synergism where "fellow workers" accomplished more by working together than if each agency, group, or church worked alone.[11]

Integrational Cross-cultural Partnership Model

I propose an integrational cross-cultural model. This model takes as the main resource the Two-Third World's missionary force. If we are to see God move on a larger scale to reach the 10/40 Window and the unreached people groups in the Arab World, we must accept the reality that the typical White-Western missionary in such areas of the world has lost credibility and influence. According to Peter Prosser, distinguished professor of Church History at Regent University, the missionary work of the White missionary has reshifted, from White colonialism to indigenous autonomy. Keeping in mind that the White's missionary work now has a different approach—that of supporting Two-Third World missionaries.[12] We still need each other, but our roles have shifted and changed. We must then seriously consider integrating Two-Third World missionaries into our missions' agenda on a greater scale.

Much has been said about such integration in the past, but little is being done in the West to accomplish such an endeavor. For example, just south of the USA we find the largest missionary force in the Latin American community, but not much is being done to mobilize them into the creative/restrictive access countries.

This model is simple; let's facilitate the sending of Two-Third World missionaries. Such integration must consider the following elements in the developmental process of the missionary force of the Two-Third World:

1 The Local Church as the Main Source of Missionaries

Most of the world is highly community-oriented, thus we must educate the Two-Third Worlds' church in the theological and practical aspects of missions. Latin Americans, for example, have a hard time detaching from their local communities. Ministries in the West must partner to bring missiological education to the Southern Hemisphere. The local church in the Southern Hemisphere must receive the missiological education needed to be able to identify, train, deploy and support their missionaries.

2 The Missionary

Two-Third World missionaries have several advantages such as language, cultural similarities and a more cross-cultural acceptance. However, they need to be properly trained for missionary service. Some Latin Americans, for example, have serious deficiences in theological and missiological education. If such Latinos want to receive high quality theological and missiological education, they can seek it in the Northern Hemisphere.

3 Educational Partners

For the missionary endeavor to be effective, the Two-Third World missionaries must receive proper education before going to the mission field. For Miguel Alvarez, "missionary training is both an academic discipline and a practical commitment."[13] Three types of educational partners must be identified:

a) *Theological Education Partner*
This is the partner responsible for providing the prospective missionaries with solid biblical and theological education. This could be a theological institution—seminary or Bible school.

b) *Missiological Education Partner*
This is the partner responsible for providing the prospective missionaries with a solid missiological education that integrates all aspects of missiology. One of the most effective methods in missiological education today is the development of Missionary Training Centers (MTC). Some of the proponents of this model of training are Open Doors Ministries International, training Latinos to reach the 10/40 Window[14], and the Asian Center for Missions, training Asians to reach Asians and beyond.

c) *Career or Skills Educational Partner*
This is the partner responsible for providing or facilitating the prospective missionaries with market place educational careers. Emerging missionaries should be motivated to pursue professional careers. The role of the pastoral leadership in motivating the youth and young adults in this area is vital. It is not my proposal that the church should pay for every member's career education, but it is the responsibility of the church to promote education with the highest regard and at all levels. Keep in mind that in creative access countries, business or some other kind of educational skill might be required to obtain a visa.

Finally, when it comes to missiological preparation, Jonathan Lewis does a substantial analysis of the outcome of missionary education in relation to its methodology and context. He describes the three learning domains that must characterize the training process: (a) the cognitive outcomes that are produced through formal methods in a school context, (b) the skill outcomes that are produced at the workplace, through non-formal methods, and (c) the affective outcomes that are produced through informal methods in a community context.[15]

4 Local Church Financial Partners

The sending church must assume the financial responsibility to provide adequate support for its missionary candidates. This can be accomplished through different methods, but keep in mind that the goal is to raise partners within the local church's community. A missionary fund, with proper accountability measures for each candidate, must be set, and there *should not* be any expectation that only churches from First World, Northern or developed countries will pay for the cost of world evangelization. Two-Third World churches must assume their responsibility in the fulfillment of the Great Commission. This does not mean that there will not be any financial involvement from other partners, but the attitude must be, "it is our call to win the lost world and it is possible."[16]

5 Foreign Partners

Foreign partners can come from a variety of sources in the broad spectrum of the Body of Christ. To be effective in world evangelization, the local church and missionary candidates must be able to identify the proper foreign partners needed for the specific goal that they want to reach. This may include evangelistic associations, medical ministries, and all kinds of holistic ministries outside of the context in which the missionary is located. At this point, it is important to note that both the Two-Third World (Southern/Non-Western) missions force and the Northern/ Western/Developed missions force must avoid the trap of dependency when establishing a partnership relationship. "It is important in a partnership to not only give but to receive, to not only teach but to learn, and to not only lead but to follow."[17]

6 International Networking and Mobilization Agencies

Though international networking and mobilization agencies might be part of the foreign partners, we give them a special place in the partnering process. They can serve as bridges between the local church with its missionaries, and the defined people group that we want to reach. These agencies can help the Two-Third World missionaries mobilize into the desired people groups. An examples is Interdev, which brings together missions groups, churches, and national leaders by helping them work together.[18]

7 The Receiving Church or Culture

In case there is already a church or group of churches working among an unreached people group (UPG), and that the missionary has been able to partner with such a church, denomination or ministry, this church or ministry will be receiving the missionary candidate in the mission field. This church must make preparations for the proper reception of the incoming missionary. Before the missionary is sent to his new field, says James Glynn, we must ensure that the cross-cultural church-to-church partnership relationship is reciprocal, intimate, ongoing, practical and spiritual. Though Glynn is referring to a West-to-West relationship, joining efforts to evangelize a people group, the principles he applies are transferable in a cross-cultural, Two-Third World-to-Two-Third World relationship.[19] It is highly recommended that exploratory short-term trips be made before the final move takes place. Some aspects that need to be considered in the partnering process with the receiving church are:

a) ***Receiving Church Financial Partnership***

It is imperative that the receiving church/ministry, who will be enjoying most of the benefits of the harvest brought through the labor of the missionary, be an active participant in the financial support process. The receiving church must understand that they should be the first investor in reaching their own people. In Two-Third World countries, a newly-planted indigenous church might not be able to provide great cash flow, but they could provide housing and board (according to the living standards of their people) and other suitable accommodations.

b) ***An Internal Ministry Task Force***

This consists of a core group of people within the receiving church/ministry that will help the missionary in the missionary task. They will become the missionary's evangelism task force. This group must be prepared in advance. The missionary should come prepared to provide training for them as well. In new church plants, where there are only a few leaders, the opportunity is appropriate, in a strong influential way, to implant a missionary heart in the entire leadership team.

c) *The No Indigenous Church Dilemma*
In case the missionary is sent to a totally unreached people group, where there is no indigenous church, he must partner with other ministries that are trying to penetrate the group, including ministries from both the Western and Two-Third Worlds. In any case, the missionary should never go without partnering with others.

8 Cultural Adaptation Partner

This partner will be responsible for facilitating the overcoming of cultural and language barriers. This could be a language or translation institution, such as Wycliffe Bible Translators, or any language school that can teach the language of the people. Keep in mind that "culture can be considered as all learned behavior, value systems, and social institutions. It is determined by the past, molded by the present events, and affected by perceptions of the future. . . . We must go behind and beyond culture to feelings, emotions, aspirations, ambitions, and perceptions that all humans share. Biblical values must determine behavior."[20] Remember, most Two-Third World cultures are group-oriented, so we must leave our Western individualistic mentality behind. A smart idea, when entering an UPG, could be to contract some of the non-Christian locals to teach the missionary the common language and culture. The receiving church should also formulate an acculturation plan. In such cases, the partner could provide the means to do so.

9 Prayer Partners

Both the sending and receiving end must set up a prayer structure that will intercede for the missionary endeavor to be fulfilled. It is important to elicit joint prayer efforts with and from as many individuals, ministries, and agencies as much as possible. These prayer partners should be trained in spiritual warfare and the missionary must keep them informed of the prayer needs and praise reports.

Implementation or Application of the Integrational Cross-cultural Partnership Model

It is now clear that the fulfillment of the Great Commission can only occur when the Body of Christ joins efforts in reaching the lost. Daryl Platt states it like this: "There must be recognition by Christian leaders, missionary agencies, and churches that the normative New Testament model for missions is one of genuine partnership by all involved. The partnership should include local congregations, training institutions, and implementing agencies."[21]

We believe that the implementation of partnership needs to happen in every aspect of missions. Phillip Butler provides us with a type of partnership model well known in the business world. Here is a brief synopsis of his concept:[22]

Horizontal and Vertical Integration Partnerships[23]

Ministry partnerships can come in two kinds: horizontally and vertically integrated. An example of horizontal integration might be:

The youth ministries in a city decide to buy and operate a youth camp in the country. It's a specialized effort—all focused on youth—but it's a long-term project with high commitment required, complex tasks, and specific outcomes planned. It's horizontal because it's all one type of ministry.

A vertical partnership is more holistic, bringing together a variety of approaches and kinds of ministries to address all facets of a problem or all needs of a community. An example might be:

If you are going to reach the community within two square miles of your church for Christ, you have to do more than focus on one group like the youth. As you look at all the needs and opportunities to share Christ, your strategy might include youth work, elderly work, single parenting workshops, drop-in centers, camp ministries, daycare and a host of other ministries linked together to reach the local community for Christ.

Vertical integration focuses on dealing with the whole task—in this case of reaching individuals for Christ and building the Church. The youth ministries in the "horizontal partnership" example are a vital element or reaching and serving the community, but they are just one element needed in a full strategy to reach and serve a community, city, or nation for Christ.

Starting from the main source for the missionary force—the local church, we must integrate and intertwine all the other elements to the evangelization of the unreached people groups. The following diagrams demonstrate the concept of this integrational cross-cultural partnership model in action:

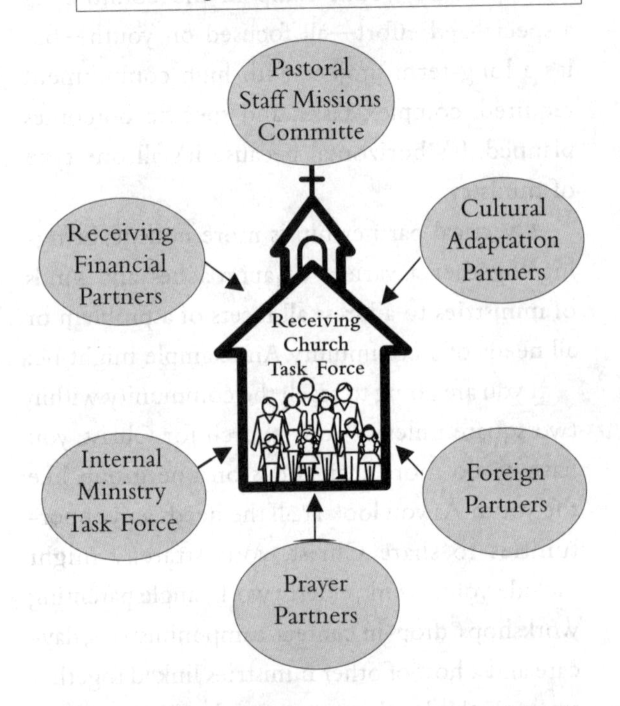

Conclusion

The answers and solutions to such dilemmas as those posted by the young native Honduran in the Introduction rely on the power of partnership within the Body of Christ, both among homogeneous and intercultural ministries.

That day, on the bus, was the beginning of a long-term partnership between ADEMIC, New Vision Ministry from Effingham, Illinois, and World Gospel Outreach, a missionary agency based in Honduras and Houston, Texas. Today the people of Yamaranguila have not only heard the Gospel, but cell groups have been planted among them and a church has been built in the city of Intibuca. A native Honduran doctor and her family moved from the capital city of Honduras to start a medical clinic in that area. Every year, medical brigades and evangelistic outreaches take place to bless the people of Yamaranguila, and other communities around them are being saturated with the Gospel of Christ.

Partnership is not only a biblical mandate, but also a heavenly cry from the Father. It is the answer to Jesus' prayer, "That they may be one . . . ." The time has come and the hour is now for the Western Missionary force to recognize the value and power that lie on the Two-Third World Missionary force. The Two-Third World Missionary force must repent from their dependence and indifference towards world evangelization. Indigenous missionaries must *go* to the harvest fields. For centuries the Western/Northern Hemisphere has sown the seed of the Gospel. God has watered that seed and honored the missionary endeavors of the North. Let the Two-Third World Church do its part by sending their best men and women to reap the harvest. We must join efforts to accomplish the Great Commission.

Finally, let's sum up this chapter with the words of Rev. Panya Baba,

> "In order to join in real partnership, there must be mutual agreement. We serve the same Lord with the same goals and destination. We are members of the same body, so mission societies should recognize their partnership in the work of evangelization. We need to contribute ourselves and share our gifts with each other, towards the completion of World Evangelization in our generation."[24]

René Arturo Gallo Gonzales, is from Honduras, where he served as Missions and Evangelism Minister for the Association of Christian Ministries (Asociación de Ministerios Cristianos—ADEMIC). He is ordained with Open Door Ministries International and has served as pastor in Central America and the USA. He is a member of Mundo de Fe Internacional in Carrollton, Texas. René and his wife, Diana, are graduates of Christ for the Nations Institute, in Dallas, Texas, and he holds credentials with the CFNI Fellowship of Ministers and Churches. He is currently a candidate for the Master of Divinity degree at Regent University, where he has received the "Who's Who Among Students in American Universities and Colleges Award" for 2001–2002.

NOTES

1 Baba, Panya. "Models in Missionary Partnership," in *Together in Mission*, 1st ed., Theodore Williams, ed. (Bangalore, India: World Evangelical Fellowship Missions Commission, 1983), p. 80.

2 *The American Heritage Dictionary of The English Language, 4th edition* (Houghton Mifflin Company, yourDictionary.com, Inc., 2000) 1996–2002. Online: http://www.yourdictionary.com/ahd/p/p0089800.html [27 April 2003].

3 Interdev, *The Power of Partnership: The Shape of Partnership*, n.p., 1/21/99. Online: http://www.ad2000.org/adoption/Coop/Partner/Pidshap.htm [27 April 2003].

4 Taylor, William D., ed. *Kingdom Partnerships for Synergy in Missions* (Pasadena, CA: William Carey Library, 1994), pp. 3–4.

5 Ricket, Daniel. *Building Strategic Relationships: A Practical Guide to Partnering with Non-Western Missions* (Pleasant Hill, CA: Kleing Graphics, Pleasant Hill Media Center, 2000), pp. 1–6.

6 Bush, Luis, and L. Lutz. *Partnering in Ministry: The Direction of World Evangelism* (Downers Grove, IL: InterVarsity Press, 1990), p. 46.

7 Rickett, p. 5.

8 All Scriptures quoted are from the *New American Standard Bible*, except when otherwise specified.

9 Butler, Phillip. "The Power of Partnership," in P*erspectives on The World Christian Movement*, 3rd ed., Ralph D. Winter and Steven C. Hawthorne, eds. (Pasadena, CA: William Carey Library, 1999), p. 754.

10 Foltz, Howard. *For Such a Time As This* (Pasadena, CA: William Carey Library, 2000), p. 36.

11 Foltz, Howard. *The Biblical Basis of Partnership* (Virginia Beach: AIMS, 2003), p. 1.

12 Prosser, Peter. "Lectures on Church History and Renewal," Regent University School of Divinity, Spring 2003 Semester.

13 Alvarez, Miguel. *Missionary Training: A Discipline*, p. 143.

14 De Venney, Kirk. "ODMI Update," email to René A. Gallo Gonzáles, April 27, 2003. See email message below:

> "Tomorrow morning, Monday the 28th of April [2003] I will be leaving with David Diaz for India. David, who is from El Salvador, graduated from the Missionary Training Center in 2000. David is the first ODMI Missionary to be planted in India. I will be gone only for 10 days. Please pray for our safety, our trip and David's new ministry in India as he establishes ODMI in that land. With David being planted we now have Missionary Training Center Graduates serving as missionaries in: Guatemala (9), Honduras (5), Bangladesh (1), Ireland (1), India (1). They are serving as evangelists, teachers, church planters, etc. What a great time to be a missionary for Jesus."

15 Lewis, Jonathan. "Matching Outcomes with Methods and Contexts," in *Training for Cross-Cultural Ministries*, Jonathan Lewis, ed., Occasional Bulletin of the International Missionary Training Fellowship (Wheaton: WEF, 1998), pp. 1–3.

16 For more on fundraising refer to the chapter in this book by Chris Jones, "Funding Missions in the Twenty-First Century," pp. 207-242).

17 Rickett, 17. For more on healthy dependency see Rickett 17–25.

18 Interdev. "The Partners," 2002. Online: http://www.interdev.org/Display.asp?Page=partners [27 April 2003]. Some of the agencies partnering with Interdev include: AD2000 and Beyond Movement, Alliance for Saturation Church Planting, Antioch Network, Arab World Ministries (AWM), Baptist General Conference, Billy Graham Evangelistic Association (BGEA), Brigada, Caleb Project, Campus Crusade for Christ, CBInternational (CBI), Child Evangelism Fellowship (CEF), ChinaSource, Christar, Christian & Missionary Alliance, Church Resource Ministries, Compassion International, Cooperative Baptist Fellowship, Development Associates International (DAI), DAWN Ministries (Discipling a Whole Nation), Evangelical Fellowship of Canada (EFC), Faith Comes by Hearing (FCBH), Frontiers, Global Connections UK, Global Mapping International, Great Commission Roundtable, International Bible Society, International Missions Board—Southern Baptist Convention, International Teams, Jesus Film Project, Joshua Project II, KidsGames, Mennonite Mission Network, MentorLink, Mission Aviation Fellowship (MAF), Mission to the World, Mission to Unreached Peoples (MUPS), Major Sports Events Partnerships (MSEP), The Network for Strategic Mission, Operation Mobilization (OM), Partners International, Presbyterian Frontier Fellowship (PFF), Scripture Union, United Bible Societies, United World Mission (UWM), US Center for World Mission (USCWM), Viva Network, WEC International, World Concern, World Evangelical Alliance (WEA), World Relief, World Team, World Vision, Wycliffe, Youth With A Mission (YWAM).

19 Glynn, James. "Church-to-Church Partnership: What? Why? How?" in *Partners in the Gospel: The Strategic Role of Partnership in World Evangelization*, James H. Kraakevik & Dotsey Welliver, eds. (Wheaton, IL: Billy Graham Center, 1991), pp. 69–70.

20 Sookhdeo, Patrick. "Cultural Issues in Partnership in Mission," in *Kingdom Partnerships for Synergy in Missions*, William D. Taylor, ed. (Pasadena, CA: William Carey Library, 1994), pp. 52–53.

21 Platt, Daryl. "A Call to Partnership in the Missionary Selection Process: Perspective of the Old Sending Countries," in *Too Valuable To Lose: Exploring The Causes and Cures of Missionary Attrition*, William D. Taylor, ed. (Pasadena, CA: William Carey Library, 1997), p. 205.

22 Butler, Philip. *Partnerships Everywhere*, n.p., Online: http://www.ad2000.org/gcowe95/partners.html [28 April 2003].

23 For more information on Horizontal and Vertical Integration Partnership also see Butler, "Why Strategic Partnerships? A Look at New Strategies for evangelism," in *Partners in the Gospel: The Strategic Role of Partnership in World Evangelization*, James H. Kraakevik and Dotsey Welliver, eds. (Wheaton, IL: Billy Graham Center, 1991).

24 Baba, Panya. "Models in Missionary Partnership," in *Together in Mission, 1st ed.*, Theodore Williams, ed. (Bangalore, India: World Evangelical Fellowship Missions Commission, 1983), p. 80.

12. The Heart's Cry of the Postmodern Missionary

The Role of Spiritual Formation Training for Missionaries in the Postmodern Era—the Need, the Method

RON DEBERRY

The Need

Realizing the Need for Spiritual Formation

Missionary trainers have long realized the need for spiritual maturity in missionary students. A. W. Tozer, speaking at the Inter-Varsity Missionary Conference in December, 1954, said, "I believe that it is a tragedy for any man or woman to take upon himself the higher responsibilities of a pastorate or of missionary work until he has met God for himself and God has become to him not an idea, nor a concept, nor a doctrine only, but a living presence, an indwelling reality."[1]

A more recent assessment comes from Ken R. Gnanakan, General Secretary of Asia Theological Association, "While I am convinced that God will continue to use all forms of attempts to accomplish His purposes, the most successful channels will always be men and women in tune with God."[2] As important as the desire to save the lost is for effective work in the missionary field, there is a need in missionary students that is of equal, or perhaps greater, importance—the need to be "in tune" with God or to know God as "a living presence." Cultivating that need is the goal of spiritual formation training.

Daniel Buechlein defines spirituality: "All spirituality is a response to God's call. He has made the initiative. It is not up to the creature to get God's attention or to win His favor. Rather he must cooperate with God's preeminent grace and respond wholeheartedly."[3] In a study of eight missionaries over different periods of history, Michael Collins Reilly concludes that some "constant marks" of missionary spirituality over the centuries were a deep love of God and a sense of a union with God.[4] It is the cultivation of this "response" as Buechlein states, or this "love/union" as Reilly states, that is the essence of development in spiritual formation.

Realizing the Need for Spiritual Formation Training

Missionary trainers have also asserted that spiritual development or formation can and should be facilitated by the training program. Marjorie Procter-Smith, speaking about ministers in general, asks the intriguing question, "If ministers-in-training do not learn the disciplines of prayer and worship as they learn their Bible and systematic theology, when will they learn them?"[5] This question can certainly be asked of missionary students. If they do not learn the disciplines of staying in tune with God as they study their Bible and missiology, when will they learn them? Kenneth B.

Mulholland asserted that one key to effective graduate education for missionaries is the orientation toward total life training—social, spiritual, and physical development. "Graduate education needs to build spiritual formation into the training process. Courses on the ministry of prayer, the history of revivals or awakenings, and principles of Christian living have a place in graduate school instruction."[6] John Kayser echoes a similar thought for Bible Institutes. "Perhaps more critical than any other factor in the establishing of missionary vision is the spiritual dynamic of a school."[7] Kayser proposes that the Bible Institute should so impart the Word of God to its students that their character would be developed, their obedience and surrender would be obvious, and their lives would demonstrate the empowerment of the Holy Spirit, prayer, and revival. He stressed the importance of a devotional life, prayer life, and personal disciplines for spiritual development. Arthur F. Glasser reported in 1990, "Fortunately, in our day there is a renewed emphasis on spiritual formation or development in virtually all missionary training schools and evangelical theological seminaries. Not that our schools can mast of anything approaching significant achievement in this regard."[8] As Glasser states, "But grow they can, and grow they must." It is doable and it is necessary.

Taking a more pessimistic view though, L. Grant McClung bemoans that much still needs to be done in the area of igniting spirituality, or "passion" as he calls it, in the mission student.[9] He suggests that the missing ingredient in much of today's missiological education is "passion—a passion for God and God's glory, and a passion for the lost." The current educational trend has several misplaced priorities with its emphases on "statistics and structures, curriculum and consultations, minutes and methodologies, news and networking . . . these misplaced priorities tend to leave us dry and wanting." He recounts the story of one of William Booth's Salvation Army officers, who wrote to General Booth and complained of his ineffectiveness. Booth replied with a two-word telegram, 'Try tears." McClung asks another searing question, "Where is Jesus in all of this cultural accommodation?" The response to this question is, of course, in the spiritual formation training that is given to missionary students. As McClung perceptively points out, the cerebral statistical methodology of current missiology must be balanced by the spiritual enhancement of the presence of God in the student.

Realizing the Need for Spiritual Formation Training from a Biblical Perspective

There are biblical foundations for spirituality in missionary training. Paul, perhaps the greatest missionary of all times, had a spiritually formative event in his conversion that was nurtured in his training period. He met the living Christ in a dramatic way and he responded (Acts 9). His letters to the various churches demonstrate his spirituality—his continual response to the call of God.

Using many references from Paul's letters (as well as other New Testament Scriptures), Lee summarizes the theology of spiritual formation as living in the presence of God and specifies ten aspects of this presence.[10] So spiritual development or formation, would be the cultivation of God's presence. Certainly, Paul was an example worthy of emulation. "The aroma of his Damascus Road experience lingered throughout his life and ministry. Where Paul was present as a gifted and yielded vessel, God was also present and working in a special way."[11] So too must we imitate Paul's example in spirituality—his passion to know God and to experience God so that God will also work in a special way in our missionary service.

The church at Antioch is another example of spirituality in action. With its strong spiritual environment, Foltz lists four unique missions characteristics of the Antioch church.

> "In humility, these believers depended on the Holy Spirit's direct revelation to administer His church, and they accepted and rejoiced in the operation of spiritual gifts. The Antioch church used those gifts to support local evangelism and discipleship, which must go hand-in-hand with a vital world missions thrust if a church is to be truly healthy."[12]

Paul and Barnabas provided the spiritual nurture and training for this Antioch church. Perhaps, their nurturing was one of the first missionary training programs that included spiritual formation training.

Realizing the Need for Spiritual Formation Training from a Missiological Perspective

There are missiological foundations for the need of spiritual formation in missionary training. Seth Anyomi suggests that missionary preparation must ground the candidate in "spiritual disciplines of prayer, Scripture memory, meditation, and fasting. These disciplines bring a release of spiritual knowledge, wisdom, and power as missionaries minister to the spirit of other people and war on behalf of that spirit to bring salvation and deliverance."[13] Lack of spiritual formation is cited as one of the reasons for missionary attrition by the ReMAP project, both in Two-Thirds World countries and Western countries. Elkins, reporting the results from the USA and Canada, ranks immature spiritual life as 12th in a rank of reasons for leaving missionary service.[14] Anyomi, reporting on missionary attrition in Ghana, concludes that spiritual emphasis in missionary preparation is a must.[15] Margaretha Adiwardana suggests that today's younger missionaries in the New Sending Countries are also prone to the postmodern aversion to the discipline of a regular devotional time.[16] She recommends that the pre-field training must address this issue in order to curb missionary attrition and suggests the model provided by the Chinese Mission Seminary in Hong Kong, which concentrates on spiritual formation during the first year of seminary. Bruce Dipple, speaking of the perspective from Old Sending Countries, echoes many of Adiwardana's recommendations, emphasizing both the need for spiritual formation and interpersonal relation training.[17]

Robert Schreiter reminds us that the theme of the 1991 annual meeting of the American Society of Missiology dealt with missionaries in violence and conflict. The Society saw the increasing dangers of missionaries as they present the Gospel to unreached people groups around the world. He suggests that missionaries are not trained and therefore are ill equipped to handle these violent situations. Interestingly enough, one of his conclusions is that missionaries need to understand that the very heart of the Gospel message is reconciliation and that this reconciliation is initiated by God and is in essence "more a spirituality than a strategy."[18] The implication can be drawn that there is a direct correlation between spiritual formation training and Schreiter's conclusions for handling these violent situations. In short, missionaries need to be trained in spiritual formation in order for them to bring the spiritual nature of God's reconciliation to the situation. Spiritual formation, then, becomes a very practical prerequisite to resolving potential life-threatening situations faced by some missionaries.

Realizing the Need for Spiritual Formation Training in this Postmodern Age

Current missiological education programs need to be adjusted to insure they enhance and cultivate the missionary candidate's "passion" for God and His presence.

The need for spiritual formation training in young Western missionaries of today is not the same as the need in Tozer's and even perhaps in Glasser's day. The recognition of this "difference" and the corresponding adjustment in training programs will determine the effectiveness of any contemporary training program.

The young missionary candidates of today who have grown up in Western societies are a product of the postmodern society. McDowell notes, "We are the first generation in 300 years to go through a distinct cultural change . . . We no longer live in a post-Judeo-Christian culture; we live in an anti-Judeo-Christian culture."[19] Western missionary training programs must understand the postmodern perspectives that have shaped the thinking and belief-systems of these young missionary candidates if we are to provide training that is relevant to their needs. Few trainers would argue that the most effective training compares the outcome objectives of the training with the needs of the trainee to determine the "gap." Stephen Hoke suggests that this "gap" then becomes the basis for developing the learning objectives and the learning activities of the training program.[20] Contemporary missionary training programs make traditional assumptions on the entry-level skill sets of young candidates that may not be normative for the postmodern candidate. A revisit of the assumptive entry-level skills is in order for all missionary training programs in Western societies.

This reassessment is particularly important in the spirituality of these postmodern candidates. Many of these young candidates have come to Christianity without the extensive church experience that was prevalent in past eras. They also have come to Christianity with personal histories of emotional and psychological pain resulting from the dysfunctional family traits that are so prevalent in Western society today. Kath Donovan and Ruth Myors reports that many missionary candidates from the "buster" generation are products of broken homes, some have been sexually abused or have been recipients of other violent abuse.[21] Dipple echoes this report, "An increasing number of missionary candidates from Old Sending countries have come out of a dysfunctional family background and broken, painful homes. Such a background often leaves them vulnerable to emotional problems and susceptible to the erosion of their personal self-esteem."[22] McDowell suggests that we are ministering to one of the most hurting generations in history because so many have experienced fractured homes and relationships.[23]

Not only are many postmodern candidates struggling with emotional and relational problems, they are coming to Christianity with a postmodern mindset that is in some respects antithetical to the Christian worldview. Earl Creps lists the traits of the postmodern philosophy as:[24]

- The centrality of community
- The primacy of experience
- The subjectivity of truth

- The complexity of human perception
- The fragility of progress
- The unreality of absolutes
- The enormity of the spiritual
- The plurality of worldviews

Two of these traits that are particularly important for understanding the need for spiritual formation training in postmodern missionary candidates are: the unreality of absolutes and the plurality of worldviews. For the postmodern, there are no absolutes and therefore there is no absolute truth. Similarly, there are no single paths to God. This postmodern mindset will make it difficult for postmodern Christians not to be skeptical of the Bible as containing absolute truths from God and to accept Jesus as the only way to salvation and God. These two postmodern mindsets mean that you have a new Christian that requires some intentional spiritual formation training. Creps characterizes the postmodern person as "biblically illiterate, skeptical, unconvinced that truth exists in absolute terms, and personally adrift."[25]

Of course, some of this spiritual formation training is occurring in the local church after conversion, and this is how it should be. The church with its nurturing community is where the postmodern should be introduced and grow in his spirituality. However, missionary trainers indicate that the need for more spiritual formation training is still needed when these candidates enter the missionary training program. Donovan and Myors conclude, "We see it as highly desirable that post-buster missionaries be given an opportunity prior to their departure for the development of spiritual disciplines."[26]

The Method

Designing Effective Learning Experiences for the Postmodern Candidate

Not only does understanding the postmodern mindset assist in determining the skill gaps in our young trainees, but it also helps determine the most effective training methods. Three of the traits identified by Creps are particularly important when planning training modules for postmodern candidates: the centrality of community, the primacy of experience, and the enormity of the spiritual. Postmoderns place a high value on community in direct defiance to the modernists' preference for individualism. They would tend to look to those around them for a frame of reference from a "tribal" view of life.[27] Added to this communal need is the value they place on experiencing life as opposed to just reading about life. These two factors in the postmodern's mindset make the traditional classroom experience outdated. Creps, speaking on the discipling of new Christians from the postmodern era, doubts that conventional teaching methods will turn this new Christian into a devoted follower of Jesus.[28] Similarly, no longer will great teaching outlines delivered from the podium be the most effective teaching method for this new generation. The postmodern will relate to strong interactive group dynamics and role-play techniques they long for strong communal relationships and they learn best by experiencing the concept themselves. They want to know the truth by experiencing it. In fact, Bevan Herangi (a Generation Xer himself) suggests that many people have left the church because it has lost "its edge in presenting the real Gospel of Jesus. The cause of the Gospel, seeing people saved, was replaced by much teaching of the theory of Christianity. This bores us, as we value an experiential faith."[29] Stephenson and others echo this assessment. The postmodern missionaries will long for "an experiential angle to their spirituality."[30] They point out that the postmodernists are bored with the didactic emphases in modern church services. This is equally true for missionary training sessions. Donovan and Myor suggest that for the buster missionary candidates more emphasis needs to be placed on experiential learning, generic orientation, and training in teams rather than training by formal lecturing.[31] The missionary student must be an active participant in the development of their spirituality. Any program must encourage this personal involvement and must involve communal relationships that foster spiritual formation.

There is one trait described by Creps that enhances spiritual formation—the enormity of the spiritual. This postmodern generation is more receptive to spirituality and spiritual formation than their rational grandparents and parents. This receptivity to things of the spiritual nature of man accounts for the rise in mysticism and New Age thought in the Western societies of today. It can also account for their hunger for the true spirituality of God. Donovan and Myor offer the assessment that busters prefer relating to God and spending time with God rather than doing things for God. Busters are contemplative, reflective, and meditative.[32] Because of these traits, postmodern candidates long for direction and mentoring in spiritual formation. The training program therefore needs to channel these tendencies toward the true spirituality of Christ.

On the other hand, the spiritual growth of the postmodern candidate is stymied by his lack of personal disciplines and self-denial. Glasser suggested that a spiritual formation program will not be effective unless it stresses the "responsible freedom and personal effort of the students. It requires of them personal asceticism and discipline, and a willingness to be accountable to themselves, to their peers, and to the church of their association."[33] In the postmodern's need to develop spiritual disciplines, Donovan and Myors suggest that missionary trainers use periods of guided retreat for post-buster candidates.[34] They suggest that this method of spiritual training would be particularly helpful for this new generation.

This postmodern generation relates to different learning techniques and methodologies than their grandparents or even parents did. To make our training programs most effective, we need to capitalize on those learning methods that most impacts our postmodern.

The Spiritual Formation Training Model

First, reassess the spirituality that is displayed in the school personnel and curriculum. This postmodern stress on community and experience means that the training environment must be a place where spirituality is valued as well. This value on spirituality must be demonstrated by example. Teachers and curriculum should be enlivened with the presence of God—spiritual vitality. Spirituality should be integrated into every subject. Each course should relate the passion of God for His people and His desire to commune with them. The words of Tite Tienou, as he addresses missionary training for the African context, resonate in all missionary trainers.

> "Missiologists trained for an African context need to have spiritual fervor and credibility. It is true, of course, that spiritual fervor and credibility

> cannot be taught or created on demand; they must be demonstrated by example. That is why the institutions of missiological training must be more than factories producing people equipped with techniques and a body of knowledge. They must be communities where spiritual fervor is valued. But the spiritual fervor must be credible. In other words, spirituality which fails to relate to the world as it is today cannot be credible."[35]

Teachers must be willing to mentor missionary candidates in spiritual disciplines; they must be willing to invest personal time in one-on-one relationships with candidates. Postmoderns need this bonding with stable, secure people.

Second, mandate that missionary candidates be involved in a church in the community where the training program is located. The school will need to purposely initiate partnerships with these local churches to assure that the community environment so necessary for postmodernists is provided. It is through this partnership where many of the mentoring and one-on-one relationships will be established and fostered. The postmodern Xers crave for this one-on-one interpersonal relationship. A Generation Xer states, "We want someone to come alongside us and have input, give directions and keep us accountable. Many Xers have an inner search for the father or boundary-setter that was never there—someone to nudge us beyond our own experiences and walk with us through places they have been."[36]

Thirdly, have available on staff or partner with local resources to assure that Christian psychologists are available for counseling sessions. The emotional hurts and pains experienced in broken childhoods need to be dealt with prior to going to the mission field. This will involve an intentional effort by the trainers to allow opportunities for the Holy Spirit to bring these hurts to the surface. Encounter weekends are excellent opportunities for this healing of emotional hurts. The backdrop is a spiritual retreat center or other locations where the candidate is removed from the school setting. Upon return, the Christian counselor or psychologist can follow up to encourage the walking out of this healing process.

Fourthly, include spiritual formation classes in the curriculum. This will intentionally teach the importance and practice of prayer, Bible study, and daily devotions. The Asian Center for Missions offers curriculum for these classes.[37] It includes a module designed to promote ministry effectiveness "through the inward disciplines of meditation, prayer, fasting, and study; the outward disciplines of simplicity, solitude, submission, and service; and the corporate disciplines of confession, worship, guidance, and celebration." They also recommend *Celebration of Discipline* by Richard J. Foster as a textbook. The postmodern candidate particularly needs this course instruction in personal discipline and spiritual "streams," as coined by Foster, in order to counter the materialistic and "me" mindset that still may linger from the modernist worldview. Buechlein agrees, "The need for self-discipline is a further concern in the face of modern psychology's emphasis on self-fulfillment as life's goal and the usual human ways of defining that goal."[38] MTI (Mission Training International) also includes training modules that develop spiritual resources within the missionary candidate.[39] Pacific Life Bible College offers 18 credit hours for the successful completion of Gateway Training's certificate program. This program includes courses in "Experiencing God" and "Spiritual Warfare."[40]

Learning activities in these spiritual formation classes should allow group interaction and role-plays. Forming teams, which will jointly review, discuss, interact with, and pray about the information presented in these classes, will enhance the learning experience of these postmodern candidates. These same teams should be maintained throughout the semester in order for relationship-bonding and team-building events to occur within the group. Projects should also be given for the joint planning and execution of the team. These projects should be themed around the spiritual disciplines being discussed in the course so that the student can live out the spirituality stream they are studying. Postmoderns need to experience their spirituality in action.

Fifthly, spiritual formation training needs to include studies and teachings on spiritual warfare. As the candidate develops his or her spiritual maturity, he also needs to understand spiritual discernment and spiritual authority. Edgar Elliston asserts that the equipping of men and women to wrestle the spiritual powers of darkness mentioned by Paul in Ephesians 6 must be at the heart of spiritual formation training.[41] Certainly the regions where many may go to reach the unreached people groups is dominated by the spiritual powers of darkness. The missionary candidate needs to be prepared to assail in prayer this darkness with the spiritual authority of Christ.

Conclusion

The postmodern missionary has a particular need for spiritual formation training. The needs of young Western missionaries for spiritual formation training today is not the same as their parents' or grandparents' needs in the past. The recognition of this "difference" and the corresponding adjustment in training programs will determine the effectiveness of any contemporary training program. Many of these young candidates have come to Christianity without the extensive church experience that was prevalent in past eras. They also have come to Christianity with personal histories of emotional and psychological pain resulting from dysfunctional families that are so prevalent in Western society today. Not only are many postmodern candidates struggling with emotional and relational problems, they are coming to Christianity with a postmodern mindset that is in some respects antithetical to the Christian worldview. The postmodern's heart cries out for spiritual formation training that will speak to their hurts and respond to their anti-Christian world-views. Any missionary training model that does not adjust to this postmodern reality will inherently be defective.

The spiritual formation model offers several steps. Firstly, reassess the spirituality that is displayed in the school personnel and curriculum. This postmodern stress on community and experience means that the training environment must be a place where spirituality is valued as well. This value on spirituality must be demonstrated by example. Secondly, mandate that missionary candidates be involved in a church in the community where the training program is located so they can foster one-on-one mentorships with mature Christians. Postmoderns need this one-on-one relationship to grow spiritually. Thirdly, have available staff or partner with local resources to insure that Christian psychologists are available for counseling sessions. The emotional hurts and pains experienced through broken childhoods need to be dealt with prior to the mission field experience. Fourthly, include spiritual formation classes in the curriculum that intentionally teach the practice of the classic spiritual disciplines: prayer, Bible study, and daily devotions. Fifthly, spiritual formation training needs to include studies and teachings on spiritual warfare.

Spiritual formation does not come without intentionality and purposeful direction. The missionary trainer welcomes this challenge, as daunting as it may seem, because he or she understands the criticality of the task. But the postmodern candidate also must accept the challenge with the realization that his or her missionary field success may very well depend on it. Elliston says it best, "Spiritual formation does not occur automatically. It requires an active commitment on the part of the learner as well as those teaching. Instruction and the building of habits of personal and corporate spiritual disciplines help. The prime mover in the midst of the process is the Holy Spirit."[42]

The goal of spiritual formation training in missionary candidates is the same for postmodern missionaries as for their parents, only the need and the method differs. The goal is to be sensitive to the leading of the Holy Spirit in all that the missionary thinks and does. This goal when attained echoes in the heart of the missionary the cry of Moses,

> "If your presence will not go, do not carry us up from here. For how shall it be known that I have found favor in Your sight, I and Your people, unless You go with us? In this way, we shall be distinct, I and Your people, from every people on the face of the earth" (Exodus 33:15–16 *NRSV*).

McClung may have summed up this matter the best. He reports the searing words from Eva Burrows at the Lausanne II conference in Manila. "She noted how, in reflection before the Lord over her many years of ministry, a clear word from the Lord came to her, 'I have seen your ministry. Now, let Me show you Mine.'"[43]

Ron DeBerry is with the US Department of Defense as an Environmental Protection Specialist. He completed his M.Div. degree from Regent University, Virginia Beach, VA. His seminary studies have ignited in him a passion for teaching missionaries in the area of spiritual formation. Ron has been called into the teaching ministry of the church and is awaiting God's plan in this area.

NOTES

1 Tozer, A. W. "Spiritual Preparation for Christian Service," in *The Alliance Weekly* (14 September 1955), p. 3.
2 Gnanakan, Ken R. "The Training of Missiologists for Asian Contexts," in *Missiological Education for the 21st Century*, J. Dudley Woodberry, Charles Van Engen, and Edgar J. Elliston, eds. (Maryknoll, NY: Orbis Books, 1996), p. 118.
3 Buechlein, Daniel. "The Status of Spiritual Formation in the Theological Seminary," CARA Seminary Forum, (March 1977), p. 3.
4 Reilly, Michael Collins. "Developing a Missionary Spirituality," in *Missiology: An International Review* VIII no. 4 (Oct 1980), p. 440.
5 Procter-Smith, Marjorie. "Daily Worship An Instituted Means of Grace," in *Christian Century* (February 6–13, 1985), p. 125.
6 Mulholland, Kenneth B. "Keys to Effective Graduate Training," in *Evangelical Missions Quarterly* 21 no. 4 (Oct 1985), p. 404.
7 Kayser, John. "How a Bible Institute Imparts Missionary Vision," in *Evangelical Missions Quarterly* 21 no. 4 (Oct 1985), p. 407.
8 Glasser, Arthur F. "Training to Go Now! Missionary Training Today and Tomorrow," in *Mission Frontiers*, accessed 07 Feb 03; available from http://www.missionfrontiers.org/1990/12/d9010.htm; Internet.

9 McClung Jr., L. Grant. "Pentecostal/Charismatic Perspectives on Missiological Education," in *Missiological Education for the 21st Century*, J. Dudley Woodberry, Charles Van Engen, and Edgar J. Elliston, eds., (Maryknoll, NY: Orbis Books, 1996), p. 58.

10 Lee, Edgar R. "Living in the Presence of God: A Theology of Spiritual Formation," in *Enrichment Journal A Journal for Pentecostal Ministry,* accessed 07 Feb 03; available from http://enrichmentjournal.ag.org/enrichmentjournal/200203/200203_086_sptlformation.cfm; Internet.

11 Ibid.

12 Foltz, Howard. *Healthy Churches in a Sick World* (Fairfax, Va: Xulon Press, 2002), p. 55.

13 Anyomi, Seth. "Mission Agency Screening and Orientation and Effect of Attrition Factors," in *Too Valuable to Lose Exploring the Causes and Cures of Missionary Attrition*, William D. Taylor, ed. (Pasadena: William Carey Library, 1997), p. 234.

14 Elkins, Phillip. "Attrition in the USA and Canada," in *Too Valuable to Lose Exploring the Causes and Cures of Missionary Attrition*, William D. Taylor, ed. (Pasadena: William Carey Library, 1997), p. 175.

15 Anyomi, Seth. "Attrition in Ghana," in *Too Valuable to Lose Exploring the Causes and Cures of Missionary Attrition*, William D. Taylor, ed. (Pasadena: William Carey Library, 1997), p. 165.

16 Adiwardana, Margaretha. "Formal and Non-Formal Pre-Field Training," in *Too Valuable to Lose Exploring the Causes and Cures of Missionary Attrition*, William D. Taylor, ed. (Pasadena: William Carey Library, 1997), p. 212.

17 Dipple, Bruce. "Formal and Non-Formal Pre-Field Training," in *Too Valuable to Lose Exploring the Causes and Cures of Missionary Attrition*, William D. Taylor, ed. (Pasadena: William Carey Library, 1997), pp. 218, 220.

18 Schreiter, Robert J. "Reconciliation as a Missionary Task," in *Missiology: An International Review* XX no. 1 (Jan 1992), p. 8.

19 McDowell, Josh. "Reaching a Postmodern Generation," in *Enrichment Journal A Journal for Pentecostal Ministry*, accessed 04 Feb 03; available from http://enrichment journal.ag.org/enrichmentjournal/19903/050_post modern_gen.cfm].

20 Hoke, Stephen. "Writing Learning Objectives," in *Establishing Ministry Training A Manual for Programme Developers*, Robert W. Ferris, ed. (Pasadena: William Carey Library, 1995), p. 70.

21 Donovan, Kath and Ruth Myors. "Reflections on Attrition in Career Missionaries: A Generational Perspective into the Future," in *Too Valuable to Lose Exploring the Causes and Cures of Missionary Attrition*, William D. Taylor, ed. (Pasadena: William Carey Library, 1997), p. 44.

22 Dipple, p. 219.

23 McDowell.

24 Creps, Earl. "Disciplemaking in a Postmodern World," in *Enrichment Journal A Journal for Pentecostal Ministry*, accessed 04 Feb 03; available from http://enrichment journal.ag.org/enrichmentjournal/200204/200204_052_discipling.cfm.

25 Ibid.

26 Donovan and Myors, 59.

27 Creps

28 Ibid.

29 Herangi, Bevan. "So, like, what's with these Xers, man?" in *Postmission World Mission by a Postmodern Generation*, Richard Tiplady, ed. (Waynesboro, GA: Paternoster Press, 2002), p. 7.

30 Stephenson, Peter, Joanne Goode and Carolyn Cole. "I Still Have Not Found What I'm Looking For," in *Postmission World Mission by a Postmodern Generation*. Richard Tiplady, ed. (Waynesboro, GA: Paternoster Press, 2002), p. 26.

31 Donovan and Myors, 58.

32 Ibid., 51.

33 Glasser.

34 Donovan and Myors, 59.

35 Tienou, Tite. "The Training of Missiologists for an African Context," in *Missiological Education for the 21st Century the Book, the Circle, and the Sandals*, J. Dudley Woodberry, Charles Van Engen, and Edgar J. Elliston (Maryknoll, NY: Orbis Books, 1996), p. 97.

36 Herangi, 8.

37 Asian Center for Missions National Office. *Asian Center for Mission Handbook*, (Makati, Philippines: July 31, 2001). More information can be obtained from their website at www. acmnet.org.

38 Buechlein, 7.

39 http://www.mti.org/splice1.htm [15 March 2003].

40 http://www.gatewaytraining.org/[15 March 2003].

41 Elliston, Edgar J. "Moving Forward from Where We Are in Missiological Education," in *Missiological Education for the Twenty-First Century the Book, the Circle, and the Sandals*, J. Dudley Woodberry, Charles Van Engen, and Edgar J. Elliston, eds. (Maryknoll, NY: Orbis Books, 1996), p. 252.

42 Ibid., p. 252.

43 McClung, p. 65.

13. So What Makes an Intercultural Training Program Successful?[1]

MIGUEL ALVAREZ

> *"One draft horse can pull four tons; two draft horses harnessed together can pull 22 tons! Are missions (agencies) ready to sacrifice self-identity and unilateral control for the possibility of such a huge playoff? Obviously the output is greater than the sum of the individual components."*[2]

Introduction

This chapter offers a comparative review of the current mission trends of both Asia and Latin America. It also expands on current issues related to regional and intercontinental missionary efforts. With this framework in mind, I would like to introduce this debate from the point of view of someone who was born and raised in Latin America. Having served in the Central American region, and later in the Asia-Pacific region, I'd like to think of myself as an apprentice in the intercultural field of service. Based on this background, I will attempt to compare some historical patterns and current trends observed in most missionary activities in Asia and Latin America.

In this presentation, I am also committed to fairness. I believe our generation must appreciate those servants of God who actually gave their lives in the mission fields of Asia and Latin America. Consequently this debate offers due honor and recognition to those men and women who unselfishly brought us the good news of the Gospel, in spite of their limitations. By no means will I attempt to undermine their historical input due to cultural or educational differences or their methodology in comparison to the current trends of missionary ministry. On the contrary, it is with a spirit of gratitude that I submit the following review.

I would also like to incorporate the issue of intentionality.[3] It is only with this attitude in mind that any negative missionary experience of the past may be overcome. Particularly it applies to situations and circumstances related to attitudes, actions and even methodology of service.[4] My line of reasoning is that if the missionary endeavor is to be improved this must be done intentionally. With all of these facts in mind, let us consider some important lessons learned from the field.

Lessons Learned from the Asians

In the early 1990s, just after arriving in Manila, I had the opportunity to participate in several mission meetings, particularly in the Philippines. The aim of these meetings was always the same, to encourage the nationals to fully participate in mission service, particularly in those areas of the so-called 10/40 Window. Those mission-meeting organizers always referred to the fact that Asians and particularly Filipinos were the right option for most missionary needs in Asia and beyond.

> "Of course, there are more than a thousand Spanish words, and may be another thousand English words in the Filipino language, which makes us indeed international people linguistically speaking. Moreover, aren't we so similar to most Southeast Asian people physically? The color of our skin and our black hair makes us so close. Besides, like most people in the region, we also eat rice. With such a natural similarity we must be the right people to reach out to them."[5]

However, after a few doses of reality in the field, Filipinos have realized there was something more required to become true missionaries. Indeed it was necessary to select carefully, and later train and equip properly, so that they would approach the field adequately and with a long-term assignment in mind.

Lessons Learned from the Latinos

Similar situations took place in Latin America. The discourse was basically the same: "This is the time for us Latinos. Aren't there are about 3,000 Arabic words in the Spanish language? Aren't we physically so similar to the people of North Africa and the Middle East? And due to our color of skin and hair we could go in and move among them unnoticed. 10/40 Window, here we go!" Well, it also took a few hard knocks of missionary reality for eager candidates to realize there was something more required to become true missionaries: adequate training and equipping.

Current Mission Trends in Asia

Consequently to be able to objectively understand the current trends on world evangelization originated in Asia and Latin America, one must evaluate some patterns observed in recent history that have reoccurred among churches, denominations and Christian leaders of both regions. Let's take a look at some of them.[6]

Inherited Patterns

The issue of the historical "colonial" mentality was there in the beginning, and today continues to be one of the most significant elements of discussion in the mission strategies affecting Asia and Latin America. This "colonial" mentality has been observed in both the sending and the receiving parties involved. Of course, more research may also register that this "colonial" mentality could be observed in other regions of the world. In recent history, this was the most predominant characteristic observed in the relationship between the sending and receiving parties. In a recent publication of the *Journal of Asian Mission*, Wonsuk Ma clearly describes how this vicious attitude developed historically:

> "It is true that in the past, missionary-sending nations and missionary-receiving countries were clearly divided. That division also coincides with

rich versus poor, developed versus underdeveloped, White versus non-White or even Western versus non-Western nations. The missionary culture and lifestyle that was always viewed as superior to their national counterparts was not entirely the missionaries' fault. Realistically, as far as Christian practices were concerned, missionaries were expected to lead nationals, particularly in evangelistic and training situations. Moreover with the missionaries' financial capability, it is common to see an "inherited pattern of dependency."[7]

Indeed the system of "colonialism" was not only established culturally, economically, politically, and sociologically, but eclessiologically as well. Incidentally, this was the context in which most current missionary efforts were initiated. Unsurprisingly this context also resulted to other attitudes such as the following:

'Dependent Forever'

I lived in the Philippines for almost a decade and I suppose that was enough time to get a glimpse of what goes on in the relationship between foreign missionaries and the nationals. Historically, most local leaders assumed a secondary role in the administration and leadership of the church. The nationals were expected to submit to the authority of those sent from overseas to manage them, without protest. Of course there have been some outstanding exceptions, but these have not been the norm.[8]

The problem has its roots in the denominational individualism and competitiveness of the West. Denominationalism eventually became the greatest obstacle in the development of strong and efficient national leaders. Denominations often overemphasized the preservation, maintenance and continuity of the institution. Thus the role of an overseer or a denominational leader was to provide these elements on behalf of the organization. Therefore people were never seen as the recipients of their service. On the contrary, people were used as instruments to protect and preserve the system. So if an individual or a group of people were not willing to submit to the rules and regulations of the establishment they were disciplined, or simply separated from the organization.

In some cases national leaders were regarded with suspicion. In the worst case scenario, the goal of the foreign overseer was actually to keep them feeble or inferior, and therefore, dependent from the mother denomination.

On the other hand, in some countries of Asia the quest for a legitimate national pride threw Christians into the other extreme. This is very much the same with most Latin American countries. Strong oppression from the past gave birth to a strong reaction of national pride that eventually led the churches to break all ties with the founding mission agencies in the region. At the end of the 20th century there was an overwhelming thrust for national pride and self-determination. A new generation of leaders emerged with a new mentality and strong commitment to the national values of their own culture and society. They saw the previous generation of church leaders as oppressors and for this reason felt that their responsibility was to break with all of those sources of archaic leadership. This attitude has provoked innumerable church splits and the establishment of numerous independent ministries.

"Colonizers Forever"

Most Western missionaries arrived in Asian countries as church planters, their presence was a justified need at that time. But later on they became well established and powerful—financially and politically. In many cases, they conveniently failed to build new and capable leaders to replace themselves. Consequently they became indispensable. They built their own kingdoms and became irreplaceable. Neither did they trust the nationals nor other fellow missionaries. Hence, these foreign workers have continued to think of the nationals as inferior or incapable of assuming such a huge responsibility as pastoring the congregation they established. This cycle has been observed in Asia, particularly in the countries where English is spoken. This result obviously denies the true nature and purpose of cross-cultural service.

Current Mission Trends in Latin America

Unlike Asians, Latinos speak either Spanish or Portuguese. However, it will be a mistake to affirm that because of the common language there are no cultural differences among them. As a matter of fact in each country people keep their own customs and traditions to preserve their particular identity. Many times Latins use this cultural norm as a way of self-protection or as an opportunity to communicate their needs among friends. With this framework in mind, let's take a look at some of the most observable issues that affect missionary efforts in Latin America.[9]

Unhealthy Interaction

Most Western missionaries arrived in Latin America under the same premises of those who went to Asia. They planted "their" congregations in the midst of persecution, primarily from the Roman Catholic Church. Catholicism had been imposed on the local cultures since the times of colonization. On the other hand the new missionaries, mostly North American and Europeans, also brought their own culture with them. They taught the nationals to submit to the foreign spiritual authority without any complaint. Moreover, only the foreign overseer had the right to exercise ecclesiastical power such as appointing the necessary subordinated authority.[10]

Another element that perpetuated dependence was the finances. Since most missionaries established their congregations among underprivileged communities, unsurprisingly the congregation and the local leaders were in financial disadvantage in relationship to the foreign leader. As a result they had no choice but to submit to him. Consequently, this relationship created a continuous cycle of economic, spiritual and political dependency.[11]

The "Transnational" Business Model

Most denominational "missionaries" were sent to Latin America following the same pattern of the transnational companies operating in the region. For most Christian denominations from the United States this was the natural American way of providing leadership to efforts overseas and the church was not the exception. They carried the title of "missionaries," however they were in fact only international administrators or representatives at the service of the denomination. Their "ministry" was to oversee the local interest of the denomination in every country where they were established. In addition this business pattern of leadership succeeded in duplicating itself by way of forming local leaders shaped with the same mentality—the most important leader in the denomination was the overseer. His most important responsibility was to preserve and maintain the system he represented. Moreover this position was the most desired by the nationals and some of them would endure the system until they were considered candidates for such a privileged position. Of course not all nationals followed this administrative way of service. This attitude was mostly observed in those who thought they had "the gift of administration."

The "Golden Rule"

The transnational mentality based its success upon needs for financial support. The denomination provided financial sustenance or maintenance of the work in the field. Hence the financial crisis of the local people, particularly during the second half of the 20th century. They were forced to remain submitted to the foreign "missionary" whose primary responsibility actually was to preserve and maintain the denominational system that he represented. In most places of Asia and Latin America today one can still observe this financial dependency, particularly among most denominationally bound congregations and ministries. This dependence is mostly observed through the leadership selection process, where foreign denominational boards will only appoint the leaders they trust.

The "Institutionalized Terrorism" Syndrome

The term "institutionalized terrorism" is used by the social sciences to define the oppressive relationship used by an individual in authority over a subordinate. The person in authority uses any mechanism that represents a threat, rejection or discipline against the subordinate, who in this case, is in a disadvantaged position and consequently is unable to defend himself.

In plain missionary language this comparison may seem awkward; nevertheless, if one digs a little deeper in recent church and missions history, there are sufficient cases out there that confirm certain levels of abuse in the exercise of authority by those in privileged position in the denominational structures. There are a number of people who have been hurt by authoritarian leaders. Most of those cases are not well known or documented due to the obvious disadvantaged position of the hurting party. Historically the church "overseas" has lost innumerable outstanding people at the hand of "untouchable" authoritarian "missionary" leaders.

Missions in the Asian and the Latin American Context

The question is, "How do Asians and Latin Americans comprehend cross-cultural missions?" Of course one must be careful not to generalize the issue. The same principle should be applied to Latinos as well: They will not have the same answer to that question. However, most Asians tend to live in monocultures and therefore each culture has its own group understanding and unique commitments to the Great Commission. In light of this allow me then to underscore some of the most pressing issues related to the missionary communities of both Asia and Latin America.

I begin with the premise that God yearns for all persons to have the opportunity to become true disciples of Jesus within their own social, cultural, and language context. Therefore, as the Church enters the third millennium, missionaries must work together in order to build a worldwide transcultural missions movement. This development should grant every person in every segment of the human mosaic an opportunity to hear, understand and respond to the Gospel during his or her lifetime. Once they accept Jesus, these new disciples should also have the opportunity to be incorporated into the life of a local congregation, and to grow in intimacy with the Holy Spirit.[12] They should be discipled to manifest the life of Christ and exhibit the fruit of the Spirit as salt and light in the world, and spiritually empowered to minister effectively both in the Church and in the world.

The Right Options

As the Gospel reaches more places and peoples and the Church grows in numbers, missionaries must seek to build up believers in nurture, discipleship, faith and knowledge. Missionaries should support every effort that provides various levels of training so that every church may have equipped and mature leaders and that every mission endeavor may have adequate pioneering leadership.[13] Asians and Latin Americans must recognize and promote the importance of a solid missiology in the context of world evangelization. Consequently churches, organizations and institutions must place cross-cultural missions at the very core of the total curriculum of Christian education and missionary training. It should be understood that the Church must include not just congregational structures, but also missiological and educational structures as well at all levels.

Regional Partnerships

Contemporary partnerships are an important part of world evangelization. Asians and Latin Americans must build relationships of trust so that they can work together in partnership. They must build and foster fellowships of believers in Christ among all peoples that worship Him.[14]

A fundamental question in missions must change, from "What can I do?" to "How do we fit in, in relationship to what others are doing?" Partnerships can help us answer this question and provide a forum for practical collaboration.[15] These partnerships will not emerge or operate without people who have the vision, skills and commitment to both the partnership purpose and process. In this way they must encourage the Church to identify, recruit, train and support partners and facilitators.

National Initiatives

At this point it is crucial that in both Asia and Latin America, nationals assume their responsibility as leaders and mobilizers. Current missionary initiatives must emphasize the importance of mobilizing indigenous resources and church structures to find and reach every unreached people group within their own countries and beyond.[16] This is the future of missions. Along these lines several models of missionary mobilization have been established in both regions.[17] Undoubtedly these efforts are already establishing a new paradigm for the new order of world evangelization. However, every effort must be strategically planned and all missionaries should receive the appropriate training. There will be no excuse for making the same mistakes of the previous generation.

Networking

As a missionary educator and mobilizer, I have had the opportunity to visit with different missionary leaders and agencies in Asia and Latin America. Most of them have shown the same attitude—the only perfect program is theirs. They do not talk to other agencies or to other missionaries. They talk about partnership and cooperation but in actuality deny them. Some of them refuse to share information and even to sit down with other fellow organizations. Missions have been permeated by selfishness. There are certain individuals who only seek after their own gain. Obviously this report represents the reality of the old paradigm.

The new paradigm however focuses on the ability to *intentionally* network and cooperate. Relational leadership must have the ability to serve as a catalyst to bring the mission community together to cooperate and coordinate toward a common goal and thereby boost the effectiveness of the overall mission force. Building networks and partnerships to accomplish this will be an essential part of the process.

Regional missionary organizations and ministries should be brought together to form specific "tracks, task forces and resource networks."[18] These ministries with similar areas of outreach should network, cooperate and coordinate their efforts. For instance, specific tracks should be formed for those involved with prayer, translation, Gospel recordings, and mobilization, church planting, women, youth and more. Hence networking leadership will bring together the adequate use of contemporary technology that will foster better communication within and between the various networks and tracks. These networks and task forces will force a much needed networking attitude among the different Christian organizations. The language and the spirit of cooperation will enfold the Christian movement.

Information-gathering and Distribution

At this time in history the missionary movement is faced with one of the most urgent elements—the proper use and distribution of information. It is no secret that the power of communication is in the collection of the best information available in the mission field. Today missionaries are sent out to collect the best information available on who the "unreached" peoples are and what God is doing to reach them. This information is necessary to mobilize both churches and mission agencies and to focus their efforts on reaching those "unreached" peoples.[19]

Another benefit of networking is the use of information to convoke national, regional and intercontinental gathering with specific missionary purposes. Equally beneficial is the use of fairness in the distribution of missionary resources available in the Body of Christ. Of course, this new paradigm points toward a new order in the mobilization of the Church for the purpose of world evangelization.[20]

Pressing Issues in Current Missionary Training

I must admit that even this "missionary training" term has already been abused, and therefore we need to establish some conceptual foundations in order to understand which kind of training we are talking about here. By missionary training we will understand the ability to provide instruction in the cross-cultural discipline, which includes spiritual foundations or practices designed to impart proficiency to undergo the cross-cultural task. This training is driven to develop missionary skills, such as behavior, spiritual habits and mental attitudes. Likewise, missionary training should cause change; it should also be action-oriented and involving. [21]

It is based upon that Asian and Latin American experience that I introduce this discussion for the sake of a sustained and long-term missionary program initiated in the Southern Hemisphere. I believe Asians and Latinos need to establish a continuous dialogue focused on common grounds of understanding and interpreting the missiological task of the Church in the South.[22] Indeed there are a number of issues that remain constant in the missiological universe of both Asia and Latin America.

Planning

There is a legitimate concern among mission agencies about the need to establish clear objectives and reachable goals, which will determine the expected level of success in a long-term assignment. Missionaries must offer clear evidence and justify why they have chosen a particular country or culture as an object of their ministry. Of course the said planning process will also include obvious organizational relationships, and sound direction, coordination and supervision.

Teamwork and Interpersonal Relationships

There is one element that makes Asians and Latinos similar. They both are capable of working as a team, unlike the individualistic attitude of some missionaries from other latitudes. However, Asians and Latinos need to learn the benefits of teamwork and how to relate properly to teammates, family, sponsors, churches and even missionary agencies. They need to develop theological and pastoral foundations that will enable them to address these issues adequately.

Spiritual Discipline

Missionary training must focus on the development of a sound individual and collective spirituality. This must be observed in the lifestyle of the missionary. The love of Christ must be their final object in all their efforts.[23] Only a solid relationship with the Holy Spirit will guarantee a successful long-term missionary service. It is no secret that the most outstanding missionaries in the history of missions evidenced a powerful passion in their love of Christ.

Pastoral Care

A successful long-term missionary assignment will be associated to a qualified pastoral care and counseling service provided to the worker in the field. This service must be planned and intentionally organized. If a missionary agency is incapable of providing pastoral care for its missionaries, it has failed to provide for one the most urgent needs in the mission field.

Strengthening the Mission Agency

The first priority of the national churches is to strengthen the missionary agency. In most negative cases of frustrating experiences the local mission agency has been identified as the weak link. This is due to lack of support from the local church. Most churches use their resources for local development thus neglecting their missionary responsibility. When this trend continues the missionary agency is forced to neglect its primary responsibility due to lack of resources. Churches have no excuse to restrain their support to the mission agency. To do otherwise only evidences lack of commitment to the Great Commission.

Synergy Built Upon the Exercise of Partnership and Cooperation

It is the purpose of this dialogue to continue to affirm that partnerships are an important part of world evangelization. Christian organizations must build relationships of trust so that they can work together in partnership, to enhance fellowships of believers in Christ among all peoples that will worship Him. Partnerships will provide a forum for practical missionary collaboration. [24] Recently there have been signs of a new day dawning among God's people everywhere to worship and work together with God's people from everywhere. There are already several dozens of international missionary partnerships emerging and operating among and for the good of the unreached peoples. Undoubtedly this effort is pleasing to God. It is true to His character and to the mission of the church. However, a major challenge is still before us. These partnerships will not emerge or operate without people who have the vision, skills and commitment to both the partnership purpose and process. Therefore this kingdom of partnership must continue to encourage the Church to identify, recruit, train and support partnership facilitators.[25]

It was William D. (Bill) Taylor who initiated this new concept of partnership at the World Evangelical Alliance Missions Commission's meeting in Manila in June 1992. In the book *Kingdom Partnerships for Synergy in Missions*, he upholds that the church and the missions community must move beyond superficial fellowship and simple networking to true partnership—cooperative ventures, strategic alliances, mutually engaged projects, and the sharing of material and human resources. The expected result is synergy—the output is greater than the sum of the individual components. [26] He says "one draft horse can pull four tons; and two draft horses harnessed together can pull 22 tons! Are mission (agencies) ready to sacrifice self-identity and unilateral control for the possibility of such a huge playoff?"[27]

A simple definition of partnership would be "using mutual gifts to accomplish tasks."[28] However the essential components of partnership are laid out in a broader definition offered by Luis Bush. He helps us to understand the idea of partnership in the context of missions as "an association of two or more autonomous bodies who have formed a trusting relationship, and fulfill agreed-upon expectations sharing complimentary strengths and resources, to reach their mutual goal."[29]

Partnership Built upon Mutual Respect and Acceptance

Recently churches in many countries have developed national strategies and processes for mobilizing the Body of Christ toward completing the unfinished task within and beyond their borders.[30] Visionary servant leaders have facilitated national initiatives that affirm existing structures and foster cooperative commitments to church planting and the goal of a pioneer church planting movement within every ethno-linguistic people.[31] It is encouraging to observe that united missionary efforts among the "unreached" people groups have already borne much fruit. And yet much work remains. Therefore, the Church must continue to pray for the hastening of the day when all persons will have a valid opportunity to experience the love, truth and saving power of Jesus Christ in fellowship with other believers of their own people. Missionary leaders must continue to encourage God's people everywhere to do their part in establishing a mission-minded church planting movement within every "unreached" people group. Providing every believer the opportunity to seek and discover God's missionary purpose for his or her life regardless of the cost.

Servant Leadership from Both the Sending and Receiving Church

This issue also must be addressed with an objective attitude. It is obvious that Asians and Latin Americans are becoming more and more sensitive to the holistic needs of the poor. In a way both the Asian and the Latin American Church represent that side of the Church, for which Jesus, the Peasant of Nazareth, showed deep concern. They were His people among the poor. Today, the majority of the Church is itself poor; consequently, ministry to the poor will therefore be a ministry by and with the poor. It is therefore encouraging that missionary organizations and fellow Christian networks are now promoting holistic, incarnational and community-transforming ministries, especially in the economically deprived areas of the world.[32] However, missionary agencies are keenly conscious of the enormous social and spiritual ills affecting millions of the poor and needy. It is also true that both the rich and the poor are guilty of covetousness, injustice and indifference leading to sins of commission and omission. Missionaries are then confronted with an overwhelming demand to join with the poor in breaking the chains of injustice and oppression, sharing all the resources that God has given them, and spreading the Gospel of the Kingdom, which is good news for the rich, and the poor alike.

Women in Missions

Today, women all over the world are experiencing God's most outstanding visitation. They are rising to their birthright and inheritance, as they trust God to fulfill all His purposes in and through them. They are committed to follow the leading of the Holy Spirit, as they realize their intrinsic value, not in cultural, geographical and generational imperatives but rather in knowing that they are made in the image of God. The Creator, who designed both male and female to reflect His likeness and glory, calls men and women to serve together as equal partners in His purpose. Missionaries therefore must continue to strengthen and pursue the ministry of reconciliation[33] and justice extending it not only to race and class but to gender as well. In consequence men and women should learn to walk and work together in the mission field with mutual and godly respect.[34]

Conclusion

In this chapter I have attempted to highlight some of the most observable elements that need to be corrected in the new order of missions of the 21st century. In the same way

I also offer some possible options that can be considered as potential solutions. There may be other indicators that could be used to demonstrate whether a missionary program is implementing the proper method of success or not. At this point what matters is that those committed to missionary service, and particularly to training, should take a close look at those indictors and find out whether they seem helpful or not.

It is also important that the missionary service in the 21st century be carried out in a cooperative and networked basis. This is especially important as more and more new missionaries and mission agencies are arising at the Four Corners of the planet. Indeed, times have changed. A new generation of missionaries and mission agencies has arisen. This generation is facing a fascinating and fast changing world. Current technology has made life different and it will continue to evolve even faster.[35] Thus more adjustments will have to be made.

What makes a missionary program successful? There is no simple answer to this question. The success of a missionary program cannot be found in the pages of an outlined handbook. We all wish that were the case; instead, we are faced with a dynamic and ever improving process. And I would like to see it continue that way—a process. It must be that way. There are many different contexts of people and societies in the world. The generation of the 21st century will have the opportunity to interact with missionaries of different cultural backgrounds: race, color, language, nationality. Indeed the Holy Spirit has been able to mobilize His people all over the world to reach out to those who are lost. This is the new context of world evangelization today.

NOTES

1 An earlier version of this article was published under the title "What Makes an Intercultural Program Effective? Lessons from Southern Hemisphere Experiences: Asian and Latin America," in *Asian Church & God's Mission,* Wonsuk and Julie C. Ma, eds. (Manila, Philippines: OMF Literature, Inc., 2003) pp. 61–78.

2 Taylor, William, ed., *Kingdom of Partnerships for Synergy in Missions* (Pasadena, CA: William Carey Library, 1994) Back cover blurb.

3 On the issue of intentionality in missions see William L. Isley Jr., "A Spirituality for Missionaries," in *Missiology. An International Review* 17:3 (July 1999) pp. 299–309 (302).

4 Padilla, C. René. "Toward the Globalization and Integrity of Mission," in *Mission in the Nineteen 90's.* Gerald H. Anderson, James B. Phillips and Robert T. Coote, eds., (Grand Rapids, Michigan: Eerdmans, 1991), pp. 30–32.

5 This is what I understood from their general speech and attitude.

6 The following Asian authors offer a clear picture and understanding of the new context of missions in Asia.

Julie C. Ma. *When the Spirit Meets the Spirits: Pentecostal Ministry Among the Kankana-ey Tribe in the Philippines* (NY: Peter Lang, 2000).

Ken Gnanakan. *The Pluralistic Predicament* (Bangalore, India: Theological Book Trust, 1992), pp.26-38.

Joseph R, Suico. "Pentecostalism: Towards a Movement of Social Transformation in the Philippines," in *Journal of Asian Mission* 1:1 (March 1999), pp. 7–19.

Choan-Seng Song. *Christian Mission in Reconstruction: An Analysis* (Maryknoll, NY: Orbis, 1977).

David S. Lim. "A Critique of Modernity In Protestant Missions in the Philippines," in *Journal of Asian Mission* 2:2 (September 2000), pp. 149-177.

Ajith Fernando. *The Christian's Attitude Toward World Religions* (Wheaton, IL: Tyndale, 1987).

Rodrigo D. Tano, "Toward an Evangelical Asian Theology," in *Biblical Theology in Asia*, Ken Gnanakan, ed. (Bangalore, India: Theological Book Trust, 1995), pp. 46–76.

John Gnanapiragasam and Felix Wilfred, eds. *Being Church in Asia, Vol. 1*, Theological Advisory Commission 1986–92 (Quezon City, Philippines: Claretian, 1994).

Wonsuk Ma, "Mission: Nine Hurdles for Asian Churches," in *Journal of Asian Mission* 2:1 (March 2000), pp. 103–124.

Jose M. De Mesa. *Solidarity with the Culture* (Quezon City, Philippines: Maryhill, 1987).

Melba P. Maggay. *The Gospel in the Filipino Context* (Manila, Philippines: OMF Literature, 1987).

Emerito P. Nacpil. "Philippines: A Gospel for the New Filipino," in *Asian Voices in Christian Theology*, Gerald H. Anderson, ed. (Mary-knoll, NY: Orbis, 1976).

Bong Rin Ro. "Urban Missions: Historical Perspective," in *ATA Journal* 3:2 (July 1995) pp. 30–48.

Hwa Yung. *Mangoes or Bananas?* (Oxford, UK: Regnum, 1997).

Titus Loong. "Equipping the Next Generation of Missionaries," in *Asian Mission* 1 (July 1998).

Met Castillo. "Missiological Education: The Missing Element in Mission Strategy," in *Asia Pulse* 1 (1973), pp. 2–5.

Met Castillo, ed., *The Asian Challenge Compendium of the Asian Missions Congress '90* (n.p.: World Evangelical Fellowship, 1991).

7 Wonsuk Ma. "Mission: Nine Hurdles for Asian Churches" in *Journal of Asian Mission* 2:1 (March 2000) pp. 103–123 (107).

8 See Samuel Escobar. "The Promise and Precariousness of Latin American Protestantism," in *Coming of Age: Protestantism in Contemporary Latin America*, Daniel R. Miller, ed. (Lanham, MD: University Press of America, 1994), pp. 26–38 (31).

9 The following authors offer a clear picture and understanding of the new context of missions in Latin America.

C. René Padilla. "The Future of Christianity in Latin America: Missiological Perspectives and Challenges," in *International Bulletin of Missionary Research* 22:3 (July 1999), pp. 105–112.

______. *Bases Bíblicas de la Misión: Perspectivas Latinoamericanas* (Grand Rapids, Michigan: Nueva Creación, 1998).

______. "Toward the Globalization and Integrity of Mission," in *Mission in the Nineteen 90's*, Gerald H. Anderson, James B. Phillips and Robert T. Coote, eds., (Grand Rapids, Michigan: Eerdmans, 1991), pp. 30–32.

Rodolfo (Rudy) Girón, "COMIBAM: Three Independent Partnerships in Latin America," William D. Taylor, ed., *Kingdom of Partnerships for Synergy in Missions* (Pasadena, CA: William Carey Library, 1994), pp. 197–204.

Darío López. *Pentecostalismo y Transformación Social. Más Allá de los Estereotipos, las Críticas se Enfrentan con los Hechos* (Buenos Aires, Argentina: Kairos Ediciones, 2000).

Lopez, La Misión Liberadora de Jesús. *Una Lectura Misiológica del Evangelio de Lucas* (Lima, Perú: Ediciones Puma, 1997).

Alexandre Araujo. "Confidence Factors: Accountability in Christian Partnerhips," William D. Taylor, ed., *Kingdom of Partnerships for Synergy in Missions* (Pasadena, CA: William Carey Library, 1994), pp. 119–130.

Samuel Escobar. "Latin America," James M. Phillips and Robert T. Coote, eds., *Toward the 21st Century in Christian Mission* (Grand Rapids, MI: Eerdmans, 1993), pp. 125–135.

Federico Bertuzzi. "A Latin American Response to Patrick Sookhdeo," William D. Taylor, ed., *Kingdom of Partnerships for Synergy in Missions* (Pasadena, CA: William Carey Library, 1994), pp. 93–99.

William D. Taylor, "Hispanic American Models of Missionary Training," in William D. Taylor, ed., *Internationalising Missionary Training: A Global Perspective* (Grand Rapids, MI: Baker Book House, 1991), pp. 121–131.

Guillermo Cook, ed., *New Face of the Church in Latin America, Between Tradition and Change* (Maryknoll, NY: Orbis Books, 1994).

Enrique Dussell, ed., *The Church in Latin America*, 1492–1992 (Maryknoll, NY: Orbis Books, 1992).

Pablo Alberto Deiros, ed., *Los Evangélicos y el Poder Político en América Latina* (Grand Rapids, MI: Eerdmans, 1986).

10 On the issue of historical "colonialism" in Latin America see Enrique Dussel, *A History of the Church in Latin America: Colonialism to Liberation* (Grand Rapids, Michigan: Eerdmans, 1981).

11 See Claudio Veliz, ed., *The Politics of Conformity in Latin America* (London, UK: Oxford University, 1967) p. 7.

12 On this subject see L. Grant McClung, Jr., "'Try to Get

People Saved.' Revisiting the Paradigm of an Urgent Pentecostal Missiology," eds., Murray W. Dempster, Byron D. Klaus, Douglas Petersen, *The Globalization of Pentecostalism: A Religion Made to Travel* (Oxford: UK: Regnum Books, 1999) pp. 31–51.

13 For a comprehensive discussion of the current worldwide missionary mobilization, see David Shibley, *A Force in the Earth: The Move of the Spirit in World Evangelization* (Lake Mary, FL: Creation House, 1997).

14 See Steve Hoke, "A Glorious Pursuit. Reflections on God's Passion for Worshipers from All Peoples" in *Mission Frontiers* 23:1 (March 2001) pp. 20–27.

15 "The Millennial Manifesto: Covenanting for the 21st Century," *Mission Frontiers*, (http://www.missionfrontiers.org/2001/02/200102.htm) (December 2001).

16 See Emilio Antonio Núñez C. and William David Taylor, *Crisis and Hope in Latin America and Evangelical Perspective* (Pasadena, CA: William Carey Library, 1996) pp. 496–498.

17 See for instance, Samuel Escobar, "Latin America" in James M. Phillips and Robert T. Coote, eds., *Toward The 21st Century in Christian Mission* (Grand Rapids, MI: Eerdmans, 1993) pp. 125–135.

18 See Gerald H. Anderson, "Christian Mission in A. D. 2000: A Glance Backward," in *Missiology: An International Review* 18:3 (July 2000) pp. 275–288 (284).

19 At GCOWE '95 in Seoul, Korea, the AD2000 Movement released, in cooperation with the Peoples Information Network a list of unreached peoples under the title, *The Least-Evangelized Peoples of the World*. See Keith Butler, "Joshua Project 2000—Unreached Peoples List," in *Mission Frontiers* 18:5-8 (May–August 1996) pp. 38–52.

20 Following GCOWE '95, the AD2000 Movement launched Joshua Project 2000 with a focus on reaching the unreached peoples with a population of 10,000 or more. Shortly after the launch of Joshua Project 2000 in November 1995, the first Joshua Project list of 1,739 unreached peoples was released in the May '96 issue of *Mission Frontiers*. This list was continually refined, as new data became available. This report can also be found in Keith Butler, "Joshua Project 2000—Unreached Peoples List," in *Mission Frontiers* 18:5–8 (May–August 1996) pp. 38–52.

21 For a broader discussion on missionary training, see Miguel Alvarez, "Missionary Training: A Discipline," in *Journal of Asian Mission* 2:1 (March 2000) pp. 91–102 (95).

22 The term "Southern Hemisphere" has been used recently to refer to that part of the world other than Western Europe, North America, Australia and New Zealand, traditionally know as, "Northern Hemisphere" nations due to their common cultural, political and economic background.

23 Cf. William L. Isley Jr. "A Spirituality for Missionaries," in *Missiology. An International Review* 17:3 (July 1999) pp. 299–309.

24 Phil Butler. "Do Strategic Partnerships Really Make a Difference," in *Mission Frontiers* 18:9–10 (September–October 1996) pp. 29–30.

25 William D. Taylor, ed., *Kingdom Partnerships for Synergy in Missions* (Pasadena, CA.: William Cary Library, 1994), pp. 1–8.

26 A thorough exposition and analysis on current trends and models of partnership can be found in William D. Taylor, ed., *Kingdom Partnerships for Synergy in Missions* (Pasadena, CA: William Cary Library, 1994).

27 Taylor, William D. *Kingdom Partnerships for Synergy in Missions*, back cover.

28 Taylor, p. 4.

29 Luis Bush, *Partnering in Ministry: The Direction of World Evangelism* (Downers Grove, IL: InterVarsity Press, 1990), p. 46.

30 Luis Bush. "The Unfinished Task," in *Mission Frontiers* 17:3–4 (March–April 1995) pp. 7–14 (12).

31 A good example of cooperative strategies in church planting is found in David Garrison, *Church Planting Movements* (Richmond, VA: International Mission Board of the Southern Baptist Convention, 1999), pp. 7–10.

32 A scenario of servant leadership in the context of a Latin American society can be found in Darío López, *Los Evangélicos y los Derechos Humanos: La Experiencia Social del Concilio Nacional Evangélico del Perú 1980–1992* (Lima, Perú: Centro Evangélico de Misiología Andino–Amazónica, 1998).

33 Cf. French L. Arrington. *Ministry of Reconciliation: A Study of 2 Corinthians.* (Grand Rapids, MI: Baker Book House, 1980).

34 For a broader discussion on the issue of women in missions see Ruth A. Tucker, "Women in Mission" in James M. Phillips and Robert T. Coote, eds., *Toward the 21st Century in Christian Mission* (Grand Rapids, MI: Eerdmans, 1993) pp. 284-293. Also in the context of Brazil see Benedicta Da Silva, *Benedicta Da Silva: An Afro-Brazilian Woman's Story of Politics and Love* as told to Medea Benjamin and Maisa Mendoca (Oakland, CA: A Food First Book, 1997), pp. 193–201.

References

Part I: Biblical and Theological Foundations

1 • Training Leadership for Intercultural Service: A New Paradigm

Burns, Barbara H. *Teaching Cross-cultural Missions Based on Biblical Theology: Implications of Ephesians for the Brazilian Church* (Deerfield, IL: Trinity Evangelical Divinity School, 1983). A thesis for the Doctor of Missiology degree.

Castillo, Met. "Let's Think Clearly about Missionary Training," in *Bridging Peoples* 8:1 (1991).

______. "Missiological Education: The Missing Element in Mission Strategy," in *Asia Pulse* 1 (1973).

Ebenezer, Sunder Raj. "The Philosophy and Ethos of OTI Training," in *The Management of Indian Missions*, Sunder Raj Ebenezerm, ed. (Bangalore, India: Indian Evangelical Mission, n.d.).

Escobar, Samuel. "The Global Scenario at the Turn of the Century," in *Global Missiology for the 21st Century: The Iguaçu Dialogue*, William D. Taylor, ed. (Grand Rapids: MI: Baker Book House, 2000).

Ferris, Robert and Lois Fuller. "Transforming a Profile into Training Goals," in *Establishing Ministry Training*, Robert Ferris, ed. (Pasadena: William Carey Library, 1995).

Foltz, Howard L. *For Such a Time as This: Strategic Missions Power Shifts for the 21st Century* (Pasadena, CA: William Carey Library, 2000).

Harley, David. *Preparing to Serve Training for Cross-Cultural Mission* (Pasadena, CA: William Carey Library, 1995).

Hopkins, Richard L. "Philosophy of Training," in *Training for Cross-Cultural Ministries*, Jonathan Lewis, ed. (Wheaton: IL: WEF, 1998).

Itioka, Neuza. "Third World Missionary Training: Two Brazilian Models," in *Internationalising Missionary Training: A Global Perspective*, William D. Taylor, ed. (Exeter, UK: Paternoster Press, 1991).

Jongeneel, Jan A. B. "Is Missiology an Academic Discipline?" *Exchange* 1 (1998).

Kayser, John. "Training and Missionary Attrition," in *Training for Cross-Cultural Ministries*, Jonathan Lewis, ed. (Wheaton, IL: WEF, 1997).

Kohls, L. R. with H. L. Brussow. *Training Know-How for Cross-Cultural and Diversity Trainers* (Duncanville, TX: Adult Learning Systems, 1995).

Lewis, Jonathan, ed. "Matching Outcomes with Methods and Contexts," in *Training for Cross-Cultural Ministries,* (Wheaton, IL: WEF, 1998).

Loong, Titus. "Equipping the Next Generation of Missionaries," in *Asian Mission* 1 (July 1998).

McKinney, Lois. "New Directions in Missionary Education," in *Internationalising Missionary Training: A Global Perspective*, William D. Taylor, ed. (Exeter, UK: Paternoster Press, 1991).

Pierson, Paul E. "A North American Missionary Trainer Responds to Two-Third World Concerns," in *Internationalising Missionary Training: A Global Perspective*, William D. Taylor, ed. (Exeter, UK: Paternoster Press, 1991).

Rickett, Daniel and Dotsey Welliver, eds. *Supporting Indigenous Ministries* (Wheaton, IL: Billy Graham Center, 1997).

Rickett, Daniel. *Building Strategic Relationships: A Practical Guide to Partnering with Non-Western Missions* (Pleasant Hill, CA: Klein Graphics, 2000).

Shubin, Russell G. "The Escalating Filipino Force for the Nations," in *Mission Frontiers* 20 (September–December 1998).

Singh, Raja B. "What Does Missionary Training Stand for?" in *The Management of Indian Missions*, Ebenezer Sunder Raj, ed. (Madras, India: India Missions Association, 1992)

Triplett, Allan R. *Introduction to Missiology* (Pasadena, CA: William Carey Library, 1987).

Winters, Roberta H. *Once More Around Jericho* (Pasadena, CA: William Carey Library, 1978).

Useful Websites

AD 2000 and Beyond Movement http://ad2000.org/.

World Evangelical Alliance Missions Commission http://world evangelical.org/missions.html/ http://www.global mission. org/.

Partnership Models http://www.interdev. org/.

2 • Getting in Cadence with God: The Goals and Objectives of Missionary Training

Keidel, Levi O. *Conflict or Connection: Interpersonal Relationships in Cross-Cultural Settings* (Chicago, Illinois: Evangel-ical Missions Information Service, 1996).

Lua, Theresa Roco. "Developing a Holistic and Contextualized Discipleship Ministry Among Filipino Urban Poor Adults in Metro Manila" in *Journal of Asian Mission* 2:1 (March 2000).

McClung, Jr., L. Grant. *Globalbeliever.com* (Cleveland, Tennessee: Pathway Press, 2000).

Nee, Watchman. *The Normal Christian Church Life* (Colorado Springs, CO: International Students Press, 1969).

Phillips, James J., and Robert T. Coote, eds. *Toward the Twenty-First Century in Christian Mission: Essays in Honor of Gerald H. Anderson* (Grand Rapids, Michigan: Eerdmans, 1993).

Strong, James. *The Exhaustive Concordance of the Bible, Dictionaries of the Hebrew and Greek Words* (Peabody, MA: Hendrickson Publishers, 1990).

Steffen, Tom A. *Business as Usual in the Missions Enterprise?* (Center for Organizational & Ministry Development, 1999).

Taylor, William D., ed. *Too Valuable to Lose: Exploring the Causes of Missionary Attrition* (Pasadena, CA: William Carey Library, 1997).

The American Heritage Dictionary, 4th Edition (New York, NY: Dell Publishing a division of Random House, Inc., 2001).

3 • Going Therefore to All People Groups: Setting up the Biblical Foundation

Alvarez, Miguel. "Missionary Training, A Discipline," in *Journal of Asian Mission* 2:1 (*March* 2000).

Foltz, Howard and Ruth Ford. *Healthy Churches In A Sick World* (Joplin, MO: Messenger Publishing House, 2000).

______. *Triumph: Missions Renewal for the Local Church* (Pasadena, CA: William Carey Library, 2000).

______. *For Such a Time As This: Strategic Missions Power Shifts for the 21st Century* (Pasadena, CA: William Carey Library, 2000).

Green, Keith. "Why Should You Go to the Mission Field?" in *Last Days Ministries* (July/September, 1984).

Horne, Herman. *Jesus the Teacher: Examining His Expertise in Education* (Grand Rapids, MI: Kregel Publications, 1998).

Jones, Marge and Jones, E. Grant, eds. *Psychology of Missionary Adjustment* (Springfield, MO: Gospel Publishing House, 1995).

Luzbetak, Louis J. *The Church and Cultures* (Techny, IL: Divine Word, 1963).

McClung, Jr., L. Grant. *Globalbeliever.com* (Cleveland, Tennessee: Pathway Press, 2000).

Schirrmacher, Thomas. "Jesus as Master Educator and Trainer," in *Training for Cross-Cultural Ministries*: 2:1 (2000).

Sorti, Craig. *The Art of Crossing Cultures* (Yarmouth, Maine: Intercultural Press Inc., 1990).

Stewart, John A., and John A. Kenyon, eds. *The Mission Handbook*, 15th Ed., (Monrovia, CA: MARC, 1995).

Taylor, William D., ed. *Too Valuable To Lose: Exploring the Causes of Missionary Attrition* (Pasadena, CA: William Carey Library, 1997).

Winters, Ralph D. and Steven C. Hawthorne, eds. *Perspectives: On the World Christian Movements*, 3rd Edition (Pasadena, CA: William Carey Library, 1999).

4 • Ecclesiological Basis for Training Intercultural Leadership

Beals, Paul A. "The Triad for Century 21," in *Evangelical Missiological Society Bulletin* (Spring 1999).

Borthwick, Paul. "A Love Affair that Must Be Cultivated Three Ways," in *Evangelical Missions Quarterly* 27 (January 1991).

Ferris, Robert. "Ten Biblical/Educational Commitments to Guide Missionary Training," in *Evangelical Missiological Society Bulletin* (Summer 1999).

Foster, Richard. "Growing Edges," in *Renovaré Perspectives* (July 1997).

Ferris, Robert and Lois Fuller, eds. *Establishing Ministry Training: A Manual for Programme Developers* (Pasadena, CA: William Carey Library, 1995).

Harley, C. David. *Preparing to Serve: Training for Cross-Cultural Mission* (Pasadena, CA: William Carey Library, 1995).

Hoke, Steve and Bill Taylor, eds. *Send Me: Your Journey to the Nations* (Pasadena, CA: William Carey Library, 1999).

Jerry Rankin. "The Southern Baptists: A Glorious Transformation in Process," in *Missions Frontiers* (July–0ctober 1997).

Johnston, Patrick J., Robyn Johnston and Jason Mandryk, eds. *Operation World: 21st Century Edition* (Carlisle, Cumbria, UK: Paternoster Lifestyle, 2001).

McConnell, C. Douglas. "Looking Back . . . Looking Forward," in *Mission Frontiers* (June 2000).

McLaren, Brian D. *The Church on the Other Side: Doing Ministry in the Postmodern Matrix* (Grand Rapids, MI: Zondervan 2000).

Newbigin, Lesslie. *The Household of God: Lectures on the Nature of the Church* (London, UK: SCM, 1953).

Niringiye, David Zac. "Jerusalem to Antioch to the World: A Biblical Missions Strategy," in *Evangelical Missions Quarterly* 26:1 (January 1990).

Peterson, Eugene. *The Message* (Colorado Springs, CO: NavPress, 2002).

Poor, Wally and Betty Poor. "Global Priority Church Models 21st Century Missions: First Baptist Church Fort Lauderdale Finds a Multicultural Setting a Perfect Incubator for Missions Involvement," in *The Commission* (August 1999).

Schirrmacher, Thomas. "Paul and His Colleagues," in *Training for Cross-Cultural Ministry: An Occasional Bulletin of the International Ministry Training Fellowship* 100:3 (2000).

Severn, Frank. "Missions Societies: Are They Biblical?" in *Evangelical Missions Quarterly* (July 2000).

Smith, Ebbie. "Four Dimensions of Leadership Training," in *Evangelical Missiological Society Bulletin* (Summer 1999).

Taylor, William D. "Partners Into the Next Millennium," in *Kingdom Partnerships for Synergy in Missions,* William D. Taylor, ed. (Pasadena, CA: William Carey Library, 1994).

Van Rheenen, Gailyn. "Doing 'Missions' Without the Local Church." http://www.missiology.org/discussion/_disc1/0000000c.htm>.

Vencer, Jun. "Control in Church/Missions Relationship and Partnership," in *Kingdom Partnerships for Synergy in Missions*, William D. Taylor, ed. (Pasadena, CA: William Carey Library, 1994).

5 • Hanging Out With the Almighty: Theological Basis for Training Intercultural Leadership

Alvarez, Miguel. "Missionary Training: A Discipline," in *Journal of Asian Mission* 2:1 (March 2000).

Anderson, Neil. *The Steps to Freedom in Christ* (USA: Gospel Light Publishers, 1996).

DeCarvalho, Levi. "Jesus' Model of Education," in *Mission Frontiers* 25:2 (March–April 2003).

Furst, Lyndon G. and Janet Mallery. *Journal of Research on Christian Education* 11:2 (Fall 2002).

Glasser, Arthur F. and Donald A. McGavran. *Contemporary Theologies of Mission* (Grand Rapids, MI: Baker Book House, 1983).

Harley, David. *Preparing to Serve; Training for Cross-Cultural Mission* (Pasadena, CA: William Carey Library, 1995).

Ireland, David. "The Courage of a Revolutionary," in *Kairos: Where Time and Destiny Meet* 4:4 (October–December 2001).

Knight III, Henry H. *Journal of the Academy for Evangelism in Theological Education* 17 (2001–2002).

Lum, Ada and Ginny Lum. *World Mission: 12 Studies on the Biblical Basis* (Chicago, IL: InterVarsity Press, 1976).

Miller, Madeleine S. and J. Lane Miller, eds. *Harper's Bible Dictionary* (New York, NY: Harper & Row Publishers, 1973).

Paik, Susan J. "Ten Strategies that Improve Learning," *Educational Horizons* 81:2 (Winter 2003).

Peters, George W. *A Biblical Theology of Missions* (Chicago, IL: Moody Press, 1972).

Pilot, Albert. "Using a Virtual Learning Environment in Collaborative Learning: Criteria For Success," in *Educational Technology* 73:2 (March–April 2003).

Shelly, Bruce L. *Church History in Plain Language* (Dallas, TX: Word Publishing, 1995).

Van Engen, Charles, Nancy Thomas and Robert Gallagher, eds. *Footprints of God: A Narrative Theology of Mission* (Monrovia, CA: MARC, 1999).

Wiersbe, Warren W. *Preaching & Teaching with Imagination* (Grand Rapids, MI: Baker Books, 1994)

Winters, Ralph D. "What's Wrong with 4,000 Pastoral Training Schools Worldwide?" in *Mission Frontiers* 25:2 (March–April 2003).

PART II — THE INDISPENSABILITY OF THE LOCAL CHURCH IN RECRUITMENT AND TRAINING

6 • Missiological Training in the Local Church

Church Mission Policy Handbook. (Wheaton, IL: ACMC, 1987).

Cunningham, William. "Training Workers Through Church Internship Programs," in *The Role of the Local Church in World Missions: Sending,* John C. Bennett, ed., (Wheaton, IL: ACMC, 1982).

Foltz, Howard L. *Triumph: Missions Renewal for the Local Church* (Joplin, MO: Messenger Publishing House, 2000).

Fuller, Lois. "Starting a Missionary Training Programme," in *Establishing Ministry Training: A Manual for Programme Developers.* Robert W. Ferris, ed., (Pasadena, CA: William Carey Library, 1995).

Hoke, Steve. "Customize Your Missions Training," http://www.urbana.org/_articles.cfm?recordid=288.

Mountainside Missionary Center in Libby, MT., http://www.internationalmessengers.org/Pages/mmt.html.

Phillips, Woodrow Jr. "Growing Missionaries in Your Church," in *The Role of the Local Church in World Missions: Sending.* John C. Bennett ed., Wheaton, IL: ACMC 1982), pp. 36–44.

Taylor, Bill. "Principles for Pre-Field Missionary Training. http://www.urbana.org/_articles.cfm?recordid=265.

Telford, Tom. *Missions in the 21st Century* (Wheaton, IL: Harold Shaw Publishers, 1998).

7 • Methods of Training Intercultural Leaders

Agnes, Michael. *Webster's New World College Dictionary,* 4th edition (New York, NY: McMillan, 1997).

AIMS. *Short-Term Missions Training: Key to Success* (Orchard Park, NY: Buffalo School of the Bible, 1989).

Carey, William. *Enquiry into the Obligations of Christians to use Means for the Conversion of the Heathens* (Leicester, UK: n.e., 1792).

Clinton, Robert. *The Making of a Leader* (Colorado Springs, CO: NavPress, 1998).

______. *Connecting: The Mentoring Relationships You Need to Succeed in Life* (Colorado Springs, CO: NavPress, 1992).

Conn, Harvie. *Missions & Theological Education in World Perspective* (Associates of Urbanus: Farmington, MI: Associates of Urbanus, 1984).

Fraser, David. *Planning Strategies for World Evangelization* (Grand Rapids, MI: Eerdmans, 1990).

Hoke, Steve and Bill Taylor, eds. *Send Me! Your Journey to the Nations* (Pasadena, CA: World Evangelical Fellowship, 1999).

Kane, Herbert. *Winds of Change in the Christian Mission.* (Chicago, IL: Moody Press, 1973).

Lerner, Alan. *Pygmalion and My Fair Lady* (New York, NY: Signet Penguin Group, 1956).

McClung, Jr., L. Grant. *Globalbeliever.com: Connecting to God's Work in Your World* (Cleveland, TN: Pathway Press, 2000).

Stoltzfus, Tony. *TLC Training Manual* (Virginia Beach, VA: TLC, 2003).

Taylor, William D. *Too Valuable to Lose: Exploring the Causes and Cures of Missionary Attrition* (Pasadena, CA: William Carey University, 1997).

Walls, Andrew. *The Missionary Movement in Christian History: Studies in the Transmission of Faith* (Maryknoll, NY: Orbis Books, 1996).

Woodberry, J. Dudley. *Missiological Education for the 21st Century* (Maryknoll, NY: Orbis Books, 1996).

8 • Missionary Selection

Alford, Deann. "Missions: Do Churches Send Wrong People?" in *Christianity Today* 42:6 (May 18, 1998).

Allen, Roland. *Missionary Methods: St. Paul's or Ours?* (London, UK: World Dominion Press, 1962).

Alvarez, Miguel. "Missionary Training: A Discipline," in *Journal of Asian Mission* 2:1 (March 2000).

Baker, Ken. "Boomers, Busters, and Missions: Things are Different Now," in *Evangelical Missions Quarterly* 33:1.

Bosch, David. *Transforming Mission: Paradigm Shifts in Theology of Mission* (Maryknoll, NY: Orbis Books, 1991).

Dixon, Janice. "Unrealistic Expectations: The Downfall of Many Missionaries," in *Evangelical Missions Quarterly* 26:4.

Dodds, Larry and Lois. "Selection, Training, Member Care and Professional Ethics: Choosing the Right People and Caring for Them with Integrity," http://www-students.biola.edu/~jay/ethicalcare.html.

Eggert, Rupert. "A Comparison of Methods Used to Identify and Select Missionaries," http://www.wls.wels.net/library/Essays/Authors/E/Eggert Methods/Eggert Methods.pdf.

Franke, Johann and Nigel Nicholson. "Who Shall We Send? Cultural and Other Influences on the Rating of Selection Criteria for Expatriate Assignments," in *International Journal of Cross Cultural Management*, 2 (2002).

Goring, Paul. *The Effective Missionary Communicator: A Field Study of the Missionary Personality* (Wheaton, IL: Billy Graham Center, 1991).

Hunter, Malcolm. "The Omega Connection," in *International Journal of Frontier Missions* 20:1 (January–March 2003).

Jones, Marge and E. Grant. *Psychology of Missionary Adjustment* (Springfield, MO: Logion Press, 1995).

Massey, Joshua. "Hometown Ministry as Pre-Field Preparation," in *Evangelical Missions Quarterly*, 38:38 (April 2002).

Reapsome, Jim. "Do You Have What It Takes?" *Great Commission Opportunities Guide* (Barrington Hills, IL: Real Media Group, 1998).

Stewart, Don. "Is a Local Church Missionary Biblical?" http://www.llano.net/baptist/localchurchmissionary.htm.

Taylor, William, ed. *Internationalising Missionary Training* (Grand Rapids, MI: Baker Book House, 1991).

Taylor, William, ed. *Too Valuable Too Lose: Exploring the Causes and Cures of Missionary Attrition* (Pasadena, CA: William Carey Library, 1997).

Terry, John Mark, Ebbie Smith and Justice Anderson, eds. *Missiology: An Introduction to the Foundations, History, and Strategies of World Missions* (Nashville, TN: Broadman & Holman Publishers, 1998).

Turner, Fennell, ed. *The Call, Qualifications and Preparation of Candidates for Foreign Missionary Service: Papers by Missionaries and Other Authorities* (New York, NY: Student Volunteer Movement, 1906).

Van Rheenen, Gailyn. "Can Local Churches Effectively Select and Care for Missionaries?" http://www.missiology.org/MMR/mmr9.htm.

Ward, Ted. "Repositioning Mission Agencies for the 21st Century," in *International Bulletin of Missionary Research* 23:4 (October 1999).

Yamamori, Tetsunao. *God's New Envoys: A Bold Strategy for Penetrating 'Closed Countries'* (Portland, OR: Multnomah Press, 1987).

9 • Organization and Planning: Maximizing Missionary Training

Alvarez, Miguel. "Missionary Training: A Discipline," in *Journal of Asian Mission* 2:1 (March 2000).

Bisoux, Tricia. "Faster, Smarter, Better," in *BizEd* (January–February 2003).

Covey, Stephen R. *The Seven Habits of Highly Effective People* (New York, NY: Simon & Schuster, 1989).

Dayton, Edward R. and David A. Fraser. *Planning Strategies for World Evangelization* (Grand Rapids: MI: Eerdmans, 1990).

Donovan, Kath and Ruth Myors. "Reflections on Attrition in Career Missionaries: A Generational Perspective Into the Future," in *Too Valuable To Lose: Exploring the Causes and Cures of Missionary Attrition,* William D. Taylor, ed. (Pasadena, CA: William Carey Library, 1997).

Ferris, Robert W. "Building Consensus on Training Commitments," in *Establishing Ministry Training: A Manual for Programme Developers*, Robert W. Ferris, ed. (Pasadena, CA: William Carey Library, 1995).

Green, Michael. *Evangelism in the Early Church* (London: UK: Hodder and Stoughton, 1970).

Harper, Stephen C. *The Forward-Focused Organization: Visionary Thinking and Breakthrough Leadership to Create Your Company's Future* (New York, NY: AMACON, 2001).

Kraakevik, James H. and Dotsey Welliver, eds. *Partners in the Gospel: The Strategic Role of Partnership in World Evangelization* (Wheaton, IL: Billy Graham Center, 1992).

Maxwell, John C. *Thinking for a Change: 11 Ways Highly Successful People Approach Life and Work* (n.a: Warner Publishing, 2003).

Ricket, Daniel. *Building Strategic Relationships: A Practical Guide to Partnering with Non-Western Missions* (Pleasant Hill, CA: Klein Graphics, 2000).

Wagner, C. Peter. "On the Cutting Edge of Mission Strategy," *Perspectives on the World Christian Movement: A Reader*, Ralph D. Winter and Steven C. Hawthorne, eds. (Pasadena, CA: William Carey Library, 1999).

PART III — Strategic Initiatives and Needed Components for Intercultural Training

10 • Funding Missions in the 21st Century

Barnhill, Carla. "Up and Comers: Fifty Evangelical Leaders 40 and Under," *Christianity Today* 40:13 (November 11, 1996).

Barrett, David B., and Todd M. Johnson. *World Christian Trends AD 30–AD2200: Interpreting the Annual Christian Megacensus* (Pasadena, CA: William Carey Library, 2001).

______. *World Christian Trends AD 30–AD2200 Companion CD.* (Pasadena, CA: William Carey Library, 2001.

Coca-Cola. "The Coca-Cola Company 2001 Annual Report." www2.coca-cola.com.

Dayton, Edward R. and David A. Fraser. *Planning Strategies for World Evangelization* (Grand Rapids, MI: Eerdmans, 1990).

Drucker, Peter F. "Managing for Business Effectiveness," in *Harvard Business Review* (May-June, 1963).

Evangelical Council for Financial Accountability. "ECFA Standards of Financial Accountability," www.ecfa.org.

Garrison, David. *Church Planting Movements,* www.IMB.org/cpm/chapter7.html.

Greenway, Roger S. "Eighteen Barrels and Two Big Crates." *EMQ* 28:2.

IMB. "Fast Facts," www.IMB.org.

Johnstone, Patrick and Jason Mandryk. *Operation World* (Waynesboro, GA: Paternoster Publishing, 2001).

Kriplalani, Manjeet. "Rural India, Have a Coke: Multinationals Target the Villages," in *Business Week Online* www.businessweek.com May 27, 2002.

Morton, Scott. *Funding Your Ministry: Whether You're Gifted Or Not* (Colorado Springs, CO: Dawson Media, 1999).

Orme, John. "This Business of Missions—What is the Bottom Line?" in *IFMA News* 51:4 (Winter 2000) www.ifmamissions.org.

Ott, Craig. "Let the Buyer Beware," in *EMQ* 29:3.

Schwartz, Glenn. "Dependency," in *Perspectives on the World Christian Movement,* Ralph D. Winter and Steven C. Hawthorne, eds. (Pasadena, CA: William Carey Library, 1999).

Van Rheenen, Gailyn. "Using Money in Missions: Four Perspectives," www.missiology.org.

11 • Understanding Partnerships Through the Eyes of a Native

Alvarez, Miguel. "Missionary Training: A Discipline," in *Journal of Asian Mission* 2:1 (March 2000).

Baba, Panya. "Models in Missionary Partnership," *Together in Mission,* Theodore Williams, eds. (Bangalore, India: World Evangelical Fellowship Missions Commission, 1983).

Butler, Phillip. "Partnerships Everywhere," http://www.ad2000.org/gcowe95/partners.html April 28, 2003.

Butler Phillip. "Why Strategic Partnerships? A Look at New Strategies for Evangelism,"

Partners in the Gospel: the Strategic Role of Partnership in World Evangelization, James H. Kraakevik and Dotsey Welliver, eds. (Wheaton, IL: Billy Graham Center, 1991).

Bush, Luis and L. Lutz. *Partnering in Ministry: The Direction of World Evangelism* (Downers Grove, IL: InterVarsity Press, 1990).

Butler, Phillip. "The Power of Partnership," in *Perspectives on The World Christian Movement*, Ralph D. Winter and Steven C. Hawthorne, eds. (Pasadena, CA: William Carey Library, 1999).

Foltz, Howard. *For Such a Time As This* (Pasadena, CA: William Carey Library, 2000).

______. *The Biblical Basis of Partnership* (Virginia Beach: AIMS, 2003).

Glynn, James. "Church-to-Church Partnership: What? Why? How?" in *Partners in the Gospel: the Strategic Role of Partnership in World Evangelization,* James H. Kraakevik and Dotsey Welliver, eds. (Wheaton, IL: Billy Graham Center, 1991).

Interdev. "The Power of Partnership: The Shape of Partnership," http://www.ad2000.org/adoption/Coop/Partner/Pidshap.htm.

Lewis, Jonathan. "Matching Outcomes with Methods and Contexts," in *Training for Cross-Cultural Ministries,* Jonathan Lewis, ed. Occasional Bulletin of the International Missionary Training Fellowship (Wheaton, IL: WEF, 1998).

Patrick Sookhdeo. "Cultural Issues in Partnership in Mission," in *Kingdom Partnerships for Synergy in Missions,* William D. Taylor, ed. (Pasadena, CA: William Carey Library, 1994).

Platt, Daryl. "A Call to Partnership in the Missionary Selection Process: Perspective of the Old Sending Countries," in *Too Valuable To Lose: Exploring the Causes and Cures of Missionary Attrition*, ed. William D. Taylor (Pasadena, CA: William Carey Library, 1997).

Rickett, Daniel. *Building Strategic Relationships: A Practical Guide to Partnering with Non-Western Missions* (Pleasant Hill, CA: Kleing Graphics, 2000).

William D. Taylor, ed. *Kingdom Partnerships for Synergy in Missions* (Pasadena, CA: William Carey Library, 1994).

12 • The Heart's Cry of the Postmodern Missionary

Adiwardana, Margaretha. "Formal and Non-Formal Pre-Field Training," in *Too Valuable to Lose Exploring the Causes and Cures of Missionary Attrition,* William D. Taylor, ed. (Pasadena: William Carey Library, 1997).

Anyomi, Seth. "Mission Agency Screening Orientation and Effect of Attrition Factors," in *Too Valuable to Lose Exploring the Causes and Cures of Missionary Attrition,* William D. Taylor, ed. (Pasadena: William Carey Library, 1997). *Asian Center for Missions Handbook.* www.acmnet.org.

Buechlein, Daniel. "The Status of Spiritual Formation in the Theological Seminary," in *CARA Seminary Forum* (March 1977).

Collins Reilly, Michael. "Developing a Missionary Spirituality," in *Missiology: An International Review* 8:4 (October 1980).

Creps, Earl. "Disciplemaking in a Postmodern World," in *Enrichment Journal. A Journal for Pentecostal Ministry* http://enrichmentjournal.ag.org/enrichmentjournal/200204/200204_052_discipling.cfm.

Dipple, Bruce. "Formal and Non-Formal Pre-Field Training," in *Too Valuable to Lose Exploring the Causes and Cures of Missionary Attrition,* William D. Taylor, ed. (Pasadena: William Carey Library, 1997).

Donovan, Kath and Ruth Myors. "Reflections on Attrition in Career Missionaries: A Generational Perspective into the Future," in *Too Valuable to Lose Exploring the Causes and Cures of Missionary Attrition,* William D. Taylor, ed. (Pasadena: William Carey Library, 1997).

Elkins, Phillip. "Attrition in the USA and Canada," in *Too Valuable to Lose Exploring the Causes and Cures of Missionary Attrition,* William D. Taylor, ed. (Pasadena: William Carey Library, 1997).

Elliston, Edgar J. "Moving Forward from Where We Are in Missiological Education," in *Missiological Education for the Twenty-First Century The Book, the Circle, and the Sandals,* J. Dudley Woodberry, Charles Van Engen, and Edgar J. Elliston, eds. (Maryknoll, NY: Orbis Books, 1996).

Foltz, Howard. *Healthy Churches in a Sick World* (Fairfax, VA: Xulon Press, 2002).

Gnanakan, Ken R. "The Training of Missiologists for Asian Contexts," in *Missiological Education for the 21st Century,* J. Dudley Woodberry, Charles Van Engen, and Edgar J. Elliston, eds. (Maryknoll, NY: Orbis Books, 1996).

Glasser, Arthur F. "Training to Go Now! Missionary Training Today & Tomorrow," in *Mission Frontiers* http://www.missionfrontiers.org/1990/12/d9010.htm.

Herangi, Bevan. "So, Like, What's with these Xers, Man?" in *Postmission World Mission by a Postmodern Generation,* Richard Tiplady, ed. (Waynesboro, GA: PaternosterPress, 2002).

Hoke, Stephen, "Writing Learning Objectives," in *Establishing Ministry Training A Manual for Programme Developers*, Robert W. Ferris, ed. (Pasadena: William Carey Library, 1995).

Kayser, John. "How a Bible Institute Imparts Missionary Vision," in *EMQ* 21:4 (October 1985).

Lee, Edgar R. "Living in the Presence of God: A Theology of Spiritual Formation," in *Enrichment Journal. A Journal for Pentecostal Ministry*, http://enrichmentjournal.ag.org/enrichmentjournal/200203 200203_086_sptlformation.cfm.

McClung, Jr., L. Grant. "Pentecostal/Charismatic Perspectives on Missiological Education," in *Missiological Education for the 21st Century*, J. Dudley Woodberry, Charles Van Engen, and Edgar J. Elliston, eds. (Maryknoll, NY: Orbis Books, 1996).

McDowell, Josh. "Reaching a Postmodern Generation," in *Enrichment Journal. A Journal for Pentecostal Ministry* http://en richmentjournal.ag.org/enrichmentjournal/19903/050_ postmodern_gen.cfm.

Mulholland, Kenneth B. "Keys to Effective Graduate Training," in *EMQ* 21:4 (October 1985).

Procter-Smith, Marjorie. "Daily Worship An Instituted Means of Grace," in *Christian Century*, (February 6-13, 1985).

Schreiter, Robert J. "Reconciliation as a Missionary Task," in *Missiology: An International Review* 20:1 (January 1992).

Stephenson, Peter, Joanne Goode and Carolyn Cole. "I Still Have Not Found What I'm Looking For," in *Postmission World Mission by a Postmodern Generation*, Richard Tiplady, ed. (Waynesboro, GA: PaternosterPress, 2002).

Tienou, Tite. "The Training of Missiologists for an African Context," in *Missiological Education for the Twenty-First Century The Book, the Circle, and the Sandals*, J. Dudley Woodberry, Charles Van Engen, and Edgar J. Elliston, eds. (Maryknoll, NY: Orbis Books, 1996).

Tozer, A. W. "Spiritual Preparation for Christian Service," in *The Alliance Weekly* (14 September 1955).

13 • So What Makes an Intercultural Training Program Successful?

Alvarez, Miguel. "Missionary Training: A Discipline," in *Journal of Asian Mission* 2:1 (March 2000).

Anderson, Gerald H. "Christian Mission in AD 2000: A Glance Backward," in *Missiology. An International Review* 18:3 (July 2000).

Araujo, Alexandre. "Confidence Factors: Accountability in Christian Partnerhips," in *Kingdom of Partnerships for Synergy in Missions,* William D. Taylor, ed. (Pasadena, CA: William Carey Library, 1994).

Arrington, French, L. *Ministry of Reconciliation: A Study of 2 Corinthians* (Grand Rapids, MI: Baker Book House, 1980).

Bertuzzi, Federico. "A Latin American Response to Patrick Sookhdeo," in *Kingdom of Partnerships for Synergy in Missions,* William D. Taylor, ed. (Pasadena, CA: William Carey Library, 1994)

Bush, Luis. *Partnering in Ministry: The Direction of World Evangelism* (Downers Grove, IL: InterVarsity Press, 1990).

______. "The Unfinished Task," in *Mission Frontiers* 17:3–4 (March–April 1995).

Butler, Keith. "Joshua Project 2000—Unreached Peoples List," in *Mission Frontiers* 18:5-8 (May–August 1996).

Butler, Phil. "Do Strategic Partnerships Really Make a Difference," in *Mission Frontiers* 18:9–10 (September–October 1996).

Castillo, Met. "Missiological Education: The Missing Element in Mission Strategy," in *Asia Pulse* 1 (1973).

______. ed. *The Asian Challenge Compendium of the Asian Missions Congress '90* (n.p.: World Evangelical Fellowship, 1991).

Cook, Guillermo, ed. *New Face of the Church in Latin America, Between Tradition and Change* (Maryknoll, NY: Orbis Books, 1994).

Da Silva, Benedicta. *Benedicta Da Silva: An Afro-Brazilian Woman's Story of Politics and Love as told to Medea Benjamin and Maisa Mendoca* (Oakland, CA: A Food First Book, 1997).

Deiros, Pablo Alberto, ed. *Los Evangélicos y el Poder Político en América Latina* (Grand Rapids, MI: Eerdmans, 1986).

De Mesa, Jose M. *Solidarity with the Culture* (Quezon City, Philippines: Maryhill, 1987).

Dussel, Enrique. *A History of the Church in Latin America: Colonialism to Liberation* (Grand Rapids, Michigan: Eerdmans, 1981).

______. ed. *The Church in Latin America, 1492-1992* (Maryknoll, NY: Orbis Books, 1992).

Escobar, Samuel. "Latin America," in *Toward the 21st Century in Christian Mission,* James M. Phillips and Robert T. Coote, eds., (Grand Rapids, MI: Eerdmans, 1993).

______. "The Promise and Precariousness of Latin American Protestantism," in *Coming of Age: Protestantism in Contemporary Latin America*, Daniel R. Miller, ed., (Lanham, MD: University Press of America, 1994).

Fernando, Ajith. *The Christian's Attitude Toward World Religions* (Wheaton, IL: Tyndale, 1987).

Garrison, David. *Church Planting Movements* (Richmond,VA: International Mission Board of the Southern Baptist Convention, 1999).

Girón, Rodolfo (Rudy). "COMIBAM: Three Independent Partnerships in Latin America," in *Kingdom of Partnerships for Synergy in Missions,* William D. Taylor, ed., (Pasadena, CA: William Carey Library, 1994).

Gnanakan, Ken. *The Pluralistic Predicament* (Bangalore, India: Theological Book Trust, 1992).

Gnanapiragasam, John and Felix Wilfred, eds. *Being Church in Asia,* Vol. 1, *Theological Advisory Commission,* 1986-92 (Quezon City, Philippines: Claretian, 1994).

Hoke, Steve. "A Glorious Pursuit. Reflections on God's Passion for Worshipers from All Peoples," in *Mission Frontiers* 23:1 (March 2001).

Isley Jr., William L. "A Spirituality for Missionaries," in *Missiology. An International Review* 17:3 (July 1999).

Lim, David S. "A Critique of Modernity in Protestant Missions in the Philippines," in *Journal of Asian Mission* 2:2 (September 2000).

Loong, Titus. "Equipping the Next Generation of Missionaries," in *Asian Mission* 1 (July 1998).

López, Dario. *La Misión Liberadora de Jesús. Una Lectura Misiológica del Evangelio de Lucas* (Lima, Perú: Ediciones Puma, 1997).

______. *Los Evangélicos y los Derechos Humanos. La Experiencia Social del Concilio Nacional Evangélico del Perú 1980-1992* (Lima, Perú: Centro Evangélico de Misiología Andino-Amazónica, 1998).

______. *Pentecostalismo y Transformación Social. Más Allá de los Estereotipos, las Críticas se Enfrentan con los Hechos* (Buenos Aires, Argentina: Kairos Ediciones, 2000).

Ma, Julie C. *When the Spirit Meets the Spirits. Pentecostal Ministry Among the Kankana-ey Tribe in the Philippines* (NY: Peter Lang, 2000).

Ma, Wonsuk. "Mission: Nine Hurdles for Asian Churches," in *Journal of Asian Mission* 2:1 (March 2000).

Maggay, Melba P. *The Gospel in the Filipino Context* (Manila, Philippines: OMF Literature, 1987).

McClung, Jr., L. Grant. *Globalbeliever.com. Connecting to God's Work in Your World* (Cleveland, TN: Pathway Press, 2000).

______. "'Try To Get People Saved.' Revisiting the Paradigm of an Urgent Pentecostal Missiology," in *The Globalization of Pentecostalism. A Religion Made to Travel,* Murray W. Dempster, Byron D. Klaus, Douglas Petersen, eds., (Oxford: UK: Regnum Books, 1999).

Nacpil, Emerito P. "Philippines: A Gospel for the New Filipino," in *Asian Voices in Christian Theology*, Gerald H. Anderson, ed., (Maryknoll, NY: Orbis, 1976).

Núñez, C. Emilio Antonio and William David Taylor, *Crisis and Hope in Latin America: An Evangelical Perspective* (Pasadena, CA: William Carey Library, 1996).

Padilla, C. Rene. *Bases Bíblicas de la Misión: Perspectivas Latinoamericanas* (Grand Rapids, Michigan: Nueva Creación, 1998).

______. "The Future of Christianity in Latin America: Missiological Perspectives and Challenges," *International Bulletin of Missionary Research* 22:3.

______. "Toward the Globalization and Integrity of Mission," *Mission in the Nineteen 90s.* Gerald H. Anderson, James B. Phillips and Robert T. Coote, eds., (Grand Rapids, Michigan: Eerdmans, 1991).

Ro, Bong-Rin. "Urban Missions: Historical Perspective," in *ATA Journal* 3:2 (July 1995).

Shibley, David. *A Force in the Earth. The Move of the Spirit in World Evangelization* (Lake Mary, FL: Creation House, 1997).

Song, Choan-Seng. *Christian Mission in Reconstruction: An Analysis* (Maryknoll, NY: Orbis, 1977).

Suico, Joseph, R. "Pentecostalism: Towards a Movement of Social Transformation in the Philippines," in *Journal of Asian Mission* 1:1 (March 1999).

Tano, Rodrigo D. "Toward and Evangelical Asian Theology," in *Biblical Theology in Asia*, Ken Gnanakan, ed., (Bangalore, India: Theological Book Trust, 1995).

Taylor, William D. Hispanic American Models of Missionary Training," in *Internationalising Missionary Training: A Global Perspective,* William D. Taylor, ed., (Grand Rapids, MI: Baker Book House, 1991).

______. ed., *Kingdom Partnerships for Synergy in Missions* (Pasadena, CA.: William Cary Library, 1994).

"The Millennial Manifesto: Covenanting for the 21st Century," *Mission Frontiers,* http://www.missionfrontiers.org/2001/02/200102.htm.

Tucker, Ruth A. "Women in Mission," in *Toward the 21st Century in Christian Mission,* James M. Phillips and Robert T. Coote, eds., (Grand Rapids, MI: Eerdmans, 1993).

Veliz, Claudio, ed. *The Politics of Conformity in Latin America* (London, UK: Oxford University, 1967).

Yung, Hwa. *Mangoes or Bananas?* (Oxford, UK: Regnum, 1997).

Subject Index

Organizational Index

Notes

Notes